New Drug Development: A Regulatory Overview
Fourth Edition

New Drug Development: A Regulatory Overview
Fourth Edition

by
Mark Mathieu

with a contribution from
Anne G. Evans, D.V.M.

PAREXEL International Corporation
Waltham, MA
Publishers

New Drug Development:
A Regulatory Overview
Fourth Edition

by
Mark Mathieu
PAREXEL International Corporation

with a contribution from
Anne G. Evans, D.V.M.

Design and Production: Blue Water Graphics
Cover Design: Art Directions
Marketing: Carolyn Newman

Acknowledgments

My sincerest thanks to the individuals who took time from their own demanding schedules to assist me in developing this text: Cori Doud; Jean Siegel, Ph.D.; Anne Evans, D.V.M.; Jonathan Fishbein, M.D.; Tomasz Sablinski, M.D., Ph.D.; James Gourzis, M.D., Ph.D.; Gary Vorsanger, M.D., Ph.D.; Alberto Grignolo, Ph.D.; David Hallinan, Ph.D.; Monica Chiu, Ph.D.; Brian Lewis; Emmanuel Bordenave; Carolyn Newman; Karleen Kelly; and Nicole Fasciano.

Special thanks to the Tufts Center for the Study of Drug Development, particularly Sheila Shulman and Peg Hewitt.

Preface

The mid-1990s have been a curious, but fascinating time for many interested observers of the Food and Drug Administration's (FDA) new drug approval process. It was a time when pharmaceutical companies, accustomed to waiting years for the agency to review their drug applications, were actually prompted by the FDA (and market forces) to speed their own regulatory processes. So rapid were some FDA drug approvals in the mid-1990s that many individuals, including some AIDS patient advocates, questioned whether agency approval decisions were being reached too quickly.

Buoyed by new staffing and driven by drug review goals established under the Prescription Drug User Fee Act of 1992 (PDUFA), the FDA's Center for Drug Evaluation and Research (CDER) established a new performance standard in 1996. During that year, the center approved an unprecedented 53 new molecular entities (NME) in a median of 14.3 months, which was also a record.

The center's building momentum under the prescription drug user fee program will be critical as CDER heads toward the millennium and perhaps more significant challenges. At this writing, CDER was facing its most daunting PDUFA-related hurdle—approving 90 percent of priority NDAs submitted in fiscal year 1997 within 6 months.

The mid-1990s also saw a shift in industry's agenda for FDA performance improvement. If the FDA's new drug review performance represented the dominant regulatory controversy of the 1980s and early 1990s, growing clinical development times had clearly supplanted it during the mid-1990s. Not surprisingly, provisions designed to stem the seemingly inexorable growth in clinical development timelines were featured prominently in drafts of PDUFA II, which was to be implemented in late 1997.

While PDUFA has been the principal driving force in drug regulation and approval in recent years, other factors have also been important. The

International Conference on Harmonization (ICH) initiative has created a new generation of regulatory guidance documents, in some cases providing recommendations in areas where none existed previously. In an effort to shield itself from a reform-minded 104th Congress, the FDA undertook a number of internal regulatory reforms that offered valuable benefits to industry.

Given the number and nature of factors constantly acting upon it, the FDA's new drug approval process evolves considerably over time. In fact, the "process" is not a single, static process, but many different processes, each designed to ensure that critical questions regarding a new drug's safety and effectiveness are addressed before approval. Today, more than ever, the development and approval paths traveled by two new products are always different, sometimes considerably so.

The new fourth edition of *New Drug Development: A Regulatory Overview* has been expanded and updated to make it the most authoritative and detailed reference available on the FDA's regulation of new drug development. The text analyzes the agency's role in the drug development process, with a particular emphasis on the emerging regulatory and reform initiatives that are both challenging and benefiting the pharmaceutical industry. The process outlined in *New Drug Development: A Regulatory Overview* applies to new molecular entities and other products classified as new drugs. It excludes biologics, generic drugs, medical devices, and animal drugs.

It is important to remember that a new drug application submitted today is evaluated by 1 of 14 new drug review divisions. Despite CDER efforts to standardize internal policies and procedures, each of these divisions has its own internal practices, philosophies, and personality. Therefore, it remains virtually impossible to provide all-encompassing descriptions of FDA policies, regulatory requirements, and review procedures that are equally relevant to each new drug or to each agency division or office. Inevitably, there are special cases and situations that make such descriptions inaccurate, and experiences and views that contradict even the most basic outlines of the drug approval process. Finally, it is important to note that this text does not necessarily, and does not claim to, represent the views of the FDA or any agency official or employee.

Contents

Chapter 1

An Introduction to the U.S. New Drug Approval Process

It is no mystery why the Food and Drug Administration's (FDA) new drug approval process is such a closely monitored government activity. After all, that process determines when and if patients are given access to new therapies that might end suffering or extend life. And as the gatekeeper to the world's most lucrative pharmaceutical market, the FDA, through that process, can determine the short-term financial destiny—in some cases, even the existence—of entire corporations.

In many ways, the FDA's role in drug development came under even greater scrutiny during the mid-1990s. An anti-regulation movement within the new Republican-led 104th Congress produced a series of regulatory reform efforts designed to overhaul the FDA's powers and drug approval standards. Meanwhile, Congress and the pharmaceutical industry scrutinized every nuance of the FDA's drug review performance against the standards established for the agency under the Prescription Drug User Fee Act of 1992.

As a function of both science and society, the drug development process evolves considerably over time. During the mid-1990s, it was the FDA's response to the two challenges cited above that has driven the latest evolutionary stages of drug regulation within the United States.

To persuade Congress to drop legislative reform proposals, the FDA and the Clinton Administration put forth their own regulatory reform agenda. Although the FDA's drug regulatory system was not affected as significantly as other program areas (e.g., biologics), important reforms were adopted.

1

Among them was a redefining of the agency's requirements for investigational new drug applications (IND) that propose Phase 1 clinical studies. Under reforms adopted in November 1995, the agency reduced IND data submission requirements by stating its willingness to accept toxicology data summaries and line listings based upon sponsors' unaudited draft toxicologic reports of completed animal studies (see Chapter 4).

Through building momentum under its prescription drug user-fee program, the FDA improved its drug review performance to the extent that then-FDA Commissioner David Kessler, M.D., proclaimed in December 1996 that the agency had become "a world leader in drug review." In fact, independent studies of global drug review times suggested that, based on median new drug approval times, the agency had become the fastest among major regulators for perhaps the first time ever. During 1996, the Center for Drug Evaluation and Research (CDER) approved 53 new molecular entities (NME) in an average of 17.8 months and a median of 14.3 months, all of which are agency records.

In addition, a variety of other factors continued to influence the FDA's drug approval process as it approached the millennium:

- *Efforts to Address Growing Clinical Development Times.* Despite shorter FDA review times, overall development time frames for new drugs continued to increase during the mid-1990s. A Tufts Center for the Study of Drug Development study indicated that average clinical development times were higher for new drugs approved in 1994 and 1995 than for drugs approved in any year since 1962. This reality helped shift the debate away from FDA review times and toward clinical development times. Not surprisingly, streamlining the clinical development process became a focus of FDA and industry discussions regarding the reauthorization of the Prescription Drug User Fee Act (PDUFA), which will expire in September 1997. In early 1997, the FDA and industry agreed to ask Congress to adopt a series of concepts in its reauthorization of PDUFA, including several targeted specifically at the clinical development process.

- *CDER Reorganization.* During 1995 and 1996, CDER reconfigured its 2 new drug evaluation offices and 10 new drug review divisions

2

into 5 new drug evaluation offices and 14 new drug review units. The objectives of this restructuring were to create smaller, more therapeutic-area-focused review groups and to expedite application reviews, both of which were seen as necessary if the center was to meet its goals under the Prescription Drug User Fee Act of 1992.

- *Cooperation Among International Regulatory Authorities.* In an effort to harmonize international technical requirements for drug and biotechnology products, American, Japanese, and European regulators and industry continued their work under the International Conference on Harmonization (ICH) initiative. The ICH program has produced a new generation of regulatory guidance documents that, in many cases, provide recommendations more current than those found in existing FDA guidelines. By April 1997, the ICH parties had harmonized more than two dozen regulatory guidelines and were seeking to harmonize several others as of this writing. In mid-1997, the ICH participants were to decide whether to embark on the most daunting and significant harmonization initiative to date—the development of a "common technical document" that would comprise a set of technical information that could be presented in marketing applications in all three ICH regions.

- *Further Integration of Computers into the Drug Review Process.* By the mid-1990s, there was growing evidence that electronic submissions could expedite the drug review process. In late 1996, the FDA also made the commitment to develop a paperless, electronic submission system for all drug and biologic submissions. Several months later, the FDA laid the regulatory foundation necessary for the agency and industry to begin to replace paper-based submissions with purely electronic filings. Specifically, the FDA published a March 1997 final regulation establishing its criteria for accepting electronic records and electronic signatures in place of paper records and handwritten signatures (see Chapter 8).

- *FDA Initiatives to Better Define and Communicate Approval Standards and Review Procedures.* Under Center for Drug Evaluation and Research Director Janet Woodcock, M.D., the drug center has undertaken a variety of initiatives to improve communications with all of its "constituents," including regulated industry. These initiatives have begun to give drug companies and others perhaps unprecedented access to the agency's requirements, internal policies, and review practices. In November 1996, for example, CDER released *Draft Reviewer Guidance: Conducting a Clinical Safety Review of a New Product Application and Preparing a Report on the Review*, a guidance that represents the first step of the center's Good Review Practices (GRP) program, which is designed to better standardize the clinical review process. Further, through a March 1997 draft guideline entitled *Providing Clinical Evidence of Effectiveness for Human Drug and Biological Products*, CDER offered what is likely its most detailed discussion ever of the efficacy data necessary to support new drug approval.

Given the number and nature of factors constantly acting upon it, the FDA's new drug approval process can never be characterized as a single, static process. Since new drugs present their own distinct risks and benefits, and because these risks and benefits are evaluated by different FDA reviewers, the development and approval paths traveled by two new products are always different, sometimes considerably so. The nature of the drug development and approval process is, in large part, a function of the drug being developed and the condition being studied, and is tailored to ensure that the key questions regarding the compound's safety and effectiveness for this indication are addressed sufficiently before approval.

The FDA and the Food, Drug and Cosmetic Act

Despite the emerging trends outlined above, the foundations of the new drug approval process remain intact within the provisions of the Federal Food, Drug and Cosmetic Act (FD&C Act). Seen by many as the most complex law of its kind, the FD&C Act has at least three provisions that continue to shape the new drug development and approval process:

1. The FD&C Act defines the term "drug," thereby identifying the universe of products subject to regulation as drugs. The statute

4

defines drugs as "articles intended for use in the diagnosis, cure, mitigation, treatment, or prevention of disease in man...." and "articles (other than food) intended to affect the structure or any function of the body of man...."

2. The FD&C Act defines "new drug," thereby identifying which products are subject to the requirements of the new drug approval process. The law defines "new drug" as: "(1) Any drug (except a new animal drug or an animal feed bearing or containing a new animal drug) the composition of which is such that such drug is not generally recognized, among experts qualified by scientific training and experience to evaluate the safety and effectiveness of drugs, as safe and effective for use under the conditions prescribed, recommended, or suggested in labeling thereof, except that such a drug not so recognized shall not be deemed to be a 'new drug' if at any time prior to the enactment of this Act it was subject to the Food and Drugs Act of June 30, 1906, as amended, and if at such time its labeling contained the same representations concerning the conditions of its use; or (2) Any drug (except a new animal drug or an animal feed bearing or containing a new animal drug) the composition of which is such that such drug, as a result of investigations to determine its safety and effectiveness for use under such conditions, has become so recognized, but which has not, otherwise than in such investigations, been used to a material extent or for a material time under such conditions."

3. The FD&C Act identifies, in the broadest possible terms, the criteria that all new drugs must meet to gain marketing approval. Before a new drug can be marketed in the United States, it must be the subject of an FDA-approved new drug application (NDA), which must contain adequate data and information on the drug's safety and "substantial evidence" of the product's effectiveness.

But as similar laws do in other areas, the FD&C Act merely establishes the basic framework and essential principles of new drug approval. The statute must be interpreted, implemented, and enforced. Since the early 1900s, these responsibilities have fallen on the FDA.

It is the interpretive and discretionary powers granted to the FDA under the FD&C Act that give the agency wide-ranging authority. Perhaps the most significant of these powers is the FDA's role in interpreting the legal requirement that a sponsor present substantial evidence of effectiveness prior to a drug's approval. While this is a statutory requirement, it is the FDA that decides what constitutes substantial evidence for each new drug. In doing so, the agency also determines what scientific testing and data are needed to obtain marketing approval.

As a drug regulator and the interpreter of the FD&C Act, the FDA has a responsibility to communicate its policies and standards so that industry may address key requirements in developing new pharmaceuticals. The agency does this primarily by developing and publishing regulations, which are compiled in the *U.S. Code of Federal Regulations* (CFR). These regulations describe pre-marketing requirements and approval procedures that are, at least in theory, binding on both the FDA and drug sponsors. Although federal regulations often provide this information in broad rather than specific detail, they are significantly more specific than the provisions of the FD&C Act.

The FDA supplements federal regulations in several ways, including by publishing guidelines. Unlike regulations, guidelines are not legally binding, but are designed to provide drug sponsors with informal and more detailed guidance on specific means through which they might satisfy regulatory requirements. Further, the FDA corresponds directly with drug applicants on specific drug testing and approval processes. To improve communications with its various constituents, particularly the pharmaceutical industry, CDER established an Office of Training and Communications in October 1995. Recent CDER communications initiatives include a CDER Internet Home Page (http://www.fda.gov/cder) and a Manual of Policies and Procedures (MaPP), which consolidates dozens of center operating procedures and policies.

New Drug Development and Approval: The Principal Steps

Despite the changes outlined above, new drugs face a reasonably well-defined development and approval process that has evolved over several decades. In fact, given CDER's commitment to better document and communicate development and approval standards, the drug approval process will likely remain the best understood of the FDA's product approval processes.

Each stage of the drug development and approval process falls within one of three classes of activities: (1) scientific testing designed to provide data on a product's safety or effectiveness; (2) the preparation and submission of these data and other information in regulatory applications; and (3) the FDA's review of regulatory submissions. While all drug development programs involve these core activities, it is important to note how fundamentally different each can be for any two products. Testing and submission requirements, for example, will be shaped by many factors, including the drug's proposed indication, the amount and nature of data already available on the drug and on compounds similar in molecular structure, and the availability of therapeutic alternatives for the target indication.

Preclinical Testing

Clearly, clinical trials represent the ultimate premarketing proving grounds for new pharmaceuticals. Because of the costs and risks inherent in using an untested drug in clinical testing, however, drug sponsors do not leap headlong into a clinical program once combinatorial chemistry, molecular modeling, or some other screening/discovery method identifies a promising compound. Prior to clinical studies, the sponsor seeks some evidence of the compound's biological activity, and both the sponsor and the FDA seek data indicating that the drug is reasonably safe for initial administration to humans.

Before initiating clinical studies, a drug sponsor must submit an application that provides information showing that the company can manufacture the drug, descriptions of the proposed clinical trials, and data establishing that the drug is reasonably safe for use in initial, small-scale clinical studies. Depending on whether the compound has been studied or marketed previously, the sponsor may have several options for fulfilling the last of these three requirements: (1) compiling existing nonclinical data derived from past *in vitro* laboratory or animal studies on the compound; (2) compiling data from previous clinical testing or marketing of the drug in the United States or another country whose population is relevant to the U.S. population; or (3) undertaking new preclinical studies designed to provide the evidence necessary to support the safety of administering the compound to humans.

For most NMEs and other drugs whose clinical safety and efficacy have not been established previously, preclinical *in vitro* and *in vivo* animal testing represents the first major step toward regulatory approval. During preclinical drug development, a sponsor evaluates the drug's toxic and pharmacologic effects. Genotoxicity screening is performed, as well as investigations on drug absorption and metabolism, the toxicity of the drug's metabolites, and the speed with which the drug and its metabolites are excreted from the body. At the preclinical stage, the FDA will generally ask, at a minimum, that sponsors: (1) develop a pharmacological profile of the drug; (2) determine the acute toxicity of the drug in at least two species of animals; and (3) conduct short-term toxicity studies ranging from two weeks to three months, depending upon the proposed use of the substance.

Once clinical trials begin, further *in vitro* and *in vivo* animal studies provide information essential to the continued clinical use and, ultimately, the approval of the drug. Long-term and specialized animal tests are needed to support the safety of testing a compound in larger patient populations and over longer periods. These tests also allow researchers to evaluate effects that are impractical or unethical to study in humans, such as drug effects over an entire life span, effects over several generations, and effects on pregnancy and reproduction.

Because preclinical drug development does not involve human exposure to an experimental compound, drug developers have considerable flexibility in manufacturing, shipping, and testing experimental drugs. Virtually the only regulatory limitations facing sponsors are the general animal welfare provisions contained in current federal and state animal protection statutes and regulations, and little more than a single FDA requirement detailed in federal regulations: "A person may ship a drug intended solely for tests in vitro or in animals used only for laboratory research purposes if it is labeled as follows: Caution: Contains a new drug for investigational use only in laboratory research animals, or for tests in vitro. Not for use in humans."

When a sponsor begins to compile safety data for submission to the FDA, however, a set of regulations called Good Laboratory Practice (GLP) apply. Because it will base important regulatory decisions on these data, the FDA uses GLP standards to ensure the quality of animal testing and the resultant data.

The Investigational New Drug Application

When a sponsor believes that it has sufficient data to show that a new drug is adequately safe for initial small-scale clinical studies, the company assembles and submits an investigational new drug application (IND). The IND is the vehicle through which a sponsor seeks an exemption from the statutory requirement that prohibits unapproved drugs from being shipped in interstate commerce. A sponsor uses the IND to alert the FDA of its intent to conduct clinical studies with an investigational new drug.

In the IND, the sponsor submits information in three principal areas: (1) the results of all preclinical testing and an analysis of what implications these results have for human pharmacology; (2) an analysis of the drug's chemical composition and the manufacturing and quality control procedures used in producing the compound; and (3) protocols describing the sponsor's plans for the initial-stage clinical studies proposed in the IND, and information describing the relevant qualifications of the investigators who will carry out these studies.

Perhaps the most significant FDA reforms implemented in the mid-1990s were those affecting IND submission requirements. In part an effort to stem the tide of Phase 1 studies moving to European countries, which generally have less demanding submission standards for initial-stage clinical research, the FDA "clarified" its IND content requirements in November 1995. Specifically, the agency stated its willingness to accept toxicology data summaries and line listings based upon sponsors' unaudited draft toxicologic reports of completed animal studies in INDs for Phase 1 studies. By accepting the summaries and listings based on unaudited draft reports, and permitting companies to update this information 120 days after trials are initiated, the FDA in effect permits sponsors to begin Phase 1 trials months earlier than in the past.

The FDA's Review of the IND

The IND review is unique among the FDA's application review processes. In many respects, this process and the FDA's treatment of INDs represents a delicate balance between the federal government's responsibility to protect clinical trial subjects from unnecessary risks and its desire to avoid becoming an impediment to the advance of medical research. Given these dual goals, the FDA must perform a safety review of an IND prior to clinical trials, but has only 30 days in which to reach an initial determination on the filing.

The FDA's review of an IND focuses on three areas:

Pharmacology/Toxicology Review. The reviewing pharmacologist examines the results of animal pharmacology and toxicology testing, and attempts to relate these results to human pharmacology.

Chemistry Review. The reviewing chemist evaluates both the sponsor's manufacturing processes and control procedures to ensure that the compound is reproducible and is stable in its pure form. If a drug is either unstable or not reproducible, then the validity of any clinical testing would be undermined and, more importantly, the studies may pose significant risks. The chemistry reviewer also evaluates the drug's characterization and chemical structure, and compares the product's structure and impurity profile to those of other drugs (i.e., drugs known to be toxic).

Clinical Review. The reviewing medical officer, who is generally a physician, evaluates the clinical protocols to ensure: (1) that subjects will not be exposed to unreasonable or unnecessary risks during clinical trials; and (2) that Phase 2 and Phase 3 trials (generally not submitted in the initial IND filing) are adequate in design to provide scientifically valid data.

If the FDA does not contact the applicant within 30 days of the IND submission, the sponsor may initiate clinical trials. In this way, the agency does not approve an IND, but allows clinical testing to proceed through its "administrative silence."

When the FDA decides that a certain clinical trial should be delayed, the agency contacts the sponsor within the 30-day period to initiate what is called a "clinical hold"—the delay of the clinical trial until potential problems or unanswered questions are addressed. Aside from the safety-related reasons mentioned above, the FDA may base a clinical hold on other grounds, including the following:

- the IND does not contain sufficient information to assess the risks of using the drug in clinical trials;

- the clinical investigators named in the IND are not qualified by reason of their training and experience to conduct the investigation described in the IND; or

- the investigator's brochure—an information package designed to inform each investigator about the drug and its benefits and risks— is misleading, erroneous, or materially incomplete.

Clinical Trials

Clinical trials clearly represent the most critical and demanding phase in the drug development process. If the drug survives the rigors of clinical testing, the FDA's ultimate approval decision will be based primarily upon data derived from these studies—the agency estimates that more than 80 percent of the average NDA for an NME consists of clinical data and analyses alone.

If the FDA's new drug review performance was the dominant regulatory controversy of the 1980s and early 1990s, growing clinical development times had clearly supplanted it during the mid-1990s. A seemingly inexorable rise in clinical development times during the past two decades, industry maintained, was making product development costs even more prohibitive, and was offsetting the benefits of the marked improvements in FDA new drug review times.

This reality and changes in the competitive environment for pharmaceuticals helped to accelerate several trends, including industry efforts to streamline their clinical development programs and to leverage their clinical trial efforts internationally. They also may have played a role in a new FDA initiative to better define the clinical trial data necessary to support drug approval. In a March 1997 draft guideline entitled *Providing Clinical Evidence of Effectiveness for Human Drug and Biological Products*, the agency provides its latest views on the "quantitative and qualitative standards" for establishing drug effectiveness.

Without question, clinical development is the most complex, time consuming, and costly element in the pharmaceutical development process. At a minimum, it requires a coordinated effort that features a sponsor willing to assume the financial, legal, and regulatory responsibilities associated with the program; the commitment and expertise of physicians, nurses, and other health-care professionals; and patients willing to take the chance that an experimental drug will do more for them than existing therapies.

Although clinical trials for different drugs can vary greatly in design, they are often similar in structure. Since researchers may know little about a new compound prior to its use in humans, testing the drug through serially conducted studies permits each phase of clinical development to be carefully designed to use and build upon the information obtained from the research phase preceding it. Clinical programs for most new drugs begin with the cautious use of an investigational compound in small, carefully selected population groups, and proceed into larger, more clinically relevant, and increasingly diverse patient pools.

While there is no statute or regulation that mandates a specific clinical trial structure or design, a clinical development program most often proceeds in three primary stages, or phases:

Phase 1: The cautious use of a drug in a few patients or normal human volunteers—20 to 80 subjects—to gain basic safety and pharmacological information. Specifically, these studies allow the sponsor to assess a drug's pharmacology and pharmacokinetics, mechanism of action in humans, side effects (of various doses), optimal route of administration, and safe dosage range.

Phase 2: The use of the compound in a small number of subjects—100 to 200 patients—who suffer from the condition that the drug is intended to treat or diagnose. Phase 2 trials provide additional safety data and the first indication of a drug's clinical effectiveness in its proposed use. Results of Phase 2 studies can establish the foundation for key aspects of Phase 3 study design (e.g., clinical endpoints, target population).

Phase 3: Use of the drug in a significantly larger group of subjects (i.e., several hundred to several thousand) who suffer from the condition that the drug is proposed to treat or diagnose to gather additional effectiveness and safety information necessary for assessments of the drug's overall risk-benefit relationship. Because certain Phase 3 trials, called "pivotal" trials, will serve as the primary basis for the drug's approval, these studies must meet more rigorous standards (e.g., controls, blinding, randomization, and size).

The dire need for therapies for AIDS, cancer, and other life-threatening illnesses has compelled the FDA to develop a variety of alternative models for clinical drug development. For medicines designed to treat life-threatening and severely debilitating illnesses, the agency works closely with sponsors to develop compressed Phase 2/3 trials designed to serve as the basis for the product's approval (see Chapter 16). In a December 1992 regulation, the agency announced its willingness to approve drugs for serious and life-threatening illnesses based on "surrogate endpoints," whose therapeutic relevance can then be verified through mandatory postmarketing clinical studies. More recently, under its March 1996 Oncology Initiative, the agency agreed to accelerate the development of cancer drugs by basing approval on surrogate endpoints such as tumor shrinkage for patients who have no satisfactory alternative therapies.

The New Drug Application

The new drug application (NDA) is the vehicle through which drug sponsors formally propose that the FDA approve a new pharmaceutical for sale and marketing in the United States. To support a drug's approval, an NDA comprises thousands of pages of nonclinical and clinical test data and analyses, drug chemistry information, and descriptions of manufacturing procedures.

The NDA is the largest and most complex premarketing application that the FDA reviews. The application must provide sufficient information, data, and analyses to permit agency reviewers to reach several key decisions, including:

1. Whether the drug is safe and effective in its proposed use(s), and whether the benefits of the drug outweigh its risks.

2. Whether the methods used in manufacturing the drug and the controls used to maintain the product's quality are adequate to preserve its identity, strength, and purity.

3. Whether the drug's proposed labeling is appropriate and, if not, what the drug's labeling should contain.

At this writing, several factors were affecting the evolution of the NDA. In mid-1997, for example, the FDA adopted a new streamlined NDA application form (Form FDA 356h) that affected several aspects of NDA content and formatting standards. Further, a March 1997 final rule provided the regulatory basis for the agency to begin accepting NDAs (and other applications) in electronic format without the previously mandatory paper-based versions.

The NDA Review Process

No other aspect of the U.S. drug development and approval system has evolved as significantly in recent years as the FDA's NDA review process. So fundamental were these changes—and the improvements in drug review times that resulted from them—that CDER's NDA review performance was transformed from one of the most harshly criticized of FDA activities into what was perhaps the agency's best defense against regulatory reform proposals advanced in the mid-1990s.

The driving forces behind this evolution, of course, were PDUFA and the changes that CDER implemented to meet the new review timelines associated with this legislation. In the early and mid-1990s, CDER instituted tight controls for managing and tracking drug reviews, and reorganized the center's drug review divisions into smaller, more therapeutically focused units.

By early 1997, as Congress began to consider reauthorizing PDUFA, there seemed little question that the prescription drug user fee program had brought much of the change that industry had long sought. In 1996, for instance, CDER approved a record 53 NMEs in a median review time of 14.3 months—the most rapid time ever.

NDAs are forwarded to one of CDER's 14 new drug review divisions—specifically, the division that handles the therapeutic area relevant to the submission. Within 45 days of the NDA's submission, FDA reviewers—including the lead medical, chemistry, and pharmacology reviewers—will meet to determine if the application is sufficiently complete for a full review. NDAs that meet minimum submission criteria are "filed" or accepted for review, while the FDA issues refuse-to-file (RTF) decisions for deficient applications, which are returned to their sponsors.

Once the review team decides that an NDA is fileable, it begins the "primary" review of the application. During this evaluation, each member of the review team sifts through volumes of research data and information applicable to his or her expertise:

Clinical Reviewer: Evaluates the data from, and analyses of, clinical studies to determine if the drug is safe and effective in its proposed use(s) and if the product's benefits outweigh its risks.

Pharmacology/Toxicology Reviewer: Evaluates the entire body of nonclinical data and analyses, with a particular focus on the newly submitted long-term test data, to identify relevant implications for the drug's clinical safety.

Chemistry Reviewer: Evaluates commercial-stage manufacturing procedures (e.g., method of synthesis or isolation, purification process, and process controls) and the specifications and analytical methods used to assure the identity, strength, purity, and bioavailability of the drug product.

Statistical Reviewer: Evaluates the pivotal clinical data to determine if there exists statistically significant evidence of the drug's safety and effectiveness, the appropriateness of the sponsor's clinical data analyses and the assumptions under which these analyses were performed, the statistical significance of newly submitted nonclinical data, and the implications of stability data for establishing appropriate expiration dating for the product.

Biopharmaceutics Reviewer: Evaluates pharmacokinetics and bioavailability data to establish appropriate drug dosing.

Microbiology Reviewer (for anti-infectives): Evaluates the drug's effects on target viruses or other microorganisms.

The filing decision also triggers a division request that the relevant FDA field office conduct what is called a "preapproval inspection" of the sponsor's manufacturing facilities. During such inspections, FDA investigators visit the applicant's production facilities to audit company statements and commitments made in the NDA against actual manufacturing practices employed by the sponsor or contract manufacturer.

When the primary technical reviews are completed, each reviewer must prepare a written evaluation of the NDA that presents his or her conclusions and recommendations regarding the application. In most cases, the medical reviewer is responsible for evaluating and reconciling the conclusions of reviewers in the other scientific disciplines. This process, and the development of what CDER calls an "institutional decision" on an NDA's approvability, is likely to involve considerable dialogue between the medical reviewer and reviewers in the other disciplines.

During the drug review process, the FDA may seek advice and comment from one of its 15 prescription drug advisory committees. When called upon, these expert committees provide the agency with independent, non-binding advice and recommendations.

Under the prescription drug user fee program, the FDA must "act on" 90 percent of "priority" NDAs submitted in fiscal year (FY) 1997 within 6 months, and 90 percent of "standard" FY1997 NDAs within 12 months. The agency fulfills this requirement by issuing one of three "action letters"—either an approval, approvable, or not-approvable letter. While an approval letter is used when a drug has been formally approved for marketing, an approvable letter will most likely indicate that the sponsor must make minor revisions or new submissions to the NDA file and probably submit final printed labeling before marketing authorization is granted. A not-approvable letter indicates that the NDA cannot be approved in its current state, and identifies the relevant deficiencies.

In each of the first several years of the user-fee program, the FDA reported that it exceeded its review performance goals. Through a December 1996 performance report to Congress, for example, the agency revealed that it had met its review target for 95 percent of FY1995 original applications for drugs and biologics, surpassing its goal of 70 percent for the FY1995 cohort.

Chapter 2

Nonclinical Drug Testing

by Anne G. Evans, D.V.M.
Director, Clinical and Regulatory Affairs
Myelos Neurosciences

For most new molecular entities (NME) and other drugs whose clinical safety and efficacy have not been established previously, preclinical *in vitro* and *in vivo* animal testing represents the first major step toward regulatory approval. According to some estimates, only one in every 1,000 compounds studied in preclinical testing progresses beyond this phase. Preclinical screening and testing shows that the remaining compounds are unsafe, are poorly absorbed, lack pharmacological activity, or have some other flaw that makes them unworthy of further development.

For those drugs that are researched further, animal studies play several roles in drug development. First, the studies provide the basic toxicological and pharmacological information needed to obtain the FDA's permission to begin clinical trials. While the FDA's decision to approve a new pharmaceutical for marketing is based largely on the results of clinical studies, the agency will not allow an entirely unknown and uncharacterized compound to be administered to human subjects. Before clinical work begins, the agency requires that the drug be administered to, and its short-term effects be studied in, laboratory animals. The FDA uses data from these studies to decide if the drug is sufficiently safe for initial administration to humans.

Once clinical trials begin, further *in vitro* and *in vivo* animal studies provide information essential to the continued clinical use and, ultimately, the approval of the drug (see exhibit below). Long-term and specialized animal tests are needed to support the safety of testing a compound in larger patient populations and over longer periods. These tests also allow researchers to evaluate effects that are impractical or unethical to study in humans, such as drug effects over an entire animal life span, effects over several generations, and effects on pregnancy and reproduction.

Although nonclinical research results are imperfect predictors of clinical responses, laboratory animals remain the best practical experimental models for identifying and measuring a compound's biological activity, and for predicting a drug's clinical effects. (Because animal studies are performed before and during clinical studies, the term "nonclinical" generally is preferable to "preclinical" when discussing the full spectrum of *in vitro* and non-human *in vivo* tests associated with drug development.) By studying a drug's dose-response characteristics, adverse and residual effects, and mechanism, site, degree, and duration of action, drug sponsors and the FDA gain valuable insights on the compound's probable action and effects in humans.

The FDA plays at least four principal roles in the nonclinical testing of drugs:

- the agency determines, sometimes on a case-by-case basis, what nonclinical test data are needed to show that a drug is sufficiently safe for initial and continued testing in humans;

- the agency, when asked, provides advice to drug sponsors on the adequacy of nonclinical testing programs developed for specific drugs before the animal studies are initiated;

- the agency provides independent analyses of nonclinical test results and conclusions; and

- the agency sets minimum standards for laboratories conducting nonclinical toxicity testing through good laboratory practice (GLP) regulations (see Chapter 3).

FDA Guidance on Nonclinical Testing Requirements

Until fairly recently, FDA nonclinical testing requirements were described only in very general terms in two now-outdated guidelines, one published in

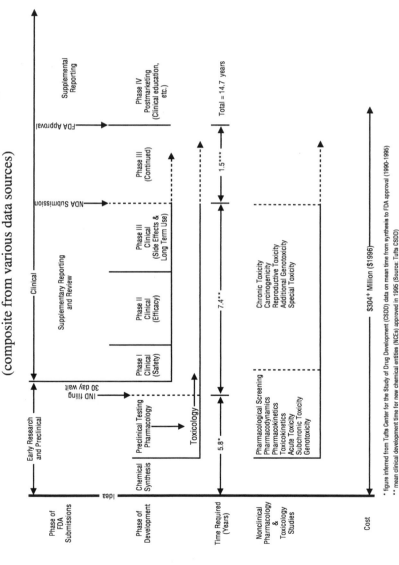

Analysis of U.S. New Drug Development Process by Average Time to Complete Each Phase of Product Development
(composite from various data sources)

1968 by the FDA and the other in 1977 by the U.S. Pharmaceutical Manufacturers Association (PMA). In the late 1980s and early 1990s, FDA toxicologists and pharmacologists were developing several guidance documents to address subjects ranging from animal-testing requirements for specific classes of drugs to the use of computer technology for nonclinical data submissions.

Concurrent with the FDA's efforts to produce updated guidance in this area, the European Community (EC) and Japan were developing testing standards that were often similar in principle but different in detail. In an effort to harmonize these and other testing standards, the regulatory authorities and pharmaceutical industries of these three regions organized the International Conferences on Harmonization (ICH).

The harmonization initiative has had fundamental effects on the FDA's own efforts to develop recommendations for nonclinical testing. Most importantly, the FDA has sought to revise its guidelines to reflect the consensus to which the agency has contributed as part of the ICH process.

The ICH process and its effects on the FDA's efforts will continue for some time. By late 1996, the FDA had accepted harmonized recommendations on single dose toxicity testing and the duration of chronic toxicity testing in rodents, as well as harmonized guidelines on reproductive toxicity studies, toxicokinetics, certain aspects of pharmacokinetics, genotoxicity testing and carcinogenicity studies. However, efforts to finalize ICH guidelines on numerous other nonclinical topics are ongoing, with various topics at different "steps" in the ICH harmonization process and with new topics destined to enter the process. In addition to outlining the FDA's nonclinical testing requirements, the following discussion analyzes the specific effects that the ICH process has had and is expected to have on these requirements.

FDA officials are always careful to stress the limitations of guidelines, no matter how current. As with any guidelines, the agency's nonclinical guidelines are designed only to provide general direction for typical situations; they cannot be applied universally to all drugs and all situations. Therefore, the FDA remains willing to advise sponsors, particularly about unusual cases. FDA staffers will discuss nonclinical testing strategies during the development of these plans, but can usually offer more useful insights if a sponsor develops a nonclinical study program and submits the plan for agency review. Recommendations obtained from such reviews supplement drug sponsors' own expertise and the more general suggestions provided by FDA and ICH guidelines.

Whether or not a sponsor chooses to initiate a dialogue with FDA reviewers, the types and amount of nonclinical testing ultimately required by the agency will depend on several factors, including:

• a drug's chemical structure, and the similarity of that structure to existing compounds with safety profiles known to the FDA;

• a drug's proposed indication in humans;

• a drug's target patient population (e.g., elderly, infants, women);

• special characteristics of a drug's use pattern (e.g., if a drug is likely to be prescribed as a concomitant medication);

• a drug's proposed route of administration; and

• a drug's proposed duration of administration (i.e., whether for chronic or short-term use).

Types of Nonclinical Studies

When drug sponsors initiate a nonclinical testing program, their first goal is to conduct the studies and collect the data necessary to support the safety of early clinical trials. In the past, these data generally have been limited to short-term animal test results. Today, however, *in vitro* and *in vivo* genotoxicity testing is assuming greater importance during the preclinical phase.

As stated above, preclinical studies represent only part of a drug's nonclinical development. The comprehensive nonclinical testing program needed to support marketing approval for most new drugs involves years of work and several different types of studies. A draft ICH consensus text entitled *Guideline on the Timing of Nonclinical Studies for the Conduct of Human Clinical Trials for Pharmaceuticals* (May 1997) discusses the timing of the various components of nonclinical testing and their relation to the conduct of clinical trials.

Although relevant comments from this ICH document are included in the discussions below, it is important to note that the draft guideline may change considerably due to pending harmonization issues and guidelines. In particular, if the ICH participants harmonize recommendations for the duration of chronic toxicology studies, the draft guideline will have to be revised to reflect these requirements.

For the purpose of analysis, nonclinical testing is often divided into two areas: pharmacology and toxicology. Together, pharmacology and toxicology studies are designed to provide an integrated overview of a drug's effects in various animal species.

Pharmacology Studies Because insights gained from pharmacological studies—particularly those regarding adverse effects—can influence the direction of later toxicological testing, pharmacologic work is generally conducted first.

Pharmacological Screening. The pharmacological study of a new drug proceeds in phases. The initial phase, pharmacological screening, is really part of the drug discovery process. It involves the use of *in vitro* and *in vivo* assays designed to determine if a compound has any pharmacological activity. Hundreds of compounds may be subjected to these screenings, with those exhibiting measurable pharmacological effects being selected as "lead chemicals" (i.e., substances to be tested further).

Pharmacodynamics. Once a lead chemical is selected, the sponsor generally begins to compile a more complete qualitative and quantitative pharmacological profile of the compound. This profile consists largely of pharmacodynamic studies, which provide an indication of the drug's action on various receptors or physiological systems in animals.

Pharmacodynamic studies, often called "safety pharmacology studies," should be sufficiently extensive to determine dose-response relationships and the drug's duration and mechanism of action. In these studies, researchers explore the drug's effects on major physiological systems and activities (i.e., neurologic, cardiovascular, respiratory, gastrointestinal, genitourinary, endocrine, anti-inflammatory, immunoreactive, chemotherapeutic, and enzymatic). The studies are designed to investigate all primary and secondary effects related or unrelated to the desired therapeutic effect, extensions of the therapeutic effect that might produce toxicity at higher doses, and effects related to interactions with other drugs. According to the ICH's draft guideline on the timing of nonclinical studies, safety pharmacology studies should be performed prior to human exposure. These assessments may be made as part of independent pharmacology studies or incorporated into appropriate toxicology studies.

Pharmacokinetics. The pharmacology component of preclinical development also includes pharmacokinetic testing, which is designed to obtain information on the extent and duration of systemic exposure to the drug. Generally, these studies are performed both *in vitro* and *in vivo* in multiple species using both radiolabelled and unlabelled test compound. The results are then compared to identify species-to-species drug-response differences that might affect later nonclinical and clinical studies or their interpretation. Today, these studies are considered to be a much more important aspect of preclinical drug development than they were previously, and serve as the basis for subsequent toxicokinetic assessments (see discussion on toxicity studies below). According to the ICH's draft guideline on the timing of nonclinical studies, exposure data in animals should be evaluated prior to human trials, with further information on absorption, distribution, metabolism and excretion available by the time early Phase 1 studies are complete.

It is worth noting that this is one area in which there is little specific international guidance available, and where the ICH regional-specific guidances differ.

Pharmacokinetic studies are designed to yield information about the drug's absorption, distribution, metabolism, and excretion (ADME) pattern. Analytical methodology employed to generate these data may include ultraviolet absorption, fluorescence, high-pressure liquid chromatography, gas chromatography, immunoassay, liquid scintigraphy, autoradiography and mass spectrometry analysis of the parent compound and/or metabolites in tissues or fluids.

Absorption studies generally involve serial determinations of drug concentration in blood and urine after dosing to indicate the rate and extent of absorption (e.g., following oral administration). Typically, studies using the intravenous route are conducted to serve as a reference. Common pharmacokinetic parameters employed in these assessments include plasma area under the curve (AUC), maximum (peak) plasma concentration (C_{max}), and plasma concentration at a specified time after administration of a given dose

($C_{(time)}$). Bioavailability (i.e., the amount of drug that reaches the systemic circulation) is dependent, in part, on the extent of absorption, but is also influenced by other factors, such as the extent of a drug's metabolism by the liver before it enters the general circulation.

Distribution studies provide information on the extent and time course of tissue accumulation and the elimination of a drug and/or its metabolites. Distribution patterns can be assessed by sacrificing animals at predetermined intervals after dosing, and then measuring the concentration of the drug and/or its metabolites in selected tissues. In general, only single dose studies of distribution are performed. However, in accordance with the adoption of the final ICH guideline entitled *Pharmacokinetics: Guidance for Repeated Dose Distribution Studies*, repeat dose distribution studies are appropriate for compounds that have: (1) an apparently long half life; (2) incomplete elimination; or (3) unanticipated organ toxicity.

The "volume of distribution" represents another parameter that is useful in assessing drug distribution. The volume of distribution relates the amount of drug in the body to the concentration of drug in the blood or plasma. For drugs that are extensively bound to plasma proteins but not to tissue components, the volume of distribution will approach that of the plasma volume.

The assessment and quantification of a drug's metabolic pattern is essential for a complete understanding of efficacy and toxicity, since species differences in toxicity may be related to differences in metabolism. To assess the metabolic profile of a drug, the concentration of the drug and its major metabolites are measured in plasma, urine, feces, bile, and/or other tissues as a function of time following dose administration. In some cases, toxicological testing of pharmacologically active metabolites may be necessary in addition to testing on the drug itself.

"Clearance" is a measure of an organism's ability to eliminate a drug. The concept represents the rate of a drug's elimination in relation to its concentration (CL = Rate of elimination/C). This excretion parameter can be determined for individual organs and, when added together, will equal total systemic clearance. In general, decreased toxic potential is associated with rapid and complete excretion.

Toxicity Studies *In vitro* and *in vivo* animal toxicity studies are undertaken to identify and measure a drug's short- and long-term functional and morphologic adverse effects. Depending on the nature of a drug, its intended use, and the extent of its proposed study in clinical trials, a toxicity testing program may consist of some or all of the following elements:

- acute toxicity studies;

- subacute or subchronic toxicity studies;

- chronic toxicity studies;

- carcinogenicity studies;

- special toxicity studies;

- reproductive toxicity studies;

- genotoxicity studies; and

- toxicokinetic studies.

Because many of the ongoing nonclinical ICH initiatives focus on toxicity testing, drug sponsors are advised to keep abreast of harmonization developments and subsequent regulatory changes as they affect these types of studies in particular.

Acute Toxicity Studies. Acute (single dose) toxicity studies are designed to measure the short-term adverse effects of a drug when administered in a single dose, or in multiple doses during a period not exceeding 24 hours. Results from acute toxicity studies should provide information on the following:

- the appropriate dosage for multiple-dose studies;

- the potential target organs of toxicity;

- the time-course of drug-induced clinical observations;

- species-specific differences in toxicity;

- the potential for acute toxicity in humans; and

- an estimate of the safe acute doses for humans.

25

To determine initial toxicity levels, researchers should study the investigational drug in at least two mammalian species, including a non-rodent species when reasonable, prior to first human exposure. These studies should involve dosages that are intended to cause no adverse effects and those intended to cause major (life-threatening) toxicity. The use of vehicle control groups should be considered.

The route(s) of administration should include an intravenous route and the route intended for human administration. When intravenous dosing is proposed in humans, use of this route alone in animal testing is sufficient. The animals are then observed for 14 days after drug administration.

The FDA indicates that investigators need to obtain more than just mortality data from acute toxicity studies. At a minimum, researchers should observe and record test animals' clinical signs, and the time of onset, the duration, and the reversibility of toxicity. Gross necropsies should be performed on all animals.

In the past, one type of data derived from acute toxicity studies was the drug's "lethal dose" (LD). LD_{50}, which is calculated using a specific statistical formula, represents the dosage level that kills 50 percent of the test animals. Since 1988, however, the FDA has recommended that classic LD_{50} studies not be conducted (*Federal Register* 53:39650). In recent years, the value of the "classic" LD_{50} has been seriously questioned internationally for ethical and scientific reasons. Today, in accordance with ICH recommendations for single dose toxicity testing, none of the ICH parties requires or recommends that sponsors determine the "classic" LD_{50}.

The LD_{50} has been replaced by single dose administration, increasing dose tolerance studies that measure toxic response as a function of dose. When relevant, major and pharmacologically significant metabolites should be tested in acute toxicity studies. The tests should employ a testing protocol that maximizes the amount of information that can be derived from the smallest number of animals.

In addition to a universal adoption of this approach by the ICH, the FDA has published a revised guideline entitled *Single Dose Acute Toxicity Testing for Pharmaceuticals* (August 1996). This new guidance document indicates that acute toxicity studies, when appropriately designed and conducted, may provide the primary safety data to support single dose pharmacokinetic studies in humans, although nonclinical studies of this nature will require a more comprehensive study design. These toxicity studies should be designed to assess dose-response relationships and pharmacokinetics. Clinical pathology and histopathology should be monitored at an early time and at termination (i.e., ideally, for maximum effect and recovery).

Subacute or Subchronic Studies. Subacute, or subchronic, toxicity testing allows investigators to evaluate a drug's toxic potential and pathologic effects over a longer period. These studies range in length from 14 to 90 days, with the duration generally dependent on the proposed term of clinical use and the duration of proposed clinical trials. According to the ICH's draft guideline on the timing of nonclinical studies, the duration of the animal toxicity studies conducted in two mammalian species (one non-rodent) should, in principle, equal or exceed the duration of the clinical trial.

Subacute studies are designed to assess the progression and regression of drug-induced lesions. However, the studies are generally of insufficient duration to identify all secondary effects that may arise during long-term clinical use or during chronic toxicity and carcinogenicity testing.

Independent studies are performed in at least one rodent and one non-rodent species. Typically, the test compound is administered daily at three or more dosage levels. The highest dose used in these studies should be selected to deliberately induce toxic reactions. The lowest dosage should be selected to identify a no-observed adverse (toxic)-effect level (NOAEL)—that is, the dose demonstrating only intended pharmacological effects. When possible, this dose should represent a multiple of the projected average daily clinical dose. Additionally, each study should employ appropriate control groups (i.e., untreated and/or vehicle, positive, comparative).

During such studies, researchers should collect the following data, as appropriate, for the specific test compound:

- observed effects;

- mortality;

- body weight;

- food/water consumption;

- physical examinations;

- hematology/bone marrow/coagulation;

- blood chemistry/urinalysis;

- organ weights;

- gross pathology; and

- histopathology.

Chronic Toxicity Testing. Chronic toxicity studies, which are tests of 180 days in duration or longer, are designed to determine the following:

- the potential risk in relation to the anticipated dose and period of drug treatment;

- the potential target organs of toxicity;

- the reversibility of any observed toxicities;

- the no-observed adverse (toxic)-effect level; and

- the maximum tolerated dose (MTD)—the dose just high enough to elicit signs of minimal toxicity without significantly altering the animal's normal life span due to effects other than carcinogenicity.

The FDA generally requires that sponsors conduct these studies in one rodent (usually rat) and one non-rodent (usually dog) species for both chronic-use drugs and drugs intended for intermittent use to treat chronic or recurrent diseases. Because there is flexibility in this requirement, sponsors should consult the relevant FDA review division for a product-specific assessment.

In accordance with an ICH consensus, the FDA has reduced its recommended maximum duration of chronic toxicity studies in rodents from 12 to 6 months. However, the agency continues to recommend 12-month studies when rodent carcinogenicity bioassays are not performed as part of the drug toxicity profile.

The recommended duration of non-rodent studies remains 12 months, although the adequacy of shorter-duration toxicity studies in non-rodents is being considered by ICH. At this writing, the ICH participants were evaluating a proposal for 9-month duration non-rodent studies, according to FDA officials. When an FDA reviewing division concludes that data from 12-month studies may not contribute significantly to the risk-benefit analysis or may not be useful to guide the clinical testing, non-rodent studies of 6 months or less may be considered appropriate.

Dose selection criteria are similar to those described for subacute and subchronic studies, and must reflect the results of these shorter-term studies, as well as structure-activity relationships, pharmacology studies, and pharmacokinetic data. Recovery, and sometimes interim sacrifice, subgroups are typically included. As specified above for subacute and subchronic studies, researchers must collect the data listed, as appropriate, for the drug under investigation.

Chronic studies are often initiated when Phase 2 trials provide indications of a drug's effectiveness, and are conducted concurrently with Phase 3 trials. Data obtained from chronic toxicity tests are used to support the safety of long-term drug administration in clinical trials and, ultimately, the approval of the drug for general marketing.

Carcinogenicity Studies. Carcinogenicity testing has been discussed as part of the ICH initiative (i.e., need, dose selection, testing approaches). As stated in ICH proceedings, "…a carcinogenicity study is one of the most resource-consuming in terms of animals and time. In the interests of decreased animal use and protection, but without prejudicing safety, such studies should only be performed once…. This could be achieved through harmonisation of the requirements of different regulatory systems."

In the past, the FDA has generally required carcinogenicity studies for any drug intended for use for 3 months or more, and for drugs intended for intermittent use where the total cumulative lifetime exposure may exceed 3 months. However, in accordance with the adoption of the final ICH guideline entitled *Final Guideline on the Need for Long-Term Rodent Carcinogenicity Studies of Pharmaceuticals* (March 1996), the agency has revised its requirements and now expects carcinogenicity studies for drugs whose use is continuous for 6 months or is intermittent to treat chronic or recurrent diseases. Completed carcinogenicity studies are not usually needed in advance of clinical trials unless there is cause for concern.

Today, the FDA generally requires carcinogenicity studies of 2 years in both the mouse and the rat. Ideally, the route of administration selected for these studies should be the intended clinical route. When there is more than one route or there is a change in the proposed clinical route, the carcinogenicity test route should be that which provides the greatest systemic exposure. Similar to chronic toxicity studies, carcinogenicity investigations are not usually initiated until a drug shows some indication of effectiveness in Phase 2 clinical trials.

Also, in accordance with the final ICH guideline entitled *Dose Selection for Carcinogenicity Studies of Pharmaceuticals* (1994) and the draft addendum entitled *Dose Selection for Carcinogenicity Studies of Pharmaceuticals: Addendum on the Limit Dose* (April 1997), the FDA no longer views dose selection based on the MTD as the only acceptable practice. As stated in this ICH document, the doses selected "should provide an exposure to the agent that (1) allows an adequate margin of safety over the human therapeutic exposure, (2) is tolerated without significant chronic physiological dysfunction and are compatible with good survival, (3) is guided by a comprehensive set of animal and human data that focuses on the properties of the agent and the suitability of the animal, and (4) permits data interpretation in the context of clinical use."

The guidance proposes that any one of several approaches may be appropriate for dose selection in carcinogenicity studies: (1) toxicity-based endpoints; (2) pharmacokinetic endpoints; (3) saturation of absorption; (4) pharmacodynamic endpoints; (5) maximum feasible dose; and (6) additional endpoints. In all cases, appropriate dose-ranging studies are necessary.

Because the approaches for dose selection adopted by ICH offer flexibility and because the factors to be considered in the use of any specific endpoint are complex, it may be prudent for sponsors to ask the agency for an assessment of appropriate dose-selection criteria in individual cases. The threat of additional revisions to recommended study designs, as well as the expense associated with this aspect of nonclinical testing, should also motivate sponsors to obtain specific FDA guidance before initiating carcinogenicity studies. CDER offers consultation on dose selection and study design issues for carcinogenicity studies through the work of the Carcinogenicity Assessment Committee.

A draft consensus text entitled *Testing for Carcinogenicity of Pharmaceuticals* (1996) is now under review by the three ICH regulatory participants. This draft guideline outlines experimental approaches that may obviate the need for the routine conduct of two long-term rodent carcinogenicity studies for those pharmaceuticals that currently require such evaluation. A basic scheme comprising one long-term rodent carcinogenicity study (generally, the rat), plus one additional study for carcinogenic activity *in vivo*, has been proposed. The additional study could be either a short- or medium-term rodent test system or a long-term carcinogenicity study in a second rodent species.

Special Toxicity Studies. Special toxicity studies include those studies appropriate for a particular formulation or route of administration (e.g., parenteral or local tolerance studies, *in vitro* hemolysis), and studies conducted in a particular animal model relevant to a human disease or age. As of this writing, formal FDA guidance pertaining to special toxicity testing is limited to a brief discussion provided in the FDA's *Guideline for the Format and Content of the Nonclinical Pharmacology/Toxicology Section of an Application.* Therefore, sponsors should ask the relevant CDER review division if special toxicity testing is considered applicable. The evaluation of local tolerance should be performed prior to human exposure, although this assessment may be part of other toxicity studies.

Reproductive Toxicity Studies. The FDA requires reproductive testing for any drug to be used in women of childbearing potential, regardless of whether the target population is pregnant women. Generally, these studies have been conducted in a three-segment testing protocol previously recommended by the FDA: (1) Segment I-fertility and general reproductive performance (involving the study of both the male and female rat); (2) Segment II-teratology (conducted in the rat and the rabbit); and (3) Segment III-perinatal and postnatal development (conducted in the rat to evaluate drug effects during the last third of pregnancy and the period of lactation).

In an effort to reduce differences in reproductive toxicity requirements between the EC, Japan, and the United States, the ICH participating parties adopted the final *Guideline on Detection of Toxicity to Reproduction for Medicinal Products* in June 1993. As stated in this guideline, "the aim of reproductive toxicity studies is to reveal any effect of one or more active substances(s) on mammalian reproduction." Therefore, the combination of studies selected should "allow exposure of mature adults and all stages of development from conception to sexual maturity." The integrated sequence of testing has been segregated into the following stages: (A) premating to conception; (B) conception to implantation; (C) implantation to closure of the hard palate; (D) closure of the hard palate to the end of pregnancy; (E) birth to weaning; and (F) weaning to sexual maturity.

The guideline suggests that the "most probable" option for investigating reproductive toxicity is a three-study design:

- Fertility and embryonic development. This study comprises stages A and B, and is conducted in at least one species, preferably the rat. Assessments should include maturation of gametes, mating behavior, fertility, preimplantation stages of the embryo, and implantation. In particular, sponsors should note that, in contrast to the previous Segment I study, this study design uses a histological evaluation of testes, epididymis, and sperm counts to assess drug effects on male fertility.

- Pre- and postnatal development, including maternal development. This phase comprises stages C to F, and is conducted in at least one species, preferably the rat. The study is designed to detect adverse effects on the pregnant/lactating female, and on the development of the conceptus and the offspring following exposure of the female from implantation through weaning. Assessments should include toxicity relative to that in nonpregnant females, pre- and postnatal death of offspring, altered growth and development, and functional deficits (e.g., behavior, maturation, and reproduction) in offspring.

- Embryo-fetal development. This study comprises stages C to D, and is usually conducted in two species: a rodent (preferably the rat) and non-rodent (preferably the rabbit). The goal is to detect adverse effects on the pregnant female and the development of the embryo and the fetus consequent to exposure of the female from implantation to closure of the hard palate. Researchers should assess toxicity relative to that in nonpregnant females, embryo-fetal death, and altered growth, including structural changes.

Subsequent to the acceptance of the above guideline, an *Addendum on Toxicity to Male Fertility* (1996) was adopted. This addendum suggests that the following be taken into account to assess effects on male fertility:

- Provided no precluding effects have been found in repeated dose toxicity studies, a premating treatment interval of four weeks for males and two weeks for females can be used.

- Histopathology of the testis has been shown to be the most sensitive method for the detection of effects on spermatogenesis. Therefore, good pathological and histopathological examination of the male reproductive organs provides a quick and direct means of detection.

- Sperm analysis can be used as a method to confirm findings by other methods and to characterize effects further.

Genotoxicity Studies. Also referred to as "mutagenicity studies," genotoxicity studies (now the preferred term) are used to assess a drug's potential to cause genomic damage that could induce cancer (i.e., somatic cell mutation) and/or heritable defects (i.e., germ cell mutation). These short-term studies include a battery of mammalian and non-mammalian, *in vitro* and *in vivo* tests designed to detect a compound's ability to cause an increase in genetic alterations (e.g., primary DNA damage, chromosomal aberrations). Although genotoxicity tests are not, at present, specifically listed by the FDA as requirements for pharmaceuticals or described in an agency guideline, these screening tests are strongly recommended by the FDA, and are required by both the EC and Japan.

Genotoxicity testing is being addressed as an ICH topic, with *Genotoxicity: Guidance on Specific Aspects of Regulatory Genotoxicity Tests for Pharmaceuticals* having been finalized in early 1996. This ICH guideline, endorsed by FDA, addresses and provides recommendations for the following issues:

- The base set of bacteria strains to be used in bacterial mutation assays;

- Acceptable bone marrow tests for the detection of clastogens *in vivo*;

- Further evaluation of compounds giving positive *in vitro* results;

- Validation of negative *in vivo* tests;

- Definition of the top concentration for *in vitro* tests; and

- Use of male/female rodents in bone marrow micronucleus tests.

Additionally, a companion draft ICH guideline entitled *A Standard Battery for Genotoxicity Testing of Pharmaceuticals* was released for comment in April 1997. This draft guideline proposes a standard set of genotoxicity tests to be conducted for pharmaceutical registration, and recommends the extent of confirmatory experimentation for *in vitro* genotoxicity tests in the standard battery. The standard test battery calls for the completion of the following tests prior to the initiation of Phase 2 studies:

- a test for gene mutation in bacteria;

- an *in vitro* test with cytogenic evaluation of chromosomal damage with mammalian cells or an *in vivo* mouse lymphoma tK assay; and

- an *in vivo* test for chromosomal damage using rodent hematopoietic cells.

Pending harmonization, however, the FDA recommends that sponsors conduct the battery of tests described in the draft revision of the FDA's *Toxicological Principles for the Safety Assessment of Direct Food Additives and Color Additives Used in Food* (Redbook). As of this writing, the genotoxicity tests recommended by the FDA include: (1) gene mutations in bacteria; (2) gene mutation in mammalian cells *in vitro*; and (3) cytogenetic damage *in vivo*. The Ames test is used to evaluate gene mutations in specified strains of

Salmonella typhimurium or *Eschericia coli.* The *in vitro* mammalian cell gene mutation assay should employ a cell line(s) capable of measuring single gene point mutations, frame-shift mutations, and chromosomal mutations. To satisfy these criteria, the FDA recommends the use of the mouse lymphoma mutation assay. Alternatively, data from other *in vitro* mammalian cell tests, which detect both site-specific and chromosome mutations, are acceptable. The *in vivo* cytogenetic assay should provide concurrent detection of micronuclei and chromosome aberrations in mouse bone marrow, although data from either mouse micronucleus or chromosome aberration tests using mouse or rat bone marrow are acceptable.

Toxicokinetic Studies. Toxicokinetics is defined "as the generation of pharmacokinetic data, either as an integral component in the conduct of nonclinical toxicity studies or in specially designed supportive studies, in order to assess systemic exposure. These data may be used in the interpretation of toxicological findings and their relevance to clinical safety issues."

A final ICH guideline entitled *Toxicokinetics: Guidance on the Assessment of Systemic Exposure in Toxicity Studies* (1994) has been adopted by FDA. As stated in this ICH guidance, the primary objective of toxicokinetics is to describe the systemic exposure achieved in animals and its relationship to the dose level and the time course of the toxicity study. Secondary objectives are:

- to relate the exposure achieved in toxicity studies to toxicological findings, and contribute to the assessment of the relevance of these findings to clinical safety;

- to support the choice of species and treatment regimen in nonclinical toxicity studies; and

- to provide information that, in conjunction with the toxicity findings, contributes to the design of subsequent nonclinical toxicity studies.

The objectives may be achieved by the derivation of one or more pharmacokinetic parameters from measurements made at appropriate time points during the course of the individual studies. These measurements usually consist of plasma (or whole blood or serum) concentrations for the parent compound and/or metabolite(s), and should be selected on a case-by-case basis. Plasma (or whole blood or serum) AUC, C_{max}, and $C_{(time)}$ are the most commonly used parameters for assessing exposure in toxicokinetic studies. For some compounds, it may be more appropriate to calculate exposure based on the (plasma protein) unbound concentration. Toxicokinetic studies should be designed to provide information that may be integrated into the full spectrum of nonclinical toxicity testing and then compared to human data.

References

Food and Drug Administration, draft revised *Toxicological principles for the safety assessment of direct food additives and color additives used in food (Redbook)*, 1993.

Food and Drug Administration, *Guideline for the format and content of the nonclinical pharmacology/toxicology section of an application.* U.S. Department of Health and Human Services, Public Health Services, Food and Drug Administration, Washington D.C., 1987.

Food and Drug Administration, *US FDA's proposed implementation of ICH safety working group consensus regarding new drug applications*; Availability. Federal Register, 1992; 57:13105.

Food and Drug Administration, International conference on harmonization; *Draft guideline on the timing of nonclinical studies for the conduct of human clinical trials for pharmaceuticals*; Notice. Federal Register, 1997; 62:24319-24323.

Food and Drug Administration, *Single dose acute toxicity testing for pharmaceuticals; Revised guidance*; Availability. Federal Register, 1996; 61:43933-43935.

Food and Drug Administration, International conference on harmonization; *Guideline on detection of toxicity to reproduction for medicinal products;* Availability. Federal Register, 1994; 59:48746-48752.

Food and Drug Administration, International conference on harmonization; *Guideline on detection of toxicity to reproduction for medicinal products; Addendum on toxicity to male fertility*; Availability. Federal Register, 1996; 61:15359-15361.

Food and Drug Administration, International conference on harmonization; *Final guideline on the need for long-term rodent carcinogenicity studies of pharmaceuticals*; Availability. Federal Register, 1996; 61:8153-8156.

Food and Drug Administration, International conference on harmonization; *Guideline on dose selection for carcinogenicity studies of pharmaceuticals*; Availability. Federal Register, 1995; 60:11278-11281.

Food and Drug Administration, International conference on harmonization; *Draft Guideline on dose selection for carcinogenicity studies of pharmaceuticals: Addendum on the limit dose.* Federal Register, 1997; 62:15715-15716.

Food and Drug Administration, International conference on harmonization; *Draft guideline on testing for carcinogenicity of pharmaceuticals.* Federal Register, 1996;61:43298-43300.

Food and Drug Administration, International conference on harmonization; *Toxicokinetics: guideline on the assessment of systemic exposure in toxicity studies*; Availability. Federal Register, 1995; 60:11264-11268.

Food and Drug Administration, International conference on harmonization; *Pharmacokinetics: guideline on repeated dose tissue distribution studies*; Availability. Federal Register, 1995; 60:11274-11275.

Food and Drug Administration, International conference on harmonization; *Genotoxicity: guidance on specific aspects of regulatory genotoxicity tests for pharmaceuticals*; Availability. Federal Register, 1996;61:18198-18202.

Food and Drug Administration, International conference on harmonization; *Draft guideline on genotoxicity: A standard battery for genotoxicity testing of pharmaceuticals*; Notice. Federal Register, 1997;62:16025-16030.

D'Arcy, PF, Harron, DWG, eds., *Proceedings of the first international conference on harmonisation*, Brussels, 1991. The Queens University of Belfast; 1992.

D'Arcy, PF, Harron, DWG, eds., *Proceedings of the second international conference on harmonisation*, Orlando, 1993. The Queens University of Belfast; 1994.

D'Arcy, PF, Harron, DWG, eds., *Proceedings of the third international conference on harmonisation*, Tokyo, 1995. The Queens University of Belfast; 1996.

Pharmaceutical Manufacturers Association, *Pharmaceutical Manufacturers Association guideline for the assessment of drugs and medical device safety in animals*, 1977; PMA, Washington, D.C.

Pharmaceutical Manufacturers Association, *Reporter's handbook for the prescription drug industry*, 1993.

Roberts SA, *Overview and history of toxicology requirements*. In: Pharmaceutical Manufacturers Association education and research institute pharmaceutical toxicology training course. Washington D.C., Nov. 14-17, 1993.

Roberts SA, *Toxicology study design (range-finding to chronic)*. In: Pharmaceutical Manufacturers Association education and research institute pharmaceutical toxicology training course. Washington D.C., Nov. 14-17, 1993.

Chapter 3

The FDA's Regulation of Nonclinical Testing: Good Laboratory Practice (GLP)

Manufacturers of drugs and other FDA-regulated products are given considerable freedom during the preclinical screening and testing of new products. Provided they comply with the U.S. Animal Welfare Act and other applicable animal welfare laws, nonclinical testing laboratories at pharmaceutical companies and private contractors are not limited in the use of animals to screen and measure the activity of drugs.

When the sponsor begins to compile safety data for submission to the FDA, however, standards called Good Laboratory Practice (GLP) apply. To ensure the quality and integrity of data derived from nonclinical testing, the FDA requires that nonclinical laboratory studies designed to provide safety data for an IND, NDA, or other regulatory submission comply with GLP standards. GLP regulations apply to product sponsor laboratories, private toxicology laboratories, academic and government laboratories, and all other facilities involved in animal testing and related analyses whose results will be submitted to the FDA in support of a product's safety.

GLP regulations establish basic standards for the conduct and reporting of nonclinical safety testing. Specifically, GLP regulations set standards in such areas as the organization, personnel, physical structure, maintenance, and operating procedures of nonclinical testing facilities.

GLP: A Short History

GLP regulations, which became effective on June 20, 1979, were the FDA's response to finding, in the mid-1970s, that some nonclinical studies submitted to support the safety of new drugs were not being conducted according to accepted standards. The FDA considered this a serious problem because data from these studies served as the basis for important regulatory decisions— specifically, whether clinical trials could be initiated or continued, and whether new drugs should be approved.

After establishing the initial GLP regulations in 1979, the FDA's confidence in the work of preclinical laboratory facilities increased markedly. As a result, in October 1987, the agency published revised GLP regulations that sought to reduce regulatory and paperwork burdens facing laboratories conducting animal studies. The FDA's 1987 GLP regulations brought changes in such areas as quality assurance, protocol preparation, test and control article characterization, and specimen and sample retention.

The Applicability of GLP

On one level, GLP applicability is fairly straightforward. According to FDA regulations, GLP applies to facilities conducting "nonclinical laboratory studies that support or are intended to support applications for research or marketing permits for products regulated by the Food and Drug Administration, including food and color additives, animal food additives, human and animal drugs, medical devices for human use, biological products, and electronic products."

What at times seems more difficult is identifying which nonclinical tests are subject to GLP requirements. The FDA states that GLP applies to "nonclinical laboratory studies," which the regulations define as "in vivo or in vitro experiments in which test articles are studied prospectively in test systems under laboratory conditions to determine their safety. The term does not include studies utilizing human subjects or clinical studies or field trials in animals. The term does not include basic exploratory studies carried out to determine whether a test article has any potential utility or to determine physical or chemical characteristics of a test article."

As currently interpreted, GLP applies to all "definitive" nonclinical safety studies, including key acute, subacute, chronic, reproductive, and carcinogenicity studies. Preliminary pharmacological screening and metabolism studies are exempt from GLP requirements, as are initial pilot studies such as dose-ranging, absorption, and excretion tests.

The use of an outside testing laboratory for nonclinical testing does not eliminate the need for GLP compliance. When using the services of a consulting laboratory, contractor, or grantee to perform an analysis or other service, the sponsor must notify the vendor "that the service is part of a nonclinical laboratory study that must be conducted in compliance with [GLP requirements]."

In some cases, sponsors may obtain exemptions from specific GLP provisions for special nonclinical laboratory studies. An FDA *Questions and Answers* document on GLP states that "not all of the GLP provisions apply to all studies and, indeed, for some special studies certain of the GLP provisions may compromise proper science. For this reason, laboratories may petition the agency to exempt certain studies from some of the GLP provisions. The petition should contain sufficient facts to justify granting the exemption."

The Major Provisions of GLP

The core provisions of GLP establish standards for the nonclinical laboratory's organization, physical structure, equipment, and operating procedures. For purposes of analysis, these standards may be grouped into seven general areas:

- organization and personnel;

- testing facility;

- testing facility operation;

- test and control article characterization;

- the protocol and conduct of the nonclinical laboratory study;

- records and reporting; and

- equipment design.

Organization and Personnel GLP regulations regarding a nonclinical laboratory's organization and personnel address four areas: general personnel, testing facility management, study director, and quality assurance unit. Aside from the general qualifications and responsibilities of personnel and management, however, this aspect of GLP focuses primarily on issues regarding the study director and quality assurance unit.

Study Director. GLP requires that the management of the testing facility conducting a nonclinical program designate a scientist or other professional to serve as the study director. This individual has overall responsibility for the "technical conduct of the study, as well as for the interpretation, analysis, documentation, and reporting of results and represents the single point of study control." The FDA does not require that the study director be technically competent in all areas of a study, however.

The study director and others involved in conducting and supervising animal experiments should possess the education, training, and experience necessary to perform their assigned functions. Current training, experience, and job description profiles must be maintained for each of these persons. The documented profiles must be stored by the facility and made available to the FDA if the agency has any questions about personnel qualifications.

Quality Assurance Unit. GLP also requires that each testing facility have a quality assurance unit (QAU) comprised of one or more persons directly responsible to facility management. The QAU monitors each study to "assure management that the facilities, equipment, personnel, methods, practices, records, and controls" are consistent with GLP. To ensure that such evaluations are made objectively, QAU members may not be involved in any animal study that they monitor.

The GLP regulations specify several major QAU responsibilities in the areas of record maintenance, study inspections, and reports to facility management. At the conclusion of a study, the QAU is required to prepare and sign a statement—to be included with the final report—that specifies the dates on which inspections were made and the findings reported to management and the study director.

Current regulations require that the QAU inspect a nonclinical study at intervals the unit considers adequate to ensure the study's integrity. However, the FDA advises that each study, regardless of its length, be inspected in-process at least once, and that, across a series of studies, all phases be inspected to assure study integrity.

In the preamble to the 1987 GLP regulations, the FDA also clarified its views on the composition and function of the QAU in the following ways:

- "FDA never has intended that the QAU necessarily has to be a separate entity or a permanently staffed 'unit'..."

- "FDA continues to believe that well-qualified and trained personnel are essential to quality assurance under the GLP regulations and that one of management's most important responsibilities in maintaining effective quality assurance is to provide an adequate number of such personnel."

- The FDA does not require that the QAU be composed of individuals whose only duties are in quality assurance. The "agency intends only that quality assurance activities be separated from study direction and conduct activities; that is, a trained and qualified person who works on one study can perform quality assurance duties on any study in which he or she is not involved."

Testing Facility Obviously, the laboratory facility in which the testing program takes place is a primary focus of GLP. Animal care and supply facilities, test substance handling areas, laboratory operation, specimen and data storage, administrative and personnel facilities, methods of dosage preparation, and test substance accountability all must meet detailed requirements. Records indicating compliance must be kept.

In general terms, a testing facility and its equipment must be of suitable size and construction to allow for the proper conduct of the nonclinical study. Animal care areas, for example, must provide for sufficient separation of species/test systems and individual projects, isolation of animals, protection from outside disturbances, and routine or specialized animal housing. Regulated environmental controls for air quality—temperature, humidity, and air changes—and sanitation are needed.

Operation of Testing Facility Each laboratory must base its operations on standard operating procedures (SOPs). SOPs, which are in some respects extensions of nonclinical protocols, are written study methods or directions that laboratory management believes are adequate to guarantee the quality and integrity of data obtained from animal tests. The description of research procedures provided by protocols and SOP documents makes possible the verification and reconstruction of studies.

The detailed written procedures specified in the SOPs must be maintained for all aspects of the study, including animal care, laboratory tests, data handling and storage, and equipment maintenance and calibration. Each laboratory area must have accessible laboratory manuals and SOPs relevant to the laboratory procedures being performed. Determining the degree to which SOPs are observed is another QAU responsibility.

Any deviations from established SOPs must be authorized by the study director and noted in the raw data. On the other hand, major changes must be approved by the laboratory's management.

Test and Control Article Characterization Under the 1987 GLP revision, testing facilities are not required to characterize test and control articles before toxicity studies begin. This allows companies to screen out many of the useless compounds before investing resources necessary to characterize them: "FDA has concluded that characterization of test and control articles need not be performed until initial toxicology studies with the test article show reasonable promise of the articles reaching the marketplace. In arriving at this conclusion, the agency considered that prior knowledge of the precise molecular structure is not vital to the conduct of a valid toxicology test. It is important, however, to know the strength, purity, and stability of a test or control article that is used in a nonclinical laboratory study." FDA officials point out that either the sponsor or the testing laboratory may perform the test and control article characterization.

The FDA also revised its stability testing requirements through the 1987 regulations. Previously, stability testing of test and control articles had to be conducted before study initiation or, if this was impossible, through periodic analyses of each batch. The 1987 GLP revisions allow facilities to choose either route.

44

The Protocol and the Conduct of Nonclinical Laboratory Studies

A protocol, or testing plan, is a vital element in both clinical and nonclinical studies. GLP states that a nonclinical program must have a written protocol that "clearly indicates the objectives and all methods for the conduct of the study."

Included in the 12-item protocol, which the sponsor must approve, should be descriptions of the experimental design and the purpose of the study as well as the type and frequency of tests, analyses, and measurements to be made. Changes made to the protocol during the course of the study must be documented by an official protocol amendment signed by the study director. The study director's approval of protocol amendments assures the FDA of the data's integrity.

Although protocols and SOPs may seem similar, the two have different purposes. The protocol is specific to the study being conducted, while laboratory SOPs are standards used for all research projects at a given facility. For example, SOPs would provide "how to" instructions on a facility's routine procedures for obtaining animal blood samples, caring for animals, and using and maintaining equipment.

In contrast, the protocol provides study-specific instructions. For a particular study, a protocol would detail how often and from what animals blood samples are to be taken, what tests are to be conducted, and the number, species, sex, age, and weight of the animals to be tested. These factors would probably differ for each nonclinical study, while the facility's SOPs would remain the same. In general terms, the protocol identifies what tests are necessary, while SOPs instruct a facility's employees how these tests should be performed.

The 1987 GLP regulations allow facilities to use "umbrella protocols." By revising the definition of "nonclinical laboratory study," the FDA permits the conduct of multiple studies using the same test article under one comprehensive protocol. According to the preamble of the 1987 GLP final rule, "under the revised definition...a single 'umbrella protocol' may be used for concurrent testing of more than one test article using a single, common procedure, e.g., mutagenicity testing, or for a battery of studies of one test article conducted in several test systems." Regarding the advantages, the regulation adds that the "agency recognizes that a longer, more complex protocol might be more difficult to manage than a simpler one; however, using an 'umbrella' protocol should be more efficient than using several closely related protocols."

Records and Reporting A final report must be prepared for each non-clinical laboratory study. Comprehensive reports typically include the summary, testing methods, results, and conclusions of a study, as well as all raw data on each of the test animals.

These final reports, as well as all raw data, documentation, protocols, and certain specimens generated during the nonclinical study, must be stored in an archive or repository to assure their safety and integrity for specific periods as designated in GLP regulations. Although these regulations state that two to five years is adequate, the FDA sometimes recommends that records be stored indefinitely and that specimens—slides, tissues, and blocks—be stored as long as they can be used to validate data.

Nonclinical testing laboratories are not required to retain wet and mutagenicity test specimens. According to current GLP requirements, "all raw data, documentation, protocols, final reports, and specimens (except those specimens obtained from mutagenicity tests and wet specimens of blood, urine, feces, and biological fluids) generated as a result of a nonclinical laboratory study shall be retained."

Equipment Design GLP regulations specify requirements for the design, maintenance, and calibration of equipment used in nonclinical tests. Equipment used for facility environmental control and automatic, mechanical, or electronic equipment used in the generation, measurement or assessment of data must be: (1) of appropriate design and adequate capacity to function according to the protocol; (2) suitably located for operation, inspection, cleaning, and maintenance; and (3) adequately tested, calibrated, and/or standardized.

SOPs are required to define, in sufficient detail, the methods, materials, and schedules to be used in the routine inspection, cleaning, maintenance, testing, calibration, and standardization of equipment. The facility must maintain written records of routine and certain nonroutine procedures involving laboratory equipment.

CDER's GLP Inspections

To monitor compliance with GLP requirements, CDER employs a program of on-site laboratory inspections and data audits. According to the FDA's Compliance Policy Guide (CPG) 7348.808, the FDA conducts two basic types of GLP compliance inspections: surveillance (or routine) inspections and directed inspections.

Representing the majority of GLP inspections, on-site surveillance inspections are periodic, routine evaluations of a laboratory's GLP compliance. Typically, these evaluations are based on either active or recently completed studies. Routine inspections for monitoring a nonclinical laboratory's GLP compliance are scheduled "approximately every two years."

In the past, CDER would preannounce routine GLP inspections approximately one week in advance. However, the agency has changed this policy and no longer preannounces any GLP inspections. CDER does make exceptions to this policy, in which case FDA inspectors may be instructed to notify the subject facility no more than about a week in advance of the inspection. In some circumstances, CDER will agree to a short postponement of the inspection.

According to CPG 7348.808, the FDA might assign a directed inspection for any of the following reasons:

- as a follow-up to the disclosure, during a routine surveillance inspection, that a facility is violating GLP regulations or that there exist significant discrepancies between a study's final reports and original data and records;

- as a follow-up to the discovery of questionable data or materials that raise suspicions during a review of a study report submitted in support of an IND or NDA;

- in response to the need to audit the data of an important or critical study submitted in support of an IND or NDA;

- in response to the need to verify a sponsor or third party's audit of a study's data and records; or

- in response to the need to review or inspect entities or studies brought to the FDA's attention by other sources (i.e., news media or other operating firms/labs).

Directed inspections are conducted when necessary. Typically, these are unannounced inspections.

The Disqualification of Nonclinical Studies

If FDA inspectors find GLP violations within a facility, agency officials review the violations and decide on a course of action. In cases involving severe compliance problems, the FDA may disqualify data from an entire nonclinical study. According to federal regulations, the purposes of the agency's right to disqualify data are: "(1) To permit the exclusion from consideration completed studies that were conducted by a testing facility which has failed to comply with the requirements of the good laboratory practice regulations until it can be adequately demonstrated that such noncompliance did not occur during, or did not affect the validity or acceptability of data generated by, a particular study; and (2) to exclude from consideration all studies completed after the date of disqualification until the facility can satisfy the Commissioner that it will conduct studies in compliance with such regulations."

Analysis of Significant GLP Violations, FY 1996			
Type of Violation	Sponsor Labs	Contract Labs	Total
Personnel/Management/ Study Director	0	3	3 (14%)
Quality Assurance Unit and Operations	0	1	1 (5%)
Animal/Testing Facilities	0	0	0 (0%)
Equipment Maintenance/Calibration	1	5	6 (29%)
Standard Operating Procedures	1	4	5 (24%)
Animal Care	1	0	1 (5%)
Test and Control Articles	0	2	2 (10%)
Protocol and Conduct	0	1	1 (5%)
Final Report	0	1	1 (5%)
Records	0	1	1 (5%)

Note: Analysis includes inspections of 11 sponsor and 10 contract laboratories

Source: CDER Office of Compliance

As implied by the second provision above, the FDA also can disqualify nonclinical laboratories. For the FDA to do this, three conditions must be met. Specifically, the agency must find that: "(a) The testing facility failed to comply with one or more of the regulations; (b) The noncompliance adversely affected the validity of the nonclinical laboratory studies; and (c) Other lesser regulatory actions (e.g., warnings or rejection of individual studies) have not been or will probably not be adequate to achieve compliance with the good laboratory practice regulations."

Chapter 4

The IND

The investigational new drug application, or IND, is a submission through which a drug sponsor alerts the FDA of its intention to conduct clinical studies with an investigational drug. The IND is a descriptive notification that the sponsor must submit to the FDA, and that the agency has a brief time to review, prior to the initiation of clinical trials.

In legal terms, the IND is a request for an exemption from the federal statute that prohibits an unapproved drug from being shipped in interstate commerce. Current federal law requires that a drug be the subject of an approved new drug application before the product is transported or distributed across state lines. Because a sponsor will probably want to ship the investigational drug to clinical sites in other states, it must seek an exemption from this legal requirement.

In many respects, the IND is a product of a successful preclinical development program. During a new drug's early preclinical development, the sponsor's primary goal is to determine if the compound exhibits pharmacological activity that justifies commercial development and if the product is reasonably safe for initial use in humans. When a product is identified as a viable candidate for further development, the sponsor then focuses on collecting the data and information necessary to establish, in the IND, that the product will not expose human subjects to unreasonable risks when used in limited, early-stage clinical studies. Generally, this includes data and information in three broad areas:

Animal Pharmacology and Toxicology Studies. Preclinical data to permit an assessment as to whether the product is reasonably safe for initial testing in humans.

Manufacturing Information. Information pertaining to the composition, manufacture, and stability of, and the controls used for, the drug substance and the drug product to permit an assessment of the company's ability to adequately produce and supply consistent batches of the drug. Further, information on the compound's structure is used to assess whether the compound is similar to drugs known to be toxic.

Clinical Protocols and Investigator Information. Detailed protocols for proposed clinical studies to permit an assessment as to whether the initial-phase trials will expose subjects to unnecessary risks. Also, information on the qualifications of clinical investigators—professionals (generally physicians) who oversee the administration of the experimental compound—to permit an assessment as to whether they are qualified to fulfill their clinical trial duties.

Federal regulations are clear regarding the purpose of the IND and the role of the FDA in the application's review. As stated in 21 CFR 312.22, "FDA's primary objectives in reviewing an IND are, in all phases of the investigation, to assure the safety and rights of subjects, and, in Phase 2 and 3, to help assure that the quality of scientific evaluation of drugs is adequate to permit an evaluation of the drug's effectiveness and safety."

Unlike NDAs, INDs are never approved by the FDA. Rather, sponsors are permitted to initiate the clinical trials proposed in an IND 30 days after the FDA receives the application, provided that the agency does not contact the applicant during this 30-day period to alert the company otherwise (see Chapter 5).

Types of INDs

This chapter focuses on submissions that are sometimes called "commercial INDs," which are applications filed principally by companies whose ultimate goal is to obtain marketing approval for new products. There are, however, at least a few types of applications that may be grouped within a second class of filings sometimes referred to as "noncommercial" INDs. Interestingly, the vast majority of INDs are for noncommercial research submissions. These include the following types of INDs:

Investigator IND (also called research IND). The investigator IND is submitted by a physician who both initiates and conducts an investigation, and under whose immediate direction the investigational drug is administered or dispensed. In most cases, an investigator IND proposes clinical studies on previously studied drugs. A physician might submit a research IND to propose studying an unapproved drug, or an approved product for a new indication or in a new patient population. Generally, however, the physician's motivation is not commercial in nature—in other words, the goal is not to develop data to support marketing approval for an unapproved product or to support new labeling for an approved product. For example, the investigator may simply want to treat patients or obtain data to publish a research paper.

Emergency Use IND. The emergency use IND is a vehicle through which the FDA can authorize the immediate shipment of an experimental drug for a desperate medical situation. According to FDA regulations, "need for an investigational drug may arise in an emergency situation that does not allow time for submission of an IND.... In such a case, FDA may authorize shipment of the drug for a specified use in advance of submission of an IND." Emergency use INDs are generally reserved for life-threatening situations in which no standard acceptable treatment is available, and in which there is not sufficient time to obtain institutional review board (IRB) approval.

Treatment IND. Although the treatment IND has a history dating back to the 1960s and 1970s, the FDA took steps to formalize the treatment IND concept in a 1987 regulation. Through the FDA's treatment IND program, experimental drugs showing promise in clinical testing for serious or life-threatening conditions are made widely available while the final clinical work is performed and the FDA review takes place (for more on treatment INDs, see Chapter 16).

The Applicability of the IND

The IND is a requirement for all persons and firms seeking to ship unapproved drugs over state lines for use in clinical investigations. However, the FDA offers exemptions from IND submission requirements for certain types of clinical testing and products, including the following:

- Clinical investigations of a drug product that is lawfully marketed in the United States, provided that all of the following conditions apply: (1) the investigation is not intended to be reported to the FDA as a well-controlled study in support of a new indication for use, or is not intended to be used to support any other significant change in the drug's labeling; (2) the investigation is not intended to support a significant change in the advertising for a prescription drug; (3) the investigation does not involve a change in the route of administration, dosage level, patient population, or other factor that significantly increases the risks (or decreases the acceptability of the risks) associated with the use of the drug product; (4) the investigation complies with institutional review board (IRB) evaluation and informed consent requirements; and (5) the study's sponsor and investigator do not represent in a promotional context that the drug is safe or effective for the purposes for which it is under investigation, or unduly prolong the study after finding that the results are sufficient to support a marketing application. The FDA has stated that this exemption is intended primarily for practicing physicians.

- Drugs intended solely for testing *in vitro* or in laboratory research animals, provided the drug labels and shipments comply with FDA regulations applicable to investigational drugs.

- Clinical investigations involving the use of a placebo, provided that the investigations do not involve the use of a new drug or otherwise trigger IND submission requirements.

- Certain *in vivo* bioavailability and bioequivalence studies in humans. FDA regulations state, however, that INDs are required for *in vivo* bioavailability or bioequivalence studies in humans if the test product is a radioactively labeled drug product, is a cytotoxic drug product, or contains a new chemical entity. Further, INDs are required for the following types of human bioavailability studies that involve a previously approved drug that is not a new chemical entity: (1) a single-dose study in normal subjects or patients when either the maximum single or total daily dose exceeds that specified in the labeling of the approved product; (2) a multiple-dose study in normal subjects or patients when either the single or total daily dose exceeds that specified in the labeling of the approved product; or (3) a multiple-dose study on a controlled-release product for which no single-dose study has been completed.

In addition to these IND exemptions, FDA regulations provide a mechanism through which individuals and firms can seek an agency waiver from IND requirements. The agency can grant a waiver if certain criteria are met, including that the sponsor's noncompliance will not pose a significant or unreasonable risk to human subjects.

IND Content and Format Requirements

Until the late 1980s, the FDA had less-than-exacting content and format requirements for INDs. A 1987 revision to federal regulations changed this, however, as the FDA sought better organized and more standardized INDs to help expedite reviews.

The latest significant change to IND content requirements came in November 1995, when the FDA clarified its IND data and data presentation requirements in a guidance entitled *Content and Format of Investigational New Drug Applications (IND) for Phase 1 Studies of Drugs, Including Well-Characterized, Therapeutic, Biotechnology-Derived Products.* Although the FDA characterized the guidance as a "clarification," it really represented a shift in policy, particularly in establishing that the agency would accept toxicology data summaries and line listings based upon sponsors' unaudited draft toxicologic reports of completed animal studies. If industry followed the reduced data requirements outlined in the November 1995 guidance, the FDA claimed that "IND submissions for Phase 1 studies should usually not be larger than two to three, three inch, 3-ring binders."

According to the current IND application form (Form FDA 1571), an IND will consist of as many as 10 principal sections:

1. Cover Sheet (Form FDA 1571).

2. Table of Contents.

3. Introductory Statement.

4. General Investigational Plan.

5. Investigator's Brochure (IB).

6. Clinical Protocols.

7. Chemistry, Manufacturing, and Control Data.

8. Pharmacology and Toxicology Data.

9. Previous Human Experience (if applicable).

10. Additional Information (if applicable).

The nature of the drug and the available product-related information affect the number of sections included in an IND submission. These and other factors also determine the quantity of information to be included in the application. "Sponsors are expected to exercise considerable discretion...regarding the content of information submitted in each section [of the IND], depending upon the kind of drug being studied and the nature of the available information," FDA regulations state. "The amount of information on a particular drug that must be submitted in an IND...depends upon such factors as the novelty of the drug, the extent to which it has been studied previously, the known or suspected risks, and the developmental phase of the drug."

The following sections discuss the content requirements for each component of the IND. Although not included in the listing of IND content requirements above, many INDs include a cover letter that briefly summarizes the purpose and content of the submission. By providing a general introduction to the submission and identifying any previously reached sponsor/FDA agreements, cover letters are often extremely useful to drug reviewers.

Cover Sheet (Form FDA 1571) Form FDA 1571, the first required element of an IND, serves as the cover sheet for the entire IND submission (see sample form below). By completing and signing, or having an authorized representative complete and sign, this form, the sponsor: (1) identifies itself, the investigational drug, the persons responsible for monitoring the clinical trial and safety-related trial information, and the phase(s) of investigation covered by the application; (2) establishes the nature of the submission (i.e., initial

DEPARTMENT OF **HEALTH AND HUMAN SERVICES** PUBLIC HEALTH SERVICE FOOD AND DRUG ADMINISTRATION **INVESTIGATIONAL NEW DRUG APPLICATION (IND)** **(TITLE 21, CODE OF FEDERAL REGULATIONS (CFR) PART 312)**	Form Approved: OMB No. 0910-0014. Expiration Date: December 31, 1999 See OMB Statement on Reverse. NOTE: No drug may be shipped or clinical investigation begun until an IND for that investigation is in effect (21 CFR 312.40).
1. NAME OF SPONSOR	2. DATE OF SUBMISSION
3. ADDRESS *(Number, Street, City, State and Zip Code)*	4. TELEPHONE NUMBER *(Include Area Code)*
5. NAME(S) OF DRUG *(Include all available names: Trade, Generic, Chemical, Code)*	6. IND NUMBER *(If previously assigned)*

7. INDICATION(S) *(Covered by this submission)*

8. PHASE(S) OF CLINICAL INVESTIGATION TO BE CONDUCTED. ☐ PHASE 1 ☐ PHASE 2 ☐ PHASE 3 ☐ OTHER _____
                                                                                            (Specify)

9. LIST NUMBERS OF ALL INVESTIGATIONAL NEW DRUG APPLICATIONS *(21 CFR Part 312)*, NEW DRUG OR ANTIBIOTIC APPLICATIONS *(21 CFR Part 314)*, DRUG MASTER FILES *(21 CFR 314.420)*, AND PRODUCT LICENSE APPLICATIONS *(21 CFR Part 601)* REFERRED TO IN THIS APPLICATION.

10. IND submissions should be consecutively numbered. The initial IND should be numbered *"Serial Number: 000."* The next submission (e.g., amendment, report, or correspondence) should be numbered *"Serial Number: 001."* Subsequent submissions should be numbered consecutively in the order in which they are submitted.	SERIAL NUMBER:

11. THIS SUBMISSION CONTAINS THE FOLLOWING: (Check all that apply)

    ☐ INITIAL INVESTIGATIONAL NEW DRUG APPLICATION (IND)   ☐ RESPONSE TO CLINICAL HOLD

PROTOCOL AMENDMENT(S):	INFORMATION AMENDMENT(S):	IND SAFETY REPORT(S):
☐ NEW PROTOCOL	☐ CHEMISTRY/MICROBIOLOGY	☐ INITIAL WRITTEN REPORT
☐ CHANGE IN PROTOCOL	☐ PHARMACOLOGY/TOXICOLOGY	☐ FOLLOW-UP TO A WRITTEN REPORT
☐ NEW INVESTIGATOR	☐ CLINICAL	

☐ RESPONSE TO FDA REQUEST FOR INFORMATION   ☐ ANNUAL REPORT   ☐ GENERAL CORRESPONDENCE

☐ REQUEST FOR REINSTATEMENT OF IND THAT IS WITHDRAWN,   ☐ OTHER _____
INACTIVATED, TERMINATED OR DISCONTINUED   *(Specify)*

CHECK ONLY IF APPLICABLE

JUSTIFICATION STATEMENT MUST BE SUBMITTED WITH APPLICATION FOR ANY CHECKED BELOW. REFER TO THE CITED CFR SECTION FOR FURTHER INFORMATION.

☐ **TREATMENT IND 21 CFR 312.35(b)**   ☐ **TREATMENT PROTOCOL 21 CFR 312.35(a)**   ☐ **CHARGE REQUEST/NOTIFICATION 21 CFR 312.7(d)**

FOR FDA USE ONLY

CDR/DBIND/OGD RECEIPT STAMP	DDR RECEIPT STAMP	DIVISION ASSIGNMENT:
		IND NUMBER ASSIGNED:

FORM FDA 1571 (1/97)   PREVIOUS EDITION IS OBSOLETE

12.

CONTENTS OF APPLICATION

This application contains the following items: *(check all that apply)*

☐ 1. Form FDA 1571 [21 CFR 312.23 (a) (1)]

☐ 2. Table of contents [21 CFR 312.23 (a) (2)]

☐ 3. Introductory statement [21 CFR 312.23 (a) (3)]

☐ 4. General investigational plan [21 CFR 312.23 (a) (3)]

☐ 5. Investigator's brochure [21 CFR 312.23 (a) (5)]

☐ 6. Protocol(s) [21 CFR 312.23 (a) (6)]

    ☐ a. Study protocol(s) [21 CFR 312.23 (a) (6)]

    ☐ b. Investigator data [21 CFR 312.23 (a) (6)(iii)(b)] or completed Form(s) FDA 1572

    ☐ c. Facilities data [21 CFR 312.23 (a) (6)(iii)(b)] or completed Form(s) FDA 1572

    ☐ d. Institutional Review Board data [21 CFR 312.23 (a) (6)(iii)(b)] or completed Form(s) FDA 1572

☐ 7. Chemistry, manufacturing, and control data [21 CFR 312.23 (a) (7)]

    ☐ Environmental assessment or claim for exclusion [21 CFR 312.23 (a) (7)(iv)(e)]

☐ 8. Pharmacology and toxicology data [21 CFR 312.23 (a) (8)]

☐ 9. Previous human experience [21 CFR 312.23 (a) (9)]

☐ 10. Additional information [21 CFR 312.23 (a) (10)]

13. IS ANY PART OF THE CLINICAL STUDY TO BE CONDUCTED BY A CONTRACT RESEARCH ORGANIZATION? ☐ YES ☐ NO

IF YES, WILL ANY SPONSOR OBLIGATIONS BE TRANSFERRED TO THE CONTRACT RESEARCH ORGANIZATION? ☐ YES ☐ NO

IF YES, ATTACH A STATEMENT CONTAINING THE NAME AND ADDRESS OF THE CONTRACT RESEARCH ORGANIZATION, IDENTIFICATION OF THE CLINICAL STUDY, AND A LISTING OF THE OBLIGATIONS TRANSFERRED.

14. NAME AND TITLE OF THE PERSON RESPONSIBLE FOR MONITORING THE CONDUCT AND PROGRESS OF THE CLINICAL INVESTIGATIONS

15. NAME(S) AND TITLE(S) OF THE PERSON(S) RESPONSIBLE FOR REVIEW AND EVALUATION OF INFORMATION RELEVANT TO THE SAFETY OF THE DRUG

I agree not to begin clinical investigations until 30 days after FDA's receipt of the IND unless I receive earlier notification by FDA that the studies may begin. I also agree not to begin or continue clinical investigations covered by the IND if those studies are placed on clinical hold. I agree that an Institutional Review Board (IRB) that complies with the requirements set forth in 21 CFR Part 56 will be responsible for initial and continuing review and approval of each of the studies in the proposed clinical investigation. I agree to conduct the investigation in accordance with all other applicable regulatory requirements.

16. NAME OF SPONSOR OR SPONSOR'S AUTHORIZED REPRESENTATIVE	17. SIGNATURE OF SPONSOR OR SPONSOR'S AUTHORIZED REPRESENTATIVE	
18. ADDRESS (Number, Street, City, State and Zip Code)	19. TELEPHONE NUMBER *(Include Area Code)*	20. DATE

(WARNING:A willfully false statement is a criminal offense, U.S.C. Title 18, Sec. 1001.)

Public reporting burden for this collection of information is estimated to average 100 hours per response, including the time for reviewing instructions, searching existing data sources, gathering and maintaining the data needed, and completing and reviewing the collection of information. Send comments regarding this burden estimate or any other aspect of this collection of information, including suggestions for reducing this burden to:

Reports Clearance Officer, PHS
Hubert H. Humphrey Building, Room 721-B
200 Independence Avenue, S.W.
Washington, DC 20201
Attn: PRA

"An agency may not conduct or sponsor, and a person is not required to respond to a collection of information unless it displays a currently valid OMB control number."

Please DO NOT RETURN this application to this address.

FORM FDA 1571 (1/97)

submission, amendment, etc.); (3) identifies any responsibilities that have been transferred to a contract research organization (CRO); and (4) agrees to comply with applicable regulations, including those requiring the sponsor to refrain from initiating clinical studies until an IND covering the investigations is in effect. A completed copy of Form FDA 1571 is also required with each amendment submitted to the IND.

If the person signing the IND form does not reside or maintain a place of business within the United States, "the IND is required to contain the name and address of, and be countersigned by, an attorney, agent, or other authorized official who resides or maintains a place of business within the United States."

Item 12 of Form 1571 is important because it identifies the various elements that must be addressed in an original IND submission. These elements are discussed below.

Table of Contents FDA regulations offer no guidance on the IND's table of contents. However, the agency does state that sponsors should follow the specified IND format "in the interest of fostering an efficient review of the application." Obviously, the table of contents should be sufficiently detailed to permit FDA reviewers to locate important elements of the application quickly and easily. The table of contents should provide the location of items by volume and page number.

Introductory Statement The IND's introductory statement should provide a description of the drug, the goals of the proposed clinical investigations, and a summary of the previous human experience with the drug. According to FDA regulations, this section should provide "a brief introductory statement giving the name of the drug and all active ingredients, the drug's pharmacological class, the structural formula of the drug (if known), the formulation of the dosage form(s) to be used, the route of administration, and the broad objectives and planned duration of the proposed clinical investigation(s)." The sponsor must also summarize all previous clinical experience with the drug (with reference to other INDs, if applicable), including "investigational or marketing experience in other countries that may be relevant to the safety of the proposed clinical investigation(s)." If a foreign regulatory authority discontinued the drug's testing or marketing for any reason related to safety or effectiveness, the sponsor must identify the country(ies) in which the withdrawal took place and must describe the reason for the withdrawal.

General Investigational Plan   The general investigational plan must provide a brief description of the clinical studies planned for the experimental drug. At a minimum, studies planned for the first year should be described. The FDA has stated that the goal of this section is to provide agency reviewers a brief overview of the scale and kind of clinical studies to be conducted during the following year. This general overview should be no more than two to three pages in length and should provide the necessary context for FDA reviewers to assess the sufficiency of technical information to support future studies and to provide advice and assistance to the sponsor.

According to federal regulations, the "plan should include the following: (a) the rationale for the drug or the research study; (b) the indication(s) to be studied; (c) the general approach to be followed in evaluating the drug; (d) the kinds of clinical trials to be conducted in the first year following the submission (if plans are not developed for the entire year, the sponsor should so indicate); (e) the estimated number of patients to be given the drug in those studies; and (f) any risks of particular severity or seriousness anticipated on the basis of the toxicological data in animals or prior studies in humans with the drug or related drugs."

The FDA does not require rigid adherence to the general investigational plan. Provided that it fulfills protocol and information amendment reporting requirements (see discussion below), a sponsor is free to deviate from the plan when necessary.

Investigator's Brochure   With the exception of investigator-sponsored applications, all INDs must include a copy of the investigator's brochure (IB)—an information package providing each participating clinical investigator with available information on the drug, including its known and possible risks and benefits. The most recent discussion of the purpose of, and content requirements applicable to, an IB appear in an addendum to the ICH's May 1997 final guideline entitled *Good Clinical Practice: Consolidated Guideline.*

"The Investigator's Brochure (IB) is a compilation of the clinical and non-clinical data on the investigational product(s) that are relevant to the study of the product(s) in human subjects," the guidance states. "Its purpose is to provide the investigators and others involved in the trial with the information to facilitate their understanding of the rationale for, and their compliance with, many key features of the protocol, such as the dose, dose frequency/interval, methods of administration, and safety monitoring procedures. The IB also provides insight to support the clinical management of the study subjects during the course of the clinical trial. The information should be presented in a concise, simple, objective, balanced, and nonpromotional form that enables a clinician, or potential investigator, to understand it and make his/her own unbiased risk-benefit assessment of the appropriateness of the proposed trial. For this reason, a medically qualified person should generally participate in the editing of an IB, but the contents of the IB should be approved by the disciplines that generated the described data."

While not as detailed as the ICH guideline's description of investigator's brochure content requirements, FDA regulations call for IBs to include the following elements:

- a brief description of the drug substance and formulation, including the structural formula (if known);

- a summary of the pharmacological and toxicological effects of the drug in animals and, to the extent known, in humans;

- a summary of the pharmacokinetics and biological disposition of the drug in animals and, if known, in humans;

- a summary of information relating to the drug's safety and effectiveness in humans obtained from prior clinical studies (reprints of published articles on such studies may be appended when useful); and

- a description of possible risks and side effects anticipated on the basis of prior experience with the drug under investigation or with related drugs, and precautions to be taken or special monitoring to be performed as part of the drug's investigational use.

The ICH's May 1997 consolidated GCP guideline offers the following example of an IB format:

Title Page
Confidentiality Statement* (optional)
Signature Page (optional)

1. Table of Contents

2. Summary

3. Introduction

4. Physical, Chemical, and Pharmaceutical Properties and Formulation

5. Nonclinical Studies

    5.1 Nonclinical Pharmacology

    5.2 Pharmacokinetics and Product Metabolism in Animals

    5.3 Toxicology

6. Effects in Humans

    6.1 Pharmacokinetics and Product Metabolism in Humans

    6.2 Safety and Efficacy

    6.3 Marketing Experience

7. Summary of Data and Guidance for the Investigator

NB: References (at the end of each section) on

    1. Publications

    2. Reports

Appendices (if any)

* a statement instructing the investigator/recipients to treat the IB as a confidential document.

As clinical trials advance, the sponsor must inform investigators "of new observations discovered by or reported to the sponsor of the drug, particularly with respect to adverse effects and safe use." Such information may be distributed to investigators by means of periodically revised IBs, reprints of published studies, reports or letters to clinical investigators, or other appropriate means. Copies of these communications should also be submitted to the IND file. According to the ICH's May 1997 consolidated GCP guideline, the IB should be reviewed at least annually and revised as necessary in compliance with a sponsor's written procedures.

Clinical Protocols FDA regulations state that, along with the general investigational plan, clinical protocols are "the central focus of the initial IND submission." Protocols are descriptions of clinical studies that identify, among other things, a study's objectives, design, and procedures. The FDA reviews clinical protocols to ensure: (1) that subjects will not be exposed to unnecessary risks in any of the clinical trials; and (2) that Phase 2 and Phase 3 clinical study designs are adequate to provide the types and amount of information necessary to show that the drug is safe and/or effective.

In the initial IND submission, the sponsor must provide only protocols for the proposed study or studies that will begin immediately after the IND goes into effect—that is, after the FDA's 30-day review period. Although initial INDs generally include just Phase 1 protocols, some may propose Phase 2 or 3 protocols, particularly if a drug has been studied in clinical trials previously (e.g., in foreign clinical studies).

As stated, the safety of initial Phase 1 studies is the FDA's principal concern in reviewing the original IND submission. Since late-phase clinical studies often are not fully developed until data from Phase 1 studies are obtained, Phase 2 and Phase 3 protocols may be submitted later in the development process.

In its November 1995 IND guidance document, the FDA highlights the regulations' more flexible approach to Phase 1 protocols. "Sponsors are reminded that the regulations were changed in 1987 specifically to allow Phase 1 study protocols to be less detailed and more flexible than protocols for Phase 2 and 3 studies. This change recognized that these protocols are part of an early learning process and should be adaptable as information is obtained, and that the principal concern at this stage of development is that the study be conducted safely. The regulations state that Phase 1 protocols should be directed primarily at providing **an outline** of the investigation: an estimate of the number of subjects to be included; a description of safety exclusions, and a description of the dosing plan, including duration, dose, or method to be used in determining dose. In addition, such protocols should specify in detail **only** those elements of the study that are critical to subject safety, such as: 1) necessary monitoring of vital signs and blood chemistries and 2) toxicity-based stopping or dose adjustment rules. In addition, the regulations state that modifications of the experimental design of Phase 1 studies that do not affect critical safety assessments are required to be reported to FDA **only** in the annual report."

In contrast, the FDA requires that Phase 2 and 3 protocols include detailed descriptions of all aspects of the studies. Federal regulations state that these protocols "should be designed in such a way that, if the sponsor anticipates that some deviation from the study design may become necessary as the investigation progresses, alternatives or contingencies to provide for such deviations are built into the protocols at the outset. For example, a protocol for a controlled short-term study might include a plan for an early crossover of nonresponders to an alternative therapy." About such contingency plans, which are optional, the FDA has commented that it "strongly encourages the submission of such plans as it believes there is much to be gained in thinking about the planning for possible alternative courses of action early in the protocol development process. Providing in the initial protocol for possible departures from the study design enhances the value or reviewability of study results. Such advance planning also permits both FDA and the sponsor to raise useful questions about study design and supporting information at the earliest possible time."

Although the components and level of detail found in a protocol will depend upon the phase covered and other factors, FDA regulations state that a protocol should include seven elements:

1. A statement of the objectives and purpose of the study.

2. The name and address of, and a statement of qualifications (curriculum vitae or other statement of qualifications) for, each investigator; the name of each subinvestigator (i.e., research fellow, resident) working under the supervision of the investigator; the names and addresses of the research facilities to be used; and the name and address of each institutional review board (IRB) responsible for reviewing the protocols (this information may be submitted on Form FDA 1572; see sample below).

DEPARTMENT OF HEALTH AND HUMAN SERVICES PUBLIC HEALTH SERVICE FOOD AND DRUG ADMINISTRATION **STATEMENT OF INVESTIGATOR** **(TITLE 21, CODE OF FEDERAL REGULATIONS (CFR) PART 312)** *(See instructions on reverse side.)*	Form Approved: OMB No. 0910-0014 Expiration Date: December 31, 1999 See OMB Statement on Reverse. NOTE: No investigator may participate in an investigation until he/she provides the sponsor with a completed, signed Statement of Investigator, Form FDA 1572 (21CFR 312.53(c)).

1. NAME AND ADDRESS OF INVESTIGATOR

2. EDUCATION, TRAINING, AND EXPERIENCE THAT QUALIFIES THE INVESTIGATOR AS AN EXPERT IN THE CLINICAL INVESTIGATION OF THE DRUG FOR THE USE UNDER INVESTIGATION. ONE OF THE FOLLOWING IS ATTACHED:

☐ CURRICULUM VITAE   ☐ OTHER STATEMENT OF QUALIFICATIONS

3. NAME AND ADDRESS OF ANY MEDICAL SCHOOL, HOSPITAL, OR OTHER RESEARCH FACILITY WHERE THE CLINICAL INVESTIGATION(S) WILL BE CONDUCTED.

4. NAME AND ADDRESS OF ANY CLINICAL LABORATORY FACILITIES TO BE USED IN THE STUDY.

5. NAME AND ADDRESS OF THE INSTITUTIONAL REVIEW BOARD (IRB) THAT IS RESPONSIBLE FOR REVIEW AND APPROVAL OF THE STUDY(IES).

6. NAMES OF THE SUBINVESTIGATORS (e.g., research fellows, residents, associates) WHO WILL BE ASSISTING THE INVESTIGATOR IN THE CONDUCT OF THE INVESTIGATION(S).

7. NAME AND CODE NUMBER, IF ANY, OF THE PROTOCOL(S) IN THE IND FOR THE STUDY(IES) TO BE CONDUCTED BY THE INVESTIGATOR.

FORM FDA 1572 (1/97)   PREVIOUS EDITION IS OBSOLETE

8. ATTACH THE FOLLOWING CLINICAL PROTOCOL INFORMATION:

☐ FOR PHASE 1 INVESTIGATIONS. A GENERAL OUTLINE OF THE PLANNED INVESTIGATION INCLUDING THE ESTIMATED DURATION OF THE STUDY AND THE MAXIMUM NUMBER OF SUBJECTS THAT WILL BE INVOLVED.

☐ FOR PHASE 2 OR 3 INVESTIGATIONS, AN OUTLINE OF THE STUDY PROTOCOL INCLUDING AN APPROXIMATION OF THE NUMBER OF SUBJECTS TO BE TREATED WITH THE DRUG AND THE NUMBER TO BE EMPLOYED AS CONTROLS, IF ANY; THE CLINICAL USES TO BE INVESTIGATED; CHARACTERISTICS OF SUBJECTS BY AGE, SEX, AND CONDITION; THE KIND OF CLINICAL OBSERVATIONS AND LABORATORY TESTS TO BE CONDUCTED; THE ESTIMATED DURATION OF THE STUDY; AND COPIES OR A DESCRIPTION OF CASE REPORT FORMS TO BE USED.

9. COMMITMENTS:

I agree to conduct the study(ies) in accordance with the relevant, current protocol(s) and will only make changes in a protocol after notifying the sponsor, except when necessary to protect the safety, rights, or welfare of subjects.

I agree to personally conduct or supervise the described investigation(s).

I agree to inform any patients, or any persons used as controls, that the drugs are being used for investigational purposes and I will ensure that the requirements relating to obtaining informed consent in 21 CFR Part 50 and institutional review board (IRB) review and approval in 21 CFR Part 56 are met.

I agree to report to the sponsor adverse experiences that occur in the course of the investigation(s) in accordance with 21 CFR 312.64.

I have read and understand the information in the investigator's brochure, including the potential risks and side effects of the drug.

I agree to ensure that all associates, colleagues, and employees assisting in the conduct of the study(ies) are informed about their obligations in meeting the above commitments.

I agree to maintain adequate and accurate records in accordance with 21 CFR 312.62 and to make those records available for inspection in accordance with 21 CFR 312.68.

I will ensure that an IRB that complies with the requirements of 21 CFR Part 56 will be responsible for the initial and continuing review and approval of the clinical investigation. I also agree to promptly report to the IRB all changes in the research activity and all unanticipated problems involving risks to human subjects or others. Additionally, I will not make any changes in the research without IRB approval, except where necessary to eliminate apparent immediate hazards to human subjects.

I agree to comply with all other requirements regarding the obligations of clinical investigators and all other pertinent requirements in 21 CFR Part 312.

INSTRUCTIONS FOR COMPLETING FORM FDA 1572
STATEMENT OF INVESTIGATOR

1. Complete all sections. Attach a separate page if additional space is needed.

2. Attach curriculum vitae or other statement of qualifications as described in Section 2.

3. Attach protocol outline as described in Section 8.

4. Sign and date below.

5. FORWARD THE COMPLETED FORM AND ATTACHMENTS TO THE SPONSOR. The sponsor will incorporate this information along with other technical data into an Investigational New Drug Application (IND). INVESTIGATORS SHOULD NOT SEND THIS FORM DIRECTLY TO THE FOOD AND DRUG ADMINISTRATION.

10. SIGNATURE OF INVESTIGATOR | 11. DATE

Public reporting burden for this collection of information is estimated to average 84 hours per response, including the time for reviewing instructions, searching existing data sources, gathering and maintaining the data needed, and completing reviewing the collection of information. Send comments regarding this burden estimate or any other aspect of this collection of information, including suggestions for reducing this burden to:

DHHS Reports Clearance Officer
Paperwork Reduction Project (0910-0014)
Humphrey Building, Room 721-B
200 Independence Avenue, S.W.
Washington, DC 20201

"An agency may not conduct or sponsor, and a person is not required to respond to a collection of information unless it displays a currently valid OMB control number."

Please DO NOT RETURN this application to this address.

FORM FDA 1572 (1/97)

3. The criteria for patient selection and exclusion, and an estimate of the number of patients to be studied.

4. A description of the study design, including the type of control group to be used, if any, and a description of the methods to be used to minimize bias on the part of subjects, investigators, and analysts.

5. The method for determining the dose(s) to be administered, the planned maximum dosage, and the duration of individual patient exposure to the drug.

6. A description of the observations and measurements to be made to fulfill the objectives of the study.

7. A description of clinical procedures, laboratory tests, or other measures to be taken in monitoring the effects of the drug in human subjects and in minimizing risk.

The ICH's May 1997 consolidated GCP guideline offers a discussion of standards for the content of clinical protocols and protocol amendments.

Chemistry, Manufacturing, and Control Information The purpose of the IND's chemistry, manufacturing and control (CMC) section is to establish that the methods used to manufacture and assay the investigational product are adequate to ensure the product's safety. Submission requirements for the IND's CMC section are a function of several factors, including the stage of the clinical trial proposed in the application.

The IND's CMC section was one of two sections affected by the FDA's 1995 IND reform initiative. Specifically, the initiative revised the CMC section in two ways: (1) it suggested that IND sponsors include a new "chemistry and manufacturing introduction;" and (2) it suggested that sponsors provide information on the drug substance and drug product in a pair of "summary reports" (see discussions below).

Based on the FDA's November 1995 guidance document, an IND proposing a Phase 1 clinical study should include CMC information consisting of the following six components:

Chemistry and Manufacturing Introduction. In this introduction, "the sponsor should state whether it believes: 1) the chemistry of either the drug substance or the drug product, or 2) the manufacturing of either the drug substance or the drug product, presents any signals of potential human risk. If so, these signals of potential risks should be discussed, and the steps proposed to monitor for such risk(s) should be described, or the reason(s) why the signal(s) should be dismissed should be discussed. In addition, sponsors should describe any chemistry and manufacturing differences between the drug product proposed for clinical use and the drug product used in the animal toxicology trials that formed the basis for the sponsor's conclusion that it was safe to proceed with the proposed clinical study. How these differences might affect the safety profile of the drug product should be discussed. If there are no differences in the products, that should be stated."

Drug Substance. The FDA states that information on the drug substance should be provided in a "summary report" comprising five elements: (1) a description of the drug substance, including its physical, chemical, or biological characteristics, along with some evidence to support its proposed chemical structure; (2) the name and address of its manufacturer; (3) a description of the general method of preparation of the drug substance (ideally presented as a detailed flow diagram), including a list of the reagents, solvents, and catalysts used; (4) a brief description of the acceptable limits and analytical methods used to assure the identity, strength, quality, and purity of the drug substance; and (5) information sufficient to support the stability of the drug substance during toxicologic studies and the proposed clinical studies (neither detailed stability data nor the stability protocol should be submitted). Reference to the current edition of the *U.S. Pharmacopeia* or *National Formulary* may satisfy relevant requirements in the drug substance subsection.

In manufacturing and packaging their products, applicants often utilize components (e.g., drug substances, nonstandard excipients, containers) manufactured by other firms, such as contract manufacturers. In such cases, the contract manufacturer is likely to want to preserve the confidentiality of its manufacturing processes. Since an IND must provide information on these processes, contract manufacturers often submit this information to the FDA in a drug master file (DMF). This allows drug sponsors using the company's products to meet submission requirements by incorporating by reference information provided in the master file. Because the drug sponsor never sees the information in the DMF, the confidentiality of the contract facility's manufacturing processes is maintained.

In the IND (or other submission), an incorporation by reference should be made in the section of the application in which the referenced information would normally appear if provided by the applicant. The incorporation by reference must identify the DMF's name and reference number, and must provide the relevant volume and page numbers to allow reviewers to locate the referenced information (i.e., the FDA stores DMFs and reviews information in the file only when referenced in a pending drug application). When the applicant is cross-referencing a DMF submitted by another firm (e.g., a bulk drug manufacturer), the IND must provide a letter of authorization from the DMF's owner in addition to the information specified above. A more detailed discussion of CDER's requirements for, and use of, DMFs can be found in the center's *Guideline for Drug Master Files* (September 1989).

Drug Product. The FDA suggests that the IND provide information on the drug product in a "summary report" comprising as many as six components: (1) a list—usually no more than one or two pages long—of all components, which may include reasonable alternatives for inactive compounds, used in the manufacture of the investigational drug product, including both those components intended to appear in the drug product and those that may not appear, but that are used in the manufacturing process; (2) where applicable, a brief summary of the quantitative composition of the investigational new drug product, including any reasonable variations that may be expected during the investigational stage; (3) the name and address of the drug product manufacturer; (4) a brief, general description of the method of manufacturing and packaging procedures for the product (ideally presented as flow diagrams); (5) a brief description of the proposed acceptable limits and analytical methods used to ensure the identity, strength, quality, and purity of the drug product; and (6) information sufficient to support the stability of the drug substance during the toxicologic studies and the proposed clinical studies (neither detailed stability data nor the stability protocol should be submitted). Reference to the current edition of the *U.S. Pharmacopeia* or *National Formulary* may satisfy certain requirements for this section.

A Brief, General Description of the Composition, Manufacture, and Control of any Placebo Used in the Controlled Clinical Trials. The FDA states that this information should be provided in "diagrammatic, tabular, and brief written" form.

Labeling. The labeling section should comprise "a mock-up or printed representation of the proposed labeling that will be provided to investigator(s) in the proposed clinical trial." Investigational labels must carry a "caution" statement required by federal regulations: "Caution: New Drug—Limited by Federal (or United States) law to investigational use."

Environmental Analysis (EA) Requirements. This section should provide either an environmental assessment, or a claim for a categorical exclusion from the requirement for an environmental assessment. In various guidelines released and initiatives undertaken during the mid-1990s, the FDA has expressed its expectation that "the great majority" of products will qualify for a categorical exclusion. In November 1995, CDER released a guideline entitled *Guidance for Industry for the Submission of Environmental Assessments for Human Drug Applications and Supplements.*

The FDA emphasizes throughout its regulations and guidelines that the amount and detail of information needed in the IND's CMC section depends on several factors, including the scope and phase of the proposed clinical investigation, the proposed duration of the study, the dosage form, and the quantity of information otherwise available. "Modifications to the method of preparation of the new drug substance and dosage form, and even changes in the dosage form itself, are likely as the investigation progresses," the agency states in its November 1995 IND guidance document. "The emphasis in an initial Phase 1 CMC submission should, therefore, generally be placed on providing information that will allow evaluation of the safety of subjects in the proposed study. The identification of a safety concern or insufficient data to make an evaluation of safety is the only basis for a clinical hold based on the CMC section."

FDA regulations add that "the emphasis in an initial Phase 1 submission should generally be placed on the identification and control of the raw materials and the new drug substance. Final specifications for the drug substance and drug product are not expected until the end of the investigational process." However, when final specifications are not established until just prior to Phase 3 studies, comparability with preceding studies may be necessary. Stability testing should support the duration of use for the proposed clinical studies.

The FDA does require that sponsors comply with Current Good Manufacturing Practices (CGMP) during clinical trials. According to the FDA's *Guideline on the Preparation of Investigational New Drug Products (Human and Animal)* (March 1991), the "FDA recognizes that manufacturing procedures and specifications will change as clinical trials advance. However, as research nears completion, procedures and controls are expected to be more specific because they will have been based upon a growing body of scientific data and documentation…. When drug development reaches a stage where the drugs are produced for clinical trials in humans…then compliance with the CGMP regulations is required. For example, the drug product must be produced in a qualified facility, using laboratory and other equipment that has been qualified, and processes must be validated. There must be written procedures for sanitation, calibration, and maintenance of equipment, and specific instructions for the use of the equipment and procedures used to manufacture the drug. Product contamination and wide variations in potency can produce substantial levels of side effects and toxicity, and even produce wide-sweeping effects on the physiological activity of the drug. Product safety, quality, and uniformity are especially significant in the case of investigational products. Such factors may affect the outcome of a clinical investigation that will, in large part, determine whether or not the product will be approved for wider distribution to the public."

As the testing and drug development process advances, sponsors must submit IND information amendments to the CMC section of the IND (see discussion below). Most importantly, the amendments must describe the effects of the transition from pilot scale production used for early clinical studies to the larger-scale production methods used for expanded clinical investigations.

In addition to the documents referenced above, the agency has published several guidelines that provide insights regarding the submission of chemistry, manufacturing, and control information in both INDs and NDAs. These include the following: *Guideline for the Format and Content of the Chemistry, Manufacturing, and Controls Section of an Application* (February 1987), *Guideline for Submitting Documentation for the Manufacture of and Controls for Drug Products* (February 1987), *Guideline for Submitting Supporting Documentation in Drug Applications for the Manufacture of Drug Substances* (February 1987), *Guideline for Submitting Documentation for Packaging for Human Drugs and Biologics* (February 1987), *Guideline for*

Submitting Documentation for the Stability of Human Drugs and Biologics (February 1987), and *Guidance for Industry for the Submission of Chemistry, Manufacturing, and Controls for Synthetic Peptide Drug Substances* (November 1994).

In February 1996, CDER released a draft guidance for industry entitled *Content and Format for Submissions of Drug Products for Investigational New Drug Application (INDs), New Drug Applications (NDAs), Abbreviated New Drug Applications (ANDAs), and Abbreviated Antibiotic New Drug Applications (AANDAs).* Although the document remains a draft, CDER reviewers have in some cases suggested that applicants refer to this guidance. Center officials point out, however, that the contents of a final guidance in this area will be a function of several factors, including ICH developments and CDER efforts to harmonize new and generic drug chemistry submission requirements.

ICH guidelines, such as the final guideline on *Stability Testing of New Drug Substances and Products* (1994), may now provide more updated guidance than is available in FDA documents. While many of the ICH's manufacturing-related guidelines apply more directly to NDA submissions, they may offer insights to IND applicants as well (see Chapter 8).

Animal Pharmacology and Toxicology Information The principal target of the FDA's 1995 IND reform initiative was the application's pharmacology and toxicology section. The agency's "clarification" of its requirements for this section have permitted sponsors to scale back data submissions and to submit INDs months earlier than they could have previously.

In the absence of data derived from previous clinical testing or marketing use, data from animal studies serve as the basis for concluding that a drug is sufficiently safe for initial administration to humans. Therefore, this IND section must include information from the preclinical pharmacology and toxicology studies (animal and *in vitro*) sufficient to establish that the investigational product is reasonably safe for initial use in clinical studies. As is true for the IND's other technical sections, the data and information necessary in the pharmacology and toxicology component depend on several factors, including the nature of the product and the nature and duration of the clinical studies proposed in the IND.

The FDA's November 1995 IND guidance document provides the most detailed and current analysis of content requirements for this section. The guideline suggests that the section comprise four elements:

Pharmacology and Drug Disposition. This section should provide, if known: (1) a description of the pharmacologic effects and mechanism(s) of actions of the drug in animals; and (2) information on the absorption, distribution, metabolism, and excretion of the drug. "A summary report, without individual animal records or individual study results, usually suffices," the agency states in the 1995 IND guidance. "In most circumstances, five pages or less should suffice for this summary. If this information is not known, it should simply be so stated. To the extent that such studies may be important to address safety issues, or to assist in evaluation of toxicology data, they may be necessary; however, lack of this potential effectiveness information should not generally be a reason for a Phase 1 IND to be placed on clinical hold."

Integrated Toxicology Summary. Requirements for the IND's integrated summary of toxicologic effects were the most significantly affected by the FDA's 1995 IND reform initiative. At that time, the agency pointed out that its regulations did not specify whether toxicology data and the study reports should be "final fully quality-assured" individual study reports or earlier, unaudited draft toxicologic reports of completed studies. The agency conceded that most sponsors had concluded that the former were required in INDs.

In clarifying its policy, the FDA stated that, "if final, quality-assured individual study reports are not available at the time of IND submission, an integrated summary report of toxicologic findings based on the unaudited draft toxicologic reports of the completed animal studies may be submitted... Usually, 10 to 15 pages of text with additional tables (as needed) should suffice for the integrated summary."

The FDA guidance document adds that the integrated summary of toxicologic findings should consist of five elements:

1. A brief description of the trial design and any deviations from the design in the conduct of the trials. In addition, the dates of the performance of the trials should be included.

2. A systematic presentation of the findings from the animal toxicology and toxicokinetic studies. This presentation may be approached from a "systems review" perspective (e.g., CNS, cardiovascular, pulmonary, gastrointestinal, renal, hepatic, genitourinary, hematopoietic and immunologic, and dermal).

3. Identification and qualifications of the individual(s) who evaluated the animal safety data and concluded that it is reasonably safe to begin the proposed human study.

4. A statement of where the animal studies were conducted and where the records of the studies are available for inspection should an inspection occur.

5. A declaration that each study subject to good laboratory practice (GLP) regulations was performed in full compliance with GLPs or, if the study was not conducted in compliance with those regulations, a brief statement of the reason for the noncompliance and the sponsor's view on how such noncompliance might affect the interpretations of the findings.

The last three information elements identified above may be supplied as part of the integrated summary or as part of the full data tabulations section.

If an IND includes an integrated summary based on unaudited draft reports, the sponsor must submit an update to the summary within 120 days of the initiation of clinical studies. This update must identify any differences found in the presentation of the final, fully quality-assured study reports and the integrated summary provided in the IND. If no differences are found, the integrated summary update should state this fact.

Full Toxicology Data Tabulation. For each animal toxicology study that is intended to support the safety of the proposed clinical investigation, the sponsor should submit a full tabulation of data suitable for a detailed review. The agency states that this section should consist of "line listings of the individual data points, including laboratory data points, for each animal in these trials along with summary tabulations of these data points." To facilitate interpretation of the line listings, they should be accompanied by "either: 1) a brief (usually a few pages) description (i.e., a technical report or abstract including a methods description section) of the study or 2) a copy of the study protocol and amendments."

Toxicology GLP Certification. A declaration that each study subject to good laboratory practice (GLP) regulations was performed in full compliance with GLPs or, if the study was not conducted in compliance with those regulations, a brief statement of the reason for the noncompliance.

Additional FDA recommendations for compiling and presenting data in this section are available in the agency's *Guideline for the Format and Content of the Nonclinical Pharmacology/Toxicology Section of an Application* (February 1987). Although the guideline is designed for NDA submissions, the agency has stated that the guideline should also shape the organization and format of IND submissions.

It is worth noting that CDER has been running a pilot program for the electronic submission of the IND's pharmacology and toxicology section since November 1994. Under its Pharmacology/Toxicology (P/T) Electronic Submissions Pilot Project, CDER has accepted computerized preclinical P/T study reports for several INDs. With the release of the agency's March 1997 final rule on electronic signatures and records, however, this program will be incorporated into CDER's larger effort to accept all types of applications in computer format (see Chapter 8).

Previous Human Experience with the Investigational Drug If an investigational drug, or any of its active ingredients, has been marketed or tested in humans previously, the sponsor must provide specific information about any such use that may be relevant to the FDA's evaluation of the safety of either the drug or the proposed investigation. In such cases, the information should be presented in an integrated summary report. If the drug has been marketed outside the United States, the IND must provide a list of the countries in which the drug has been marketed or withdrawn.

Additional Information Any other information that would aid in the evaluation of the proposed clinical study should be included in this section. For example, the section might include information on a drug's dependence and abuse potential (if applicable), or data from special tests on radioactive drugs. Often, the section contains published literature, scientific meeting abstracts, etc.

75

Submitting the IND

FDA regulations state that "the sponsor shall submit an original and two copies of all submissions to the IND file, including the original submission and all amendments and reports." In some cases, additional copies may be needed.

The sponsor must provide an accurate and complete English translation for any information originally written in a foreign language. In addition, the applicant must submit the original foreign language document or literature article on which the translation is based.

Maintaining the IND

Given that clinical development takes place over a multi-year period, a single IND may be "in effect," or "active," for several years or even decades. Because of this, the IND is a "living document" that must be updated continually so that the safety of ongoing and upcoming clinical trials may be periodically reassessed in light of the latest information.

Any document submitted to an active IND (i.e., after FDA receipt of an original submission) is referred to as an IND amendment. Each amendment must be accompanied by a completed and signed Form 1571, which identifies the purpose and contents of the submission.

Federal regulations require sponsors of active INDs to update their filings through four types of amendments: protocol amendments, information amendments, IND safety reports, and annual reports.

Protocol Amendments Protocol amendments are necessary when a sponsor wants to change a previously submitted protocol or to add a study protocol not submitted in the original IND. New protocols and most protocol changes must have been submitted to the FDA and have received IRB approval before being initiated. However, some sponsors may choose to obtain FDA comments before implementing new protocols or protocol changes.

Protocol amendments that introduce a new protocol should contain the protocol itself along with a brief description of the most clinically significant differences between the new and previous protocols. In explaining this requirement, the FDA writes that "...a detailed and undiscriminating enumeration of the differences would defeat the purpose of this requirement, which is to identify the most important differences between the old and new protocols and to alert FDA reviewers to major changes that may require additional supporting data, such as changes in dose, route of administration, or indication."

Amendments that specify changes to previously submitted protocols are required when a sponsor seeks: (1) to modify a Phase 1 protocol in a manner that significantly affects the safety of clinical subjects; or (2) to modify a Phase 2 or Phase 3 protocol in a manner that significantly affects the safety of the subjects, the scope of the investigation, or the scientific quality of the study. Federal regulations provide the following examples of protocol changes requiring amendments:

- any increase in drug dosage or the duration of individual subject exposure to the drug beyond that in the current protocol, or any significant increase in the number of study subjects;

- any significant change in the design of a protocol, such as the addition or deletion of a control group;

- the addition of a new test or procedure that is intended to improve monitoring for, or reduce the risk of, a side effect or adverse event, or the elimination of a test intended to monitor safety;

- the elimination of an apparent, immediate hazard to subjects (such a change may be implemented prior to an amendment submission, provided that the FDA is subsequently notified through a protocol amendment and that the IRB is properly notified); and

- the addition of a new investigator to carry out a previously submitted protocol (the investigational drug may be shipped to the investigator and the investigator may participate in the study prior to the submission of the amendment, provided the sponsor notifies the FDA within 30 days of the investigator's first participation in the study).

Amendments for changes to existing protocols must provide a "brief description of the change and reference (date and number) to the submission that contained the protocol." Amendments for a new investigator must include "the investigator's name, the qualifications to conduct the investigation, refer- ence to the previously submitted protocol, and all additional information as is required [for other investigators]."

For certain protocol amendments, the FDA requires sponsors to reference the specific technical information that supports the new protocol or protocol change. According to FDA regulations, a protocol amendment must contain a "reference, if necessary, to specific technical information in the IND or in a concurrently submitted information amendment to the IND that the sponsor relies on to support any clinically significant change in the new or amended protocol. If the reference is made to supporting information already in the IND, the sponsor shall identify by name, reference number, volume, and page num- ber the location of the information." The FDA has written that "the intent of the provision...is to elicit reference to technical information supporting the clini- cally significant aspects of the proposed change. Thus, if a sponsor intends to change the dosage form of the investigational drug, appropriate animal tests that would support this increased human exposure are required. To the extent that FDA is apprised of the basis for a change in a protocol, it can move quickly and comprehensively to review the change. Of course, if the change is one that plainly does not require specific technical support, the sponsor would not be expected to reference any supporting technical information."

Protocol amendments must be prominently identified in one of three ways: "Protocol Amendment: New Protocol," "Protocol Amendment: Change in Protocol," or "Protocol Amendment: New Investigator." Amendments for new protocols or changes in existing protocols must be submitted to the FDA before their implementation. The FDA states, however, that "when several submissions of new protocols or protocol changes are anticipated during a short period, the sponsor is encouraged, to the extent feasible, to include these all in a single submission." Amendments to add new investiga- tors or to provide additional information about investigators may be batched and submitted at 30-day intervals.

IND Safety Reports Sponsors must submit IND safety reports to inform the FDA of any adverse experience (AE) that is associated with the use of a product and that is both serious and unexpected. The goal of this requirement is to "ensure timely communication of the most important new information about experiences with the investigational drug."

The FDA's current AE and IND safety reporting requirements will be revised in several important ways through a series of final regulations that were pending at this writing. These regulatory changes, which were first outlined in an October 1994 omnibus proposed rule, will include a modification in the reporting time frames for IND safety reports and revised definitions for key AE-related terms (see discussion below).

FDA regulations require sponsors to review all information that might represent a possible adverse experience: "Sponsors must promptly review all information relevant to the safety of the drug from any source, foreign or domestic, including information derived from clinical investigations, animal investigations, commercial marketing experience, reports in the scientific literature, and unpublished scientific papers." Once a sponsor's employee has knowledge of safety-related data, the sponsor is considered to have received that information. Therefore, sponsors must develop efficient mechanisms to ensure that such information is communicated internally (e.g., from subsidiaries, other departments within the company, and CROs).

The reporting requirements applicable to an adverse experience are based on the nature, severity, probable cause, and frequency of the experience. In determining reporting requirements, three definitions are important:

Serious Adverse Experience. A serious adverse experience is any experience that suggests a significant hazard, contraindication, side effect, or precaution. Current FDA regulations define a serious clinical AE as "any experience that is fatal or life-threatening, is permanently disabling, requires inpatient hospitalization, or is a congenital anomaly, cancer, or overdose." Regarding AEs found in animal testing, a serious adverse drug experience includes any experience suggesting "a significant risk for human subjects, including any finding of mutagenicity, teratogenicity, or carcinogenicity."

Unexpected Adverse Experience. An unexpected adverse event is "any adverse experience that is not identified in nature, severity, or frequency in the current investigator's brochure." If an investigator's brochure is not required for the study, this requirement would apply to any adverse experience that is not identified in nature, severity, or frequency in the risk information provided in the general investigational plan or elsewhere in the IND or its amendments.

Associated with the Use of the Drug. The phrase "associated with the use of the drug" is interpreted by the regulations to mean that there is a reasonable possibility that the experience may have been caused by the drug.

For each unexpected fatal or life-threatening experience associated with a drug's use during clinical trials, the sponsor is required to notify the FDA initially through a telephone report made within three working days after the sponsor receives information on the reaction.

Written IND safety reports are required for any clinical or nonclinical "adverse experience associated with the use of the drug that is both serious and unexpected." These reports must be submitted to the FDA (and all participating investigators) no later than ten working days after the sponsor's initial receipt of the information. Also, the reports must identify all safety reports previously filed with the IND concerning a similar adverse experience, and must provide an analysis of the adverse experience's significance in light of the previous, similar reports. Adverse reactions that require the three-day telephone alert must also be the subject of a written safety report.

In cases in which ten working days are not sufficient to determine conclusively whether an adverse event should be reported, the agency advises that sponsors submit preliminary information within ten days. Applicants should then supplement this initial report with whatever more definitive information they obtain after the original report.

Applicants should submit follow-up information to a safety report "as soon as the relevant information is available."

A safety report to an IND does not necessarily represent the sponsor's concession that there is a relationship between the product and the adverse experience. In fact, the sponsor may state this fact explicitly in the safety report.

The agency may request that a sponsor submit IND safety reports in a particular format or at a frequency different than that required by regulations. The sponsor is also free to adopt its own reporting format or frequency, provided that CDER agrees to this in advance.

As stated, a series of pending final regulations will affect IND safety reports in several significant ways:

- *Alteration of Reporting Time Frames for IND Safety Reports.* The FDA is expected to alter the time frame for submitting written IND safety reports from 10 working days to 15 calendar days and for making telephone safety reports from 3 working days to 7 calendar days. The agency is also expected to permit telephone safety reports to be made by "facsimile transmission."

- *Redefinition of "Serious" AE.* The FDA will redefine the term "serious" AE to be consistent with the MedWatch Form (Form 3500A) and with international standards. In its October 1994 proposal, the FDA proposed the following new definition: "an adverse experience occurring at any dose that is fatal or life-threatening, results in persistent or significant disability/incapacity, requires or prolongs inpatient hospitalization, necessitates medical or surgical intervention to preclude permanent impairment of a body function or permanent damage to a body structure, or is a congenital anomaly." In the expected final rule, however, the FDA is likely to adopt language that is closer to the definition of serious AE included in the ICH's March 1995 final guideline entitled *Clinical Safety Data Management: Definitions and Standards for Expedited Reporting.* This document defines a serious AE as "any untoward medical occurrence that at any dose: results in death, is life-threatening, results in persistent or significant disability/incapacity, or is a congenital anomaly/birth defect."

- *Definition of Other Key Terms.* To help companies determine what comprises a "serious" AE, the FDA will also define two terms used in the proposed definition: disability, which the agency proposed would mean "a substantial disruption of one's ability to carry out normal life functions;" and life threatening, which the agency proposed would mean "that the patient was, in the view of the initial reporter, at immediate risk of death from the adverse experience as it occurred."

- *Codification of the New MedWatch Form.* The final rule will codify the use of FDA Form 3500A, which will be used to report postmarketing AEs (see Chapter 12) and which the agency has proposed for IND safety reports.

In mid-1997, the FDA had developed a final regulation based on the proposed rule, and was awaiting final clearance for the regulation. Agency officials hoped to implement the final rule in the second half of 1997.

Another pending FDA proposal would require that sponsors submit a clinical trial "semiannual death and serious adverse experience report" and make a series of other modifications that would reduce investigator and sponsor interpretations in AE reporting, and affect trial protocol development, study design, and clinical monitoring. Because these additional proposals have been highly controversial, however, they will not be implemented with the changes specified above.

Annual Reports Within 60 days of the anniversary date on which the initial IND "went into effect," the sponsor must submit an overview of information collected on the subject product during the previous year. Described by regulations as "a brief report of the progress of the investigation," the annual report should provide the following:

Information on Individual Studies. The FDA requires "a brief summary of the status of each study in progress and each study completed during the previous year. The summary must include the following information on each study: (1) the title of the study (with any appropriate study identifiers such as protocol number), its purpose, a brief statement identifying the patient population and a statement as to whether the study is completed; (2) the total number of subjects initially planned for inclusion in the study, the number entered into the study to date, the number whose participation in the study was completed and planned, and the number who dropped out of the study for any reason; and (3) if the study has been completed or if the interim results are known, a brief description of any available study results."

Summary Information. This section should include all additional product-related information collected during the previous year, as well as summary data from all clinical studies:

- a narrative or tabular summary showing the most frequent and most serious adverse experiences by body system;

- a summary of all IND safety reports submitted during the past year;

- a list of subjects who died while participating in the investigation, with the cause of death for each subject (this list must identify all deaths, including those persons whose cause of death is not believed to be product related);

- a list of subjects who dropped out during the study due to an adverse experience, regardless of whether the experience is thought to be drug related;

- a brief description of any information that is pertinent to an understanding of the drug's actions (e.g., information from controlled trials and information about bioavailability);

- a list of the preclinical studies (including animal studies) completed or in progress during the past year, and a summary of the major preclinical findings; and

- a summary of any significant manufacturing or microbiological changes made during the past year.

General Investigational Plan. A brief description of the general investigational plan for the coming year must be provided. This plan should be as descriptive as the earlier plans submitted in the original IND and subsequent annual reports. If the plans are not yet formulated, the sponsor must indicate this fact in the report.

Investigator's Brochure Revisions. When the investigator's brochure has been revised, the sponsor must include a description of the revision and a copy of the new brochure.

Phase 1 Modifications. The sponsor must describe any significant Phase 1 protocol modifications that were implemented during the previous year and that were not reported previously to the FDA through a protocol amendment.

Foreign Marketing Developments. According to the IND regulations, this section should provide a "brief summary of significant foreign marketing developments with the drug during the past year, such as approval of marketing in any country or withdrawal or suspension from marketing in any country."

Request for an FDA Response. If the sponsor requests an FDA meeting, reply, or comment, a log of any relevant outstanding business with respect to the IND should be included.

Information Amendments Often representing the majority of IND amendments, information amendments are used to report to the FDA new information that would not ordinarily be included in a protocol amendment or IND safety report, and information whose importance dictates that it must be reported before the next IND annual report. Information amendments commonly include new data from animal studies, changes or additions to the IND's chemistry, manufacturing, and controls section, and reports on discontinued clinical trials. Such information is more immediately critical than that included in the annual report. The amendments can also be used to provide administrative information, including responses to CDER requests, changes in IND contact persons, and letters of cross reference. Information amendments should be submitted as necessary, but preferably not more frequently than every 30 days.

The principal content requirements for information amendments are: (1) a statement of the nature and purpose of the amendment; (2) an organized submission of the data in a format appropriate for scientific review; and (3) a request for FDA comment on the information amendment (i.e., if the sponsor seeks agency comment).

Chapter 5

CDER and the IND Review Process

Although most analyses of the U.S. Food and Drug Administration (FDA) focus on the agency's authority to decide which new treatments reach the American market, the FDA plays a regulatory gatekeeper role at another key point in the drug development process. In reviewing INDs, the FDA determines which experimental therapies advance from the preclinical to the clinical development phase.

When a drug sponsor submits an IND, the FDA assumes an important role in the development of a new product. From this point forward, the sponsor can do little without at least submitting documents to, and in some cases awaiting the review and approval of, the FDA.

In fact, most sponsor activities beyond the preclinical development phase are subject to some form of FDA oversight. This reality is highlighted in the following statement that a sponsor must sign in the IND: "I agree not to begin clinical investigations until 30 days after FDA's receipt of the IND unless I receive earlier notification by FDA that the studies may begin. I also agree not to begin or continue clinical investigations covered by the IND if those studies are placed on clinical hold. I agree that an Institutional Review Board (IRB) that complies with [federal regulations] will be responsible for the initial and continuing review and approval of each of the studies in the proposed clinical investigation. I agree to conduct the investigation in accordance with all other applicable regulatory requirements."

The FDA's Center for Drug Evaluation and Research (CDER) is the regulatory and scientific body that oversees the development and marketing of all new drugs. Therefore, before outlining the IND review process, it is appropriate to profile CDER, one of the FDA's several primary program centers.

The FDA's Center for Drug Evaluation and Research (CDER)

CDER has functioned in many forms during the past several years. The center's current structure is the product of a series of reorganizations in the mid-1990s. The most important of these was a sweeping center-wide restructuring initiative that fundamentally changed the offices and divisions responsible for reviewing INDs and NDAs. Center management stated in 1995 that the initiative was designed to flatten what had become a "pyramidal system" of drug review and approval, to create smaller and more focused and cohesive review teams, and to facilitate intra-center communication.

This October 1995 reorganization created what CDER officials have called two "super offices" within the center:

Office of Review Management. Within its Office of Review Management (ORM), CDER has concentrated virtually all the offices and units essential for new drug reviews. In addition, the center has reconfigured its 10 previous new drug review divisions into 14 review units, and spread these over 5 Offices of Drug Evaluation, instead of the previous 2 (see organizational chart below). This chapter focuses largely on these 14 new drug review divisions and their activities related to IND reviews. ORM also houses the Office of Epidemiology and Biostatistics, which is responsible for providing biostatistical expertise for new drug reviews and for processing and evaluating adverse experience reports.

Office of Pharmaceutical Science. The Office of Pharmaceutical Science (OPS) was created, in part, to bring all of CDER's generic and new drug review chemists under a single management structure, thereby promoting a greater degree of consistency in chemistry reviews, policies, and approaches. In addition to the Office of New Drug Chemistry, to which CDER's new drug review chemists report, OPS comprises three offices: the Office of Generic Drugs, which reviews generic drug and antibiotic products; the Office of Clinical Pharmacology and Biopharmaceutics, which supports new drug reviews by providing research expertise and evaluating pharmacokinetic and bioavailability data used to establish drug dosing; and the Office of Testing and Research, which conducts research into product quality and examines research methods for shortening drug development time.

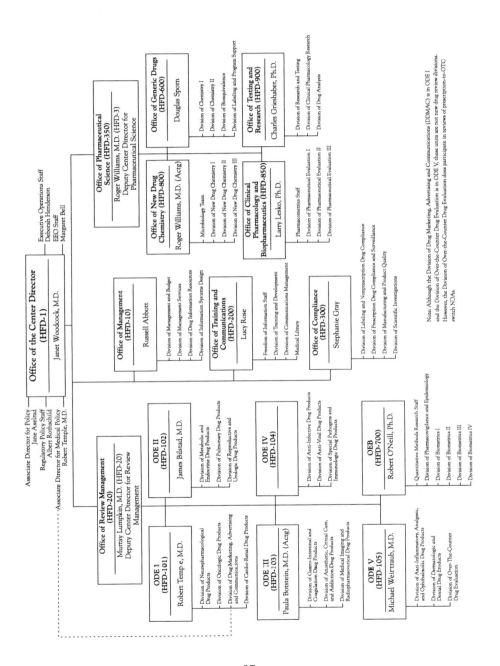

CDER itself comprises three principal offices in addition to ORM and OPS:

Office of Compliance. CDER's Office of Compliance monitors the quality of marketed drugs through product testing, surveillance inspections, and compliance programs; develops policies and standards for drug labeling, current good manufacturing practice (CGMP), good clinical practices (GCP), and good laboratory practice (GLP); coordinates actions between CDER's center and field offices; and directs CDER's Bioresearch Monitoring Program (see Chapter 15).

Office of Training and Communications. The Office of Training and Communications was created during the 1995 restructuring to spearhead CDER's various training/personnel development and internal and external communications programs.

Office of Management. The Office of Management leads the center's planning, budgeting, facilities management, program management, and information systems activities.

CDER's Drug Review Divisions

Although the offices profiled above each play an essential role in drug regulation, this chapter focuses on ORM's five Offices of Drug Evaluation (ODE), which house the 14 new drug review divisions that process and evaluate INDs and NDAs. Since their decisions determine the fates of therapeutically and commercially significant new drugs, these divisions are certainly among the most closely monitored and highly pressured offices within the FDA. With the advent of the prescription drug user fee program, the industry, congressional, and public scrutiny under which the divisions have traditionally operated has intensified considerably in the mid-1990s. To meet the review goals established under the Prescription Drug User Fee Act (PDUFA), these divisions have absorbed a few hundred additional staffers since 1992.

As the division titles (cardio-renal, antiviral, etc.) indicate, the reviewing responsibilities are apportioned to CDER's 14 drug review divisions by therapeutic area. Each unit has its own areas of expertise, and reviews all new drugs proposed for use in these areas. As one would expect, this separation of responsibility creates a disparity in the workloads facing each division and fundamental differences in the scientific and medical issues that each division addresses in reviewing new drugs.

Maintaining manageable divisional workloads and creating review groups that evaluate "more focused groups of products" were among CDER's primary motivations in its 1995 restructuring and in several divisional shifts that have taken place since. The most recent of these reorganizations brought not only structural change within ODE IV, but a shift in the drug regulation and review paradigm for this office. In May 1997, CDER created the Division of Special Pathogens and Immunologic Drug Products, which took responsibilities from the Division of Antiviral Drug Products and the Division of Anti-Infective Drug Products, two divisions that had been among the center's busiest according to several measures. At the same time, however, ODE IV created a series of new office-level coordinating teams that comprised a new CDER model for addressing certain early development and postapproval tasks (see discussion below).

CDER's 14 drug review divisions differ in other ways. Although the groups function under the same legal and regulatory framework, each division traditionally has had considerable autonomy to establish its own policies and procedures within this general framework.

While the center's drug review groups continue to function independently, at least some of their autonomy has been minimized in recent years by CDER efforts to standardize policies and processes. In 1995, for example, the center implemented a Manual of Policies and Procedures (MaPP) that now includes dozens of new and more detailed center-wide policies on issues ranging from meetings management to clinical hold procedures. Under its Good Review Practices (GRP) initiative (see Chapter 9), the center has also begun to develop guidances to add consistency to its reviews of clinical data submitted in drug applications.

The following sections provide brief profiles of CDER's drug review divisions, with particular emphasis on the therapeutic categories of drugs that each unit regulates.

Division of Cardio-Renal Drug Products The Division of Cardio-Renal Drug Products was one of only three new drug review units that were not either split or relocated as part of CDER's October 1995 reorganization. Since 1986, the division has been headed by Division Director Raymond Lipicky, M.D., an internist and 18-year FDA veteran.

The primary classes of drugs for which the division is responsible include antihypertensives, catecholamines, drugs for congestive heart failure, antianginals, antiarrhythmics, diuretics, and miscellaneous vasoactive drugs. These drug groups include angiotensins, renin inhibitors, ACE inhibitors, vasodilators (except for uses related to memory), non-glycoside inotropic agents, diuretics, free radical scavengers, hypotension and shock drugs, agents used for intermittent claudication, nitroglycerin products, beta blockers, cardiovascular diagnostics, nitric oxide, calcium channel blockers, centrally acting alpha-agonists, potassium channel openers, potassium salts, angiographic diagnostic adjuncts (e.g., adenosine, dipyridamole), and EDTA (chelation therapy for intermittent claudication).

In May 1997, the division also took over responsibility for certain antiplatelet drugs, which were previously regulated by CDER's Division of Gastrointestinal and Coagulation Drug Products. Specifically, the division assumed responsibility for IIb/IIIa fibrinogen receptor antagonists because of the role of such products in preventing serious cardiovascular events, such as myocardial infarctions. At this writing, CDER was considering whether other antiplatelet drugs, such as thromboxane inhibitors, would be shifted to the cardio-renal unit as well.

During the mid-1990s, the Division of Cardio-Renal Drug Products was one of CDER's more productive in terms of new drug approvals, and was one of the center's most improved in terms of average new drug review times. In 1995 and 1996, the unit approved a total of nine new molecular entities (NME), the third highest within CDER. During this same two-year period, the unit more than halved its average new drug review times (see Chapter 9).

Division of Oncologic Drug Products The Division of Oncologic Drug Products was formed under CDER's 1995 reorganization initiative, which separated the oncology and pulmonary drug groups that had comprised the Division of Oncology and Pulmonary Drug Products.

Today, the division reviews all oncology drugs, including drugs to treat AIDS patients with Kaposi's sarcoma and lymphoma, drugs to treat graft-versus-host disease, immunomodulators, and chemoprotective agents.

Since October 1995, the division has been headed by Robert DeLap, M.D. DeLap, who had specialty training in internal medicine and medical oncology, joined the agency as a medical officer in 1993.

In early 1996, the division was at the center of a controversy that ultimately brought a greater focus on cancer drug reviews. Cancer patient advocacy groups and Congress had begun to question why the agency was expending so many more resources on the review of AIDS treatments than on drugs for cancer or heart disease, which kill far more Americans each year. Then-FDA Commissioner David Kessler, M.D., promised to evaluate the issue and consider ways to expedite cancer drug reviews.

The product of this effort was the FDA's Oncology Initiative, which the Clinton Administration estimated would reduce cancer drug development times by at least a year and cut oncology NDA review times from an average of 12.4 months to 6 months (see Chapter 16). Under this program, the FDA announced that, to expedite the development and approval of cancer therapies, it would "rely on partial response (such as measurable but incomplete shrinkage of a tumor) to a therapy, in addition to the current criteria such as a patient's survival and improved quality of life." During the Oncology Initiative's first year, the division granted accelerated approvals to two drugs: Taxotere (docetaxel) and Camptosar (irinotecan).

The division's pilot oncology IND review project is an unrelated initiative that began in 1993. Under the current program, some drug and biological INDs are cross-reviewed by medical officers in the Division of Oncology Drug Products and the Oncologic Products Group within the Center for Biologics Evaluation and Research (e.g., CDER reviewers evaluate biological INDs and CBER reviewers evaluate drug INDs). In addition to promoting consistency in cancer drug reviews, the primary long-term objective of this pooling of oncology reviewers is the formation of a single oncology review group, with drug and biologic applications being assigned to CBER and CDER medical reviewers regardless of their center affiliations.

Division of Neuropharmacological Drug Products Like the cardio-renal unit, the Division of Neuropharmacological Drug Products was unaffected by CDER's 1995 restructuring and the minor reorganizations undertaken more recently. Since 1981, the division has been headed by Paul

Leber, M.D. Board certified in psychiatry and pathology, Leber joined the FDA as a medical reviewer in 1978.

The division's current responsibilities can be divided into two general therapeutic categories:

Neurology Drugs. Anticonvulsants, antiemetics, antinauseants, anti-Parkinson agents, antispasticity agents, cerebral stimulants, vascular agents, drugs to assist memory (Alzheimer's/senility/dementia), and drugs to treat migraine, movement disorders, multiple sclerosis, narcolepsy/sleep apnea, stroke, and tardive dyskinesia.

Psychiatric Drugs. Anorexigenic agents/CNS stimulants, antianxiety agents/anxiolytics, antidepressants, antimanics, antipsychotics, hypnotics, sedatives, and drugs to treat schizophrenia, eating disorders, learning disorders (dyslexia), minimal brain dysfunction, obsessive compulsive disorder, and panic.

By several measures, the division faces one of CDER's most challenging workloads (see table below). The unit ranks among CDER's busiest new drug review divisions in terms of active IND and pending NDA workloads.

The division has made great strides in terms of both new drug approval productivity and review performance in recent years. The unit approved 7 NMEs in 1996, after having approved only 9 in the previous 3 years combined. Perhaps even more impressive was the fact that the division approved these 7 NMEs in an average of 15.2 months, virtually half of its overall NME average review time—28.9 months—from 1991 through 1995.

Division of Metabolic and Endocrine Drug Products Because its workload and staffing levels were among CDER's highest, the Division of Metabolic and Endocrine Drug Products was restructured somewhat in 1996. Specifically, the division's reproductive health and urologic drugs review staff was split off from the unit to form the Division of Reproductive and Urologic Drug Products (see discussion below).

The division's review responsibilities now include the following: Adrenal/ACTH, androgens/anabolic steroids, bone calcium and phosphorus

Breakdown of CDER Drug Review Divisions' Active IND and Pending NDA Review Workload (As of Year-End 1996)

Division	Active INDs (commercial)	Pending NDAs
Cardio-Renal Drug Products	723 (293)	11
Neuropharmacological Drug Products	1444 (408)	15
Oncology Drug Products	1043 (377)	5
Pulmonary Drug Products	275 (199)	12
Medical Imaging and Radiopharm. Drug Products	775 (91)	6
Gastrointestinal and Coagulation Drug Products	463 (189)	16
Metabolism and Endocrine Drug Products	1638 (303)	12
Anti-Infective Drug Products	1474 (208)	12
Anesthetic, Critical Care, and Addiction Drug Products	589 (162)	3
Antiviral Drug Products	1556 (243)	8
Dermatological and Dental Drug Products	766 (300)	16
Anti-Inflammatory, Analgesic,and Ophthalmologic Drug Products	820 (347)	9
Reproductive and Urologic Drug Products	753 (232)	11
TOTAL	12,319 (3,352)	136

Note: Table does not account for new Division of Special Pathogens and Immunologic Drug Products. Pending refers to applications currently under FDA review and does not imply overdue.

Source: FDA

metabolism, drugs for diabetes (miscellaneous), dopamine agonists, growth hormone and analogs, hyperglycemic agents, oral hyperglycemic agents, insulin, lipid-altering agents, metabolic agents, nutrients/amino acids, somatostatin, thyroid agents, vasopressin, and vitamins (other than vitamin D).

Since 1979, the Division of Metabolic and Endocrine Drug Products has been headed by Division Director Solomon Sobel, M.D. Board certified in internal medicine with a specialty in infectious diseases, Sobel has been with the FDA since 1977, when he joined the Division of Anti-Infective Drug Products as a medical officer.

More than any other CDER review division, the Division of Metabolism and Endocrine Drug Products has seen the most consistent year-to-year reductions in NME review times since the early 1990s. The unit took an average of 19.2 months to approve 7 NMEs in 1996.

Division of Reproductive and Urologic Drug Products As noted above, the Division of Reproductive and Urologic Drug Products was created in mid-1996 as part of CDER's continuing efforts to maintain smaller divisions that review "more focused groups of products." CDER named Lisa Rarick, M.D., an obstetrician and formerly a medical officer and deputy director within the Division of Metabolic and Endocrine Drug Products, as the division's director.

The unit's product responsibilities include contraceptives, estrogens, oxytocics, progestins, uterine-acting agents, drugs for sexual dysfunction, drugs for treatment of preterm labor, IUDs, sclerosing agents, prostaglandins (abortifacients), drugs for premenstrual syndrome, subdermal pellets (testosterone and estrogen), and androgens/anabolic steroids.

Division of Pulmonary Drug Products The Division of Pulmonary Drug Products was formed under CDER's 1995 restructuring. Under this reorganization, the center separated the oncology and pulmonary drug groups that had comprised the Division of Oncology and Pulmonary Drug Products. In reality, however, the Division of Pulmonary Drug Products had been functioning largely as an independent review group prior to this time.

The Division of Pulmonary Drug Products is responsible for reviewing a wide variety of pulmonary and antiallergic drugs. These include antiasthmatics (nonsteroidal), bronchodilators, bronchoconstrictors, cough-cold-allergy preparations, antihistamines, antitussives, decongestants, mucolytic agents, pulmonary surfactants, and drugs for cystic fibrosis.

The division is led by John Jenkins, M.D. Board certified in internal medicine and pulmonology, Jenkins joined the FDA in 1992 as a medical officer.

Division of Gastrointestinal and Coagulation Drug Products

Many individuals inside and outside the FDA were stunned to learn in May 1997 that Stephen Fredd, M.D., the director of the Division of Gastrointestinal and Coagulation Drug Products since 1987, left the unit to take a position elsewhere in CDER. During Fredd's tenure, the Division of Gastrointestinal and Coagulation Drug Products was considered by many to be one of CDER's best and most tightly managed review divisions.

Upon Fredd's departure, CDER announced that responsibility for certain antiplatelet drugs would be shifted to the Division of Cardio-Renal Drug Products, a unit that center officials maintained was better suited to review these products. The fact that the Division of Gastrointestinal and Coagulation Drug Products had the center's highest pending NDA workload at year-end 1996 might have been another motivation for the shift.

The division's review responsibilities can be broken down into two principal therapeutic areas:

Coagulation Drugs. Anticoagulants, antifibrinolytics, chelating agents, coagulants, fibrinolytics, hematologics, prostaglandins, postoperative thromboembolic agents, and thromboxane antagonists.

Gastrointestinal Drugs. Antacids, anticholinergics, anticolitis and anti-ileitis agents, antiemetics, antiflatulents, gastrointestinal antimotility and antispasmodics, antiulcer agents, cholecystokinetic agents, choleretics and hydrocholeretics, gastrointestinal diagnostics, gallstone solvents, hemorrhoidal preparations, laxatives, liver agents, motility stimulants, pancreatic agents, and gastrointestinal prostaglandins.

As noted above, the division surrendered responsibility for certain antiplatelet drugs to the Division of Cardio-Renal Drug Products in May

1997. Specifically, IIb/IIIa fibrinogen receptor antagonists were shifted because of the role these drugs play in preventing serious cardiovascular events, such as myocardial infarction. At this writing, CDER was considering whether other antiplatelet drugs, such as thromboxane inhibitors, should be shifted to the cardio-renal unit as well.

Division of Medical Imaging and Radiopharmaceutical Drug Products The Division of Medical Imaging and Radiopharmaceutical Drug Products was created in 1995 when CDER split off responsibilities for surgical and dental drugs from the former Division of Medical Imaging, Surgical and Dental Drug Products.

Today, the division oversees a relatively homogeneous group of imaging and therapeutic products, including magnetic resonance image enhancement agents, radioactive diagnostic agents, radioactive therapeutic agents, radiopaque agents, ultrasound agents, and adjuvants used with all of these products (e.g., potassium perchlorate).

In terms of gains in reviewing resources, perhaps no single group of drugs has benefited more from CDER reorganization and user-fee hirings than medical imaging and radiopharmaceutical drug products. In 1993, the products were regulated by a division that had more than two pending NDAs per medical officer—a commonly used staffing-to-workload measure. In 1996, however, the newly formed Division of Medical Imaging and Radiopharmaceutical Drug Products had a far more favorable ratio of 1.1 pending NDAs per medical officer. Also, the division had CDER's lowest active commercial IND workload and one of the center's lowest pending NDA workloads as of year-end 1996.

The division is led by Patricia Love, M.D. A rheumatologist, Love had served as a medical officer within CDER's former Pilot Drug Evaluation Staff (PDES).

Division of Anesthetic, Critical Care, and Addiction Drug Products Created in 1995, the Division of Anesthetic, Critical Care, and Addiction Drug Products represents a patchwork quilt of two former CDER divisions. From the now-defunct Pilot Drug Evaluation Staff (PDES), the division inherited responsibility over two drug groups—scheduled/abusable drugs and anesthetic drugs; from the unit known previously as the Division of

Medical Imaging, Surgical, and Dental Drug Products, the division inherited responsibility over surgical/critical care drugs.

The division's current responsibilities can be categorized into three general product groups:

Abusable Drugs. Drugs to treat alcoholism, encephalin analgesics, hallucinogenic agents, methadone and other addictives, narcotic antagonist/agonists/analgesics, narcotics in addiction research, and drugs to treat nicotine addiction.

Anesthetic Drugs. Epidural and intrathecal analgesics, lidocaine for cardiac arrhythmia, neuromuscular blocking agents, preanesthetic sedatives, and general, local, and regional anesthetic agents.

Surgical/Critical Care Drugs. Burn treatment agents, peritoneal dialysis solutions, osmotic diuretics, injectable surgical adjunct enzymes, and irrigating fluids.

In both 1995 and 1996, the division had one of CDER's better average NME review times, hovering near the 12.0-month mark. As of year-end 1996, the unit also had the center's lowest backlog of pending NDAs.

Division of Anti-Infective Drug Products At this writing, the Office of Drug Evaluation IV had announced a reorganization that pulled some drug product responsibilities from the two divisions within ODE IV—the Division of Anti-Infective Drug Products and the Division of Antiviral Drug Products—and placed them under a new third division, the Division of Special Pathogens and Immunologic Drug Products (see profile below). The creation of the third division within ODE IV was designed largely to lighten the considerable workload facing the anti-infectives group, and to allow the antivirals unit to focus even more on AIDS drug reviews.

By most measures, CDER's Division of Anti-Infective Drug Products was the busiest of the center's drug review divisions through the early and mid-1990s. During this time, the division faced what was one of CDER's largest NDA workloads and what was easily the center's most daunting backlog of efficacy supplements. At year-end 1995, for example, the unit had 45 pending efficacy supplements, more than three times the number within any other CDER division.

In May 1997, the Division of Anti-Infective Drug Products shifted responsibility for several products and product categories to the new review group, the most significant of which was the quinolones (i.e., other than those for ear/nose/throat indications). Also moved to the new group were antimycobacterials (tuberculosis), vaginal antifungals, tropicals (e.g., anti-malarials), anthelmintics, and *H. pylori* treatments.

Currently, the division's responsibilities can be divided into three broad therapeutic groupings:

- cephalosporins, aminoglycosides, sulfonamides, clindamycins/lincomycins, glycopeptides.

- macrolides, tetracyclines, monobactams, penicillins.

- sepsis immunomodulators, topical antimicrobials, antiresistance antimicrobials, and ear/nose/throat-indicated quinolones.

The May 1997 reorganization had other significant implications for the three divisions within ODE IV. Along with the founding of the new division, ODE IV also created three office-level teams to coordinate certain activities within ODE IV's review divisions. According to an internal CDER memo, ODE IV created "three cross-cutting teams that will be responsible—for the entire office—for overseeing and coordinating (1) the pre-IND work, (2) the post-approval safety, labeling and advertising work with [the Division of Drug Marketing, Advertising and Communication] and [the Office of Epidemiology and Biostatistics] and (3) the line extension-biopharm only applications." In addition, an information-technology group and research laboratory will support the work of all three ODE IV divisions. CDER officials characterized the ODE IV structure as a "forum for innovation" that, if successful, could be a model for the way CDER's other offices and divisions manage their work.

At this writing, CDER had not staffed the new office-level coordinating teams. According to ODE IV staffers, the Pre-IND Team will be staffed by a project manager and a microbiologist, and will serve as a clearinghouse for the office's pre-IND activities, in part by ensuring that pre-IND materials and issues are tracked and addressed.

Division of Antiviral Drug Products Since it was founded in 1983, the Division of Antiviral Drug Products has labored with a nation peering over its shoulder. Buoyed by influxes of resources and staffing and driven by rigorous review goals that make weekend and late-evening reviews of new AIDS treatments a virtual necessity, the Division of Antiviral Drug Products continues to set the standard for drug review and approval.

During a 13-day stretch in early 1996, for example, the division set two new records for drug approval speed. First, during a 72-day period from December 22, 1995 to March 1, 1996, the division managed to review, hold an advisory committee meeting for, and approve an NDA for Abbott's protease inhibitor Ritonavir, bettering CDER's all-time best NME approval time of 87 days for Alcon's Iopidine. Less than two weeks later, the division approved Merck's protease inhibitor Crixivan (indinavir sulfate) in just 42 days.

Due to the nature of its primary mission, the division has been isolated from reviewing responsibilities as diverse as those found in many other divisions. CDER took steps to further sharpen the division's focus when it established the Division of Special Pathogens and Immunology Drug Products in May 1997 (see discussion below). Under this reorganization, the Division of Antiviral Drug Products shifted responsibility for several non-AIDS drugs and drug classes to the new unit, including solid organ transplantation drugs, drugs for non-viral opportunistic infections in AIDS patients, and wasting agents.

Division of Special Pathogens and Immunologic Drug Products The Division of Special Pathogens and Immunologic Drug Products was created in May 1997 as part of CDER's continuing effort to maintain smaller, more therapeutically focused review groups during the user-fee era.

The division assumed responsibility for several drugs and drug groups previously handled by the two other ODE IV review groups (see profiles above): systemic antifungals (including liposomal amphotericin products), antimycobacterial drugs (tuberculosis), vaginal antifungals, quinolone antibiotics not intended for ear/nose/throat indications, anti-parasitics, *H. pylori* treatments, solid organ transplantation drugs, drugs for non-viral opportunistic infections in AIDS patients, vaginal drugs for HIV, immunomodulating drugs (including some uses for thalidomide), and wasting agents.

Mark Goldberger, M.D., formerly a medical team leader within the Division of Antiviral Drug Products, was named the acting director for the new division.

Division of Dermatologic and Dental Drug Products The Division of Dermatologic and Dental Drug Products is the product of three CDER reorganizations since 1994. Formerly the Division of Topical Drug Products, the division currently regulates two broad drug categories:

Dermatological Drugs. Anti-acne drugs, antiperspirants, topical antipruritics, topical astringents, topical aural drugs, topical corticosteroids, topical and systemic retinoids, topical antifungals, dermatophytes, pediculocides, and miscellaneous topical and systemic immunosuppressants.

Dental Drugs. Anticaries preparations, antiplaque agents, mouthwashes, and periodontal treatments.

Since its founding, the division has been led by Jonathan Wilkin, M.D., formerly a member of CDER's Dermatologic Drug Products Advisory Committee.

Division of Anti-Inflammatory, Analgesic and Ophthalmic Drug Products The Division of Anti-Inflammatory, Analgesic, and Ophthalmic Drug Products is also the product of multiple CDER reorganizations in recent years.

Today, the division is responsible for the three drug categories identified in its title:

Anti-Inflammatory Drugs. Inhalant corticosteroids, systemic corticosteroids, nonsteroidal anti-inflammatory agents, anti-gout drugs, and immunomodulators for rheumatic diseases.

Analgesics. Non-narcotic analgesics, antipyretics, and muscle relaxants.

Ophthalmics. Alpha adrenergic agonist/blockers, antibiotics, antiprotozoals, antivirals, beta adrenergic blockers, corticosteroids, and nonsteroidal anti-inflammatory agents.

Inside the FDA's Drug Review Divisions

Although CDER's 14 new drug review divisions differ in many ways, they are similar in nature and structure. Each unit is led by a division director who is generally a physician. Most divisions have deputy directors as well.

At the core of each division is a three- or four-discipline review structure. IND and NDA reviews are conducted by individuals from each of three or four technical disciplines: medical/clinical; nonclinical pharmacology/toxicology; chemistry; and microbiology (i.e., for anti-infective drugs).

Medical/Clinical Discipline Often called medical officers, medical/clinical reviewers are almost exclusively physicians. In some instances, such as in the review of psychiatric and dental products, non-physicians are used as medical officers to evaluate drug efficacy.

Medical reviewers are responsible for evaluating the clinical sections of submissions, such as the safety of the clinical protocols in an IND or the results of clinical testing as submitted in an NDA. Within most divisions, clinical reviewers take the lead role in IND and NDA reviews, and are responsible for reconciling the results of the chemistry, pharmacology, and clinical reviews to formulate the basis upon which a drug will be approved or used in early clinical testing.

In most divisions, medical reviewers are assigned to one of two or more drug groups. The Division of Metabolic and Endocrine Drug Products has three medical review teams, for example: an Endocrine/Adrenal Medical Team, a Metabolism/Obesity Medical Team, and a Lipid/Nutrient/Thyroid/Vasopressor Medical Team. Typically, such groups are headed by a team leader, and are staffed by physicians who possess expertise in a specific drug category/disease state.

Chemistry Discipline Each review division has a team of chemists responsible for reviewing the chemistry, manufacturing, and control sections of drug applications. In general terms, chemistry reviewers address issues related to drug identity, manufacturing and control, and analysis.

Technically, CDER's chemists report into the center's Office of New Drug Chemistry rather than the review divisions in which they work. For practical reasons, however, the chemists are physically located within the respective review divisions.

Pharmacology Discipline The pharmacology review team is staffed by pharmacologists and toxicologists who evaluate the results of animal studies in attempting to relate nonclinical drug effects to potential effects in humans.

Microbiology Discipline Within the Division of Anti-Infective Drug Products and the Division of Antiviral Drug Products, there is a fourth technical review discipline—microbiology. Since antimicrobial and antiviral drug products are designed to affect microbial or viral, rather than human, physiology, the groups employ microbiologists to evaluate the products' effects on viruses or other microorganisms.

Project Management Staff/Consumer Safety Officers There is at least one other group of individuals who are critical to the application review process—project management staff. Traditionally called consumer safety officers (CSO), these individuals are increasingly being called project managers to better reflect their role in the review management process.

CDER's project managers serve as a drug sponsor's primary contact with a division during the product development and application review processes. In addition to a scientist/physician from each of the primary technical disciplines, a project manager is assigned to each IND and NDA upon its submission.

Since most project managers/CSOs have scientific backgrounds (i.e., primarily in pharmacy), they can provide informed reports of technical issues that arise during the application review process. Their real expertise, however, is their knowledge of the drug review process, and of the policies, procedures, and idiosyncracies of their respective divisions.

The IND Review Process

The IND review is unique among the FDA's application review processes. In many respects, this process and the FDA's treatment of INDs represent a delicate balance between the federal government's responsibility to protect clinical trial subjects from unnecessary risks and its desire to avoid becoming an impediment to the advance of medical research. Given these dual goals, the FDA must perform a safety review of an IND prior to clinical trials, but is given only 30 days in which to reach an initial decision on the application.

The FDA's principal goals during the IND review are: (1) to determine if the preclinical test data show that the drug is reasonably safe for administration to humans; and (2) to determine if the protocol for the proposed clinical studies will expose clinical subjects to unnecessary risks (assuming the protocol proposes only Phase 1 studies).

Initial Processing of the IND The FDA's early processing of the IND depends on the manner in which the application is shipped to the agency. INDs arriving by regular mail, for example, are forwarded to the general FDA mail room, while applications shipped by courier are sent directly to CDER's Central Document Room.

Once within CDER's Central Document Room, the IND is stamped with the date of receipt, an extremely important event since it starts the 30-day review clock. Staffers within this office assign an identification number to the IND, and then log information about the filing into a computer database—the sponsor's name, the drug's name, and the application's identification number. Finally, before sending the application to a review division, staffers package the application (e.g., in review jackets if necessary).

Given the tight IND review time frame, this initial processing occurs extremely quickly. INDs arriving in CDER's Central Document Room during the morning will be forwarded to the review division within the same day in most cases. For treatment INDs, however, the staffers attempt to forward the applications within an hour of their receipt.

The IND within the Review Division Once within the relevant review division, the IND is sent to a file or document room where a staffer creates a history card containing the applicant's name, the IND's date of receipt and identification number, and other information. The division then develops and forwards an "acknowledgement letter," which tells the applicant that the FDA has received the IND. The letter also specifies the IND's identification number and receipt date, and provides the name of the project manager/CSO who will act as the FDA contact person on matters involving the application.

The assigned project manager/CSO will then act as the unofficial coordinator of the review, seeing that the application is forwarded to the relevant individuals. At this stage, the project manager/CSO may choose to review the contents of the IND to identify any deficiencies.

As previously discussed, an IND faces reviews by the three or four technical review disciplines within a division—medical/clinical, pharmacology, chemistry, and, in two divisions, microbiology. The first copy of the IND is usually forwarded to a supervisory medical officer, sometimes called a "group leader," who has expertise in the subject drug's therapeutic category. In some review divisions, it is the group leader who analyzes the results of the medical, pharmacology, and chemistry reviews, and recommends whether or not the contents of the IND are adequate to allow the initiation of clinical trials.

Obviously, each review discipline focuses on the aspect of the IND relevant to its expertise:

Pharmacology Review. The reviewing pharmacologist focuses on the results of animal pharmacology and toxicology testing, and attempts to relate these test results to human pharmacology.

Chemistry Review. The reviewing chemist evaluates the manufacturing and processing procedures for a drug to ensure that the compound is adequately reproducible and stable in its pure form. If the drug is either unstable or not reproducible, then the validity of any clinical testing would be undermined and, more importantly, the studies may pose significant risks. The chemistry reviewer also evaluates the drug's characterization and chemical structure, and compares the product's structure and impurity profile to those of other drugs (i.e., drugs known to be toxic).

Clinical Review. The medical reviewer evaluates the clinical trial protocol to determine: (1) if the subjects will be protected from unnecessary risks; and (2) if the study design will provide relevant data on the safety and effectiveness of the drug. Since the late 1980s, FDA reviewers have been instructed to provide drug sponsors with greater freedom during Phase 1, as long as the investigations do not expose subjects to undue risks. In evaluating Phase 2 and 3 investigations, however, FDA reviewers also must ensure that these studies are of sufficient scientific quality, and that they are capable of yielding data that can support marketing approval.

Microbiology Review. The microbiologist evaluates data on the drug's *in vivo* and *in vitro* effects on the physiology of the target virus or other microorganism.

During the drug evaluation process, reviews in the three or four technical areas are supplemented by what are called "consultative reviews" in biostatistics and biopharmaceutics. At the IND review stage, agency biostatisticians may evaluate animal data to determine the statistical significance of drug effects in animals, including tumor rates and dose-response relationships. And, while FDA biopharmaceutics staffers may not become directly involved in the IND review (except for AIDS drugs and other critical therapies), these staffers can review biopharmaceutics and pharmacokinetic data (i.e., drug concentrations in blood and urine) from initial clinical studies to provide advice on dosing, dosing intervals, and other drug administration issues for later trials.

When the reviewers complete their evaluations, they each submit a report summarizing their findings to the group leader, who is left to synthesize these findings and to make a final recommendation to the division director. Recommendations made by group leaders are rarely overturned by the division director.

While a division must complete a safety evaluation within the 30-day period, reviewers may continue to evaluate the IND after the period expires. If new safety concerns arise from this continuing review, the FDA may order that ongoing clinical trials be discontinued until these concerns are addressed and resolved.

The 30-Day Review Clock The FDA has no uniform procedures for informing applicants about the results of IND reviews. Most drug review divisions, for instance, do not contact the sponsor if no problems are found with drug safety and the proposed clinical trials. Rather, the divisions just allow the 30-day review period to expire, thereby permitting the sponsor to initiate clinical studies immediately. In this way, INDs are never formally approved, but are passively approved through the center's "administrative silence." Although they are not required to do so, sponsors should contact the agency before beginning clinical trials to confirm that the studies may be initiated.

CDER staffers caution that a firm that has not received an acknowledgement letter should not initiate trials, no matter how long the company believes that an IND has been at the agency. Because INDs can be lost during shipment or misplaced at the agency, applicants should contact the FDA if they have not received an acknowledgement letter within a reasonable period.

When deficiencies are found in an IND, the FDA may take one of two actions. If the review division decides that an IND deficiency is not serious enough to justify delaying clinical studies, the division may either telephone, or forward a deficiency letter to, the sponsor. In either case, the division informs the sponsor that it may proceed with the planned clinical trials, but that additional information is necessary to complete or correct the IND file.

The Clinical Hold

When CDER discovers serious deficiencies that cannot be addressed before or during the IND review process, the center will contact the sponsor within the 30-day review period to delay the clinical trial. The clinical hold is the mechanism that CDER uses to accomplish this.

Through a clinical hold order, the agency can delay the initiation of an early-phase trial on the basis of information submitted in the IND. Later, clinical hold orders can be used to suspend an ongoing study based on either a re-review of the original IND or a review of newly submitted clinical protocols, safety reports, protocol amendments, or other information. When a clinical hold is issued, a sponsor must address the issue that is the basis of the hold before it is removed.

The FDA's authority regarding clinical holds is outlined in federal regulations. The regulations specify the clinical hold criteria that the FDA applies to the various phases of clinical testing. In addition, CDER has developed a policy guide entitled *IND Process and Review Procedures* (MaPP 6030.1) to describe the center's policies and procedures for issuing IND clinical holds.

Clinical Holds and Phase 1 Trials One of the principal goals of the FDA's 1987 IND regulations was to give sponsors "greater freedom" during the initial stages of clinical research. Therefore, the regulations state that the FDA should not place a clinical hold on a Phase 1 study "unless it presents an unreasonable and significant risk to test subjects." In the regulation's preamble, the FDA establishes that it will "defer to sponsors on matters of Phase 1 study design," and will not consider a Phase 1 trial's scientific merit in deciding whether it should be allowed to proceed.

The regulation specifies four situations in which the FDA can either delay a Phase 1 study proposed in an IND or discontinue an ongoing Phase 1 trial:

- if human subjects are or would be exposed to an unreasonable and significant risk of illness or injury;

- if the clinical investigators named in the IND are not qualified by reason of their scientific training and experience to conduct the investigation described in the IND;

- if the investigator's brochure (i.e., material supplying drug-related safety and effectiveness information to clinical investigators) is misleading, erroneous, or materially incomplete; or

- if the IND does not contain sufficient information as required under federal regulations to assess the risks that the proposed studies present to subjects.

Clinical Holds and Phase 2 and 3 Studies The FDA has greater discretionary powers to delay and discontinue Phase 2 and Phase 3 trials. Current regulations allow the agency to place a clinical hold on a Phase 2 or Phase 3 trial if: (1) any of the four Phase 1 clinical hold criteria outlined above are met; or (2) the "plan or protocol for the investigation is clearly deficient in design to meet its stated objectives."

How Clinical Holds Work The FDA acknowledges that the imposition of a clinical hold is a relatively informal and flexible process. Given the nature of product development, the agency has resisted suggestions that it formalize the clinical hold process.

Current regulations state that the hold process will, in many cases, begin with an FDA-sponsor discussion: "Whenever FDA concludes that a deficiency exists in a clinical investigation that may be grounds for the imposition of a clinical hold, FDA will, unless patients are exposed to immediate and serious risk, attempt to discuss and satisfactorily resolve the matter with the sponsor before issuing the clinical hold order." The agency claims that most potential holds, particularly those based on inadequate patient monitoring, can be resolved through such discussions.

In certain situations, a division may ask sponsors, on an informal basis, to voluntarily agree to an extension of the 30-day review to avoid a clinical hold order. For example, if a reviewing pharmacologist is unable to complete a review of an IND's preclinical data within the 30-day limit, the division may ask the sponsor to delay its clinical studies for a brief time so a more thorough review can be completed. Called an "informal clinical hold," this mechanism allows the FDA and the sponsor alike to avoid complications associated with formal clinical hold orders (e.g., paperwork). In such cases, the division typically promises to contact the sponsor as soon as a decision is reached.

Federal regulations make clear, however, that the FDA is not obligated to initiate a dialogue or to pursue alternative means before issuing a hold: "While the agency is committed to making a good faith attempt to discuss and satisfactorily resolve deficiencies in an IND before considering the need to impose a clinical hold, it does not believe that it is obligated to establish procedural...[requirements obligating the agency to take such action]. The nature of the agency contact with sponsors will depend on the imminence of hazard to human subjects, on the availability of key agency and sponsor personnel, and on a variety of other factors. For similar reasons, FDA believes that it cannot in the abstract specify the extent of notice that can approximately be given before making a hold effective."

CDER's MaPP 6030.1 defines two types of clinical holds:

Complete clinical hold: "A clinical hold that represents a hold of all clinical work requested under an IND."

Partial clinical hold: "A clinical hold of only part of the clinical work requested under the IND [e.g., a specific protocol is not allowed to proceed; however, other protocols are allowed to proceed under the IND]. If only part of a protocol is allowed to be conducted, with progress to the next part contingent upon FDA review/approval of additional data, this is a partial hold. In contrast, if the division has told a sponsor that the sponsor needs to review results of a clinical study (or preclinical data) before proceeding, there is no hold."

Under CDER policy, the division medical team leader (i.e., the reviewing medical officer's supervisor) is responsible for leading discussions of safety concerns regarding the planned protocol. If these concerns cannot be resolved through the discussions, however, the review division director must be involved in the decision to impose a clinical hold.

According to CDER's MaPP 6030.1, "clinical holds of commercial INDs should be communicated to the appropriate sponsor representative by a telephone call from the division director (or acting division director)." A letter clearly identifying the reasons for the clinical hold must be sent to the sponsor within five working days of this telephone call.

When the hold order is issued, identified studies must be delayed or discontinued immediately. If the study has not yet begun, no subjects may be administered the investigational drug. Ongoing studies placed on clinical hold must be discontinued immediately, and no new subjects may be recruited to the study or placed on the treatment. CDER may, however, permit subjects already on the treatment to continue receiving the experimental drug.

Under the terms of some clinical hold orders, sponsors may be allowed to begin or to continue the affected investigations when the required modification is instituted and without the prior notification of CDER. In many other cases, the investigation may proceed only after the sponsor has notified CDER, and after the company has received the center's authorization to begin or resume the clinical program.

To facilitate CDER's timely review of sponsor responses to clinical holds, applicants should forward their responses by overnight mail to the division document room and forward a copy of the cover letter to the division project manager responsible for the IND. This communication should be clearly identified as an "IND Clinical Hold Response."

Current CDER policy calls for divisions to respond to complete sponsor responses within 30 calendar days of their receipt. If the division is not able to do so, the division director is required to telephone the sponsor and discuss "the review progress to date and what is being done to facilitate completion of the review." Division directors make the final decisions on issuing and lifting all clinical holds.

IND Clinical Hold Rates Within CDER CDER's clinical hold rates on commercial INDs have declined dramatically in the mid-1990s. In 1996, the center issued holds on an estimated 6 percent of initial IND submissions, compared to 16 percent in 1991. It is important to note, however, that hold

CDER Holds on Commercial IND Submissions, 1990-1996

	Holds**	INDs Received	Percent Placed on Hold
1990	60	364	16%
1991	59	358	16%
1992	46	361	13%
1993	44	372	12%
1994	43	333	13%
1995*	38	358	11%
1996*	23	376	6%

* Data in 1995 and 1996 are Fiscal Year (FY) statistics

** Holds column for 1995 and 1996 represents the number of INDs received in FY that were placed on hold (full or partial) at any point (data as of 2/28/97). Holds in previous years represent holds issued on initial IND filings.

Source: Food and Drug Administration

rates can vary considerably from division to division. This variability is at least partially influenced by the nature of the drugs that the various divisions review.

There are several possible reasons for the downturn in IND hold rates. Some maintain that all industry submissions have improved in recent years. Others point to CDER's establishment of its Clinical Holds Peer Review Committee, which meets quarterly to review all of the center's IND hold decisions. Divisions that issue IND holds must now be prepared to discuss and defend these decisions before the committee, which is comprised largely of senior CDER officials. In addition, sponsors are given the opportunity to appear before the committee to discuss clinical holds placed on their INDs.

IND Status

Once the FDA's 30-day review period expires and clinical investigations are initiated, an IND may be classified into any one of five status categories:

Active Status. Generally, an active IND is one under which clinical investigations are being conducted—in other words, the FDA has decided not to delay or suspend the clinical studies proposed under the initial IND or subsequent protocol amendments. However, an IND may remain on active status for extended periods even though no trials are being conducted under the application. In such cases, clinical studies may be re-initiated under the IND without further notification to the FDA.

Inactive Status. An IND on inactive status is one under which clinical investigations are not being conducted. There are two ways through which an IND can be put on inactive status. First, the IND sponsor may ask CDER to place the application on inactive status, thereby eliminating the IND updating and submission requirements applicable to the sponsor. Also, the FDA may place the application on inactive status if the agency finds either: (1) that no subjects are entered into an IND's clinical studies for a period of two years or more, or (2) that all investigations under an application remain on clinical hold for one year or more. CDER may seek to terminate INDs that remain on inactive status for five years or more (see discussion below).

Clinical Hold. As previously discussed, a clinical hold is an FDA order to delay a proposed investigation or to suspend an ongoing investigation. If all investigations covered by an IND remain on clinical hold for one year or more, CDER may place the IND on inactive status.

Withdrawn Status. The sponsor of an IND can withdraw an IND at any time and for any reason. When the sponsor withdraws an IND, all clinical investigations under the IND must be discontinued, the FDA and all investigators must be notified, and all stocks of the drug must be returned to the sponsor or otherwise disposed of at the request of the sponsor.

IND Termination. The FDA will seek to terminate an IND if the agency is unable to resolve deficiencies in an IND or in the conduct of an investigation through a clinical hold order or through a more informal alternative. For example, the agency would pursue IND termination if a sponsor failed to delay a proposed investigation under an IND that had been placed on clinical hold. Except when continuing an investigation will present an immediate danger to clinical subjects, the FDA will issue a proposal to terminate and will offer the sponsor an opportunity to respond before finalizing a termination.

Likely Changes to the FDA's IND Process

The FDA's IND and clinical trial processes were a focus of early agency/industry efforts to develop a legislative package for the reauthorization of the Prescription Drug User Fee Act of 1992 (PDUFA), which will expire in September 1997. This is principally the case because clinical development times have continued to escalate despite marked improvements in the FDA's drug approval times.

In early 1997, FDA/industry talks on PDUFA II produced agreement on a series of legislative concepts that, if implemented by Congress, could reduce drug development times by an estimated 10 to 16 months. These legislative concepts would put into place several FDA performance measures in the IND/clinical development process, including the following:

- The FDA would be required to establish a meetings-management system under which the agency would meet with sponsors within a defined period following a meetings request (e.g., within 60 days for a pre-IND meeting).

- The agency would be required to respond within 30 days of a company's response to a clinical hold order.

- The FDA would be called upon to develop a paperless, electronic application submission system for all applications, including INDs.

Chapter 6

The Clinical Development of New Drugs

Virtually all preclinical work—animal pharmacology/toxicology testing and the development of the IND—is undertaken to obtain the FDA's permission to initiate clinical trials, the ultimate premarketing testing ground for unapproved drugs. During these trials, an investigational compound is administered to human subjects and is evaluated for its safety and efficacy in treating, preventing, or diagnosing a specific disease or condition. The results of this testing will comprise the single most important factor in the FDA's approval or disapproval of a new drug.

If the FDA's new drug review performance represented the dominant regulatory controversy of the 1980s and early 1990s, growing clinical development times had clearly supplanted it during the mid-1990s. A seemingly inexorable rise in clinical development times during the 1980s and 1990s, industry maintained, was making product development costs even more prohibitive, and was offsetting gains from the marked improvements in FDA drug review times.

There was a growing body of data to support these contentions. Recent studies, for instance, pegged the cost of developing a new drug at anywhere from $300 to $600 million expressed in 1996 dollars. Further, a 1996 study by the Tufts Center for the Study of Drug Development showed that, while the FDA's drug review times dropped 23 percent from the period 1990 through 1992 compared to the period 1993 through 1995, clinical development times rose 16 percent over these same time frames. The study also showed that average clinical development times were longer for new drugs approved in 1994 and 1995 (6.8 years and 7.4 years, respectively) than for drugs approved in any year since at least 1962.

This issue and a variety of other factors, including the fact that clinical development is the most complex and costly element in the drug development process, served as the backdrop for several emerging developments on the clinical testing landscape:

- *New FDA Guidance on Clinical Standards for Drug Approval.* Although the clinical testing process has long been the focus of the plurality of FDA guidelines, the agency added several important guidance documents to this corpus in the mid-1990s. Principal among these is a March 1997 draft guideline entitled *Providing Clinical Evidence of Effectiveness for Human Drug and Biological Products*, which offers the agency's latest views regarding the "quantitative and qualitative standards" for establishing drug effectiveness (see discussion below). Perhaps because it provides the agency's most detailed discussion to date on situations in which a single pivotal trial can support drug approval, the guidance was greeted by immediate praise from industry groups, which said that it would help companies better focus their research efforts. At the same time, the agency released a sister guideline entitled *FDA Approval of New Cancer Treatment Uses for Marketed Drug and Biological Products*.

  Supplementing these new FDA guidance documents are about a dozen clinically oriented guidelines developed under the International Conference on Harmonization (ICH) initiative (see discussion below). Among the more recent are two ICH draft guidelines, entitled *General Considerations for Clinical Trials* (May 1997), which describes internationally accepted principles for the conduct of clinical studies, and *Statistical Principles for Clinical Trials* (May 1997), which provides recommendations on trial design, conduct, analysis, and evaluation.

- *Globalization of Clinical Testing Programs.* Faced with the rising costs of product development, pharmaceutical companies have moved to leverage their clinical trials internationally. In fiscal year 1996, for example, CDER inspected more than double the number of foreign clinical trial sites than it had in fiscal year 1995. This is a clear sign that far more pivotal clinical trial data used for U.S. approval are being derived from foreign-based studies. Center inspectional statistics also provide clear indications of where most of the data were being developed: Canada (48 inspections), United Kingdom (27), France (18), Germany (14), The Netherlands (13), and Sweden (12).

- *Industry Efforts to Streamline Clinical Development.* Seeing their product development costs spiral and the pharmaceutical marketplace become increasingly competitive (i.e., managed care, generic competition), major companies quickly undertook initiatives to streamline the drug development process. These included the reduction of research and development staffs, the implementation of aggressive project timelines designed to slash clinical development times by as much as a third or more at some firms, and the increased use of contract research organizations (CRO) in managing clinical trials.

The clinical development program remains, without question, the most complex, time consuming, and costly element in the pharmaceutical development process. At a minimum, it requires a coordinated effort that features a sponsor willing to assume the financial, legal, and regulatory responsibilities associated with the program, the commitment and expertise of physicians, nurses, and other health-care professionals, and patients willing to take the chance that an experimental drug will do more for them than existing therapies.

The FDA's Role in Clinical Trials

The FDA plays at least three major roles in the clinical testing of a drug. As it does for animal studies, the FDA sets general standards for clinical studies to ensure that data derived from clinical trials are accurate. The agency accomplishes this goal essentially by maintaining and enforcing a set of related

115

guidelines and regulations called Good Clinical Practices, or GCP (see Chapter 7). These documents define the responsibilities of the key figures involved in clinical trials.

The FDA's second role is to protect, to the degree possible, the rights and safety of subjects participating in clinical trials. Obviously, since such testing involves the administration of pharmacologically active drugs to humans, the agency cannot guarantee the safety of clinical subjects. The FDA's role, then, is to ensure: (1) that clinical subjects are not exposed to any unnecessary risks; (2) that clinical subjects are exposed to the least possible risk given the benefit anticipated from the use of the drug; and (3) that all clinical subjects give their informed consent before entering a trial. The FDA does this not only through GCP regulations, but also by reviewing all proposed clinical protocols and all proposed changes to the protocols that may affect the safety of the subjects.

Lastly, by deciding the nature and quantity of clinical data necessary to establish a drug's safety and effectiveness, the FDA determines what testing is necessary in a clinical development program. Because the scientific and medical issues differ so significantly between drugs and medical conditions, the agency reaches such determinations on a case-by-case basis.

FDA and ICH Clinical Guidelines To help drug sponsors design clinical trials that are based upon sound scientific principles and that provide for the protection of clinical subjects, the FDA developed a guideline entitled *General Considerations for the Clinical Evaluation of Drugs*. Released in September 1977, the guidance document outlines the major elements of the clinical testing process, details acceptable approaches to meeting FDA requirements, and discusses study planning and design.

More recently, however, the FDA has released a spate of new draft clinical guidelines that were necessitated by the evolution of the science and practice of drug development and clinical evaluation. From 1977 to 1997, the FDA has published dozens of guidelines and other guidance documents on the clinical testing process and the clinical evaluation of specific types of drugs (see exhibit below).

Other CDER guidelines currently under development will supplement existing clinical guidances. For example, the center's Good Review Practices

FDA Clinical Guidelines, Points to Consider, and Related Guidelines

- *General Considerations for the Clinical Evaluation of Drugs* (1977)
- *General Considerations for the Clinical Evaluation of Drugs in Infants and Children* (1977)
- *Guidelines for the Clinical Evaluation of Antidepressant Drugs* (1977)
- *Guidelines for the Clinical Evaluation of Antianxiety Drugs* (1977)
- *Guidelines for the Clinical Evaluation of Anti-Infective Drugs (Systemic) (1977)*
- *Guideline for the Clinical Evaluation of Anti-Inflammatory and Antirheumatic Drugs (Children)* (May 1993)
- *Guideline for the Study and Evaluation of Gender Differences in the Clinical Evaluation of Drugs* (July 1993)
- *Draft Guideline for the Clinical Evaluation of Anti-Anginal Drugs* (January 1989)
- *Draft Guidelines for the Clinical Evaluation of Anti-Arrhythmic Drugs* (July 1985)
- *Guidelines for the Clinical Evaluation of Antidiarrheal Drugs* (1978)
- *Guidelines for the Clinical Evaluation of Gastric Secretory Depressant (GSD) Drugs* (1978)
- *Guidelines for the Clinical Evaluation of Hypnotic Drugs* (1978)
- *Guidelines for the Clinical Evaluation of Antacid Drugs* (1978)
- *Guidelines for the Clinical Evaluation of Motility-Modifying Drugs*
- *Guidelines for the Clinical Evaluation of Laxative Drugs* (1978)
- *Guidelines for the Clinical Evaluation of Psychoactive Drugs in Infants and Children* (1979)
- *Guidelines for the Clinical Evaluation of Bronchodilator Drugs* (1979)
- *Guidelines for the Clinical Evaluation of Drugs to Prevent, Control, and/or Treat Periodontal Disease* (1979)
- *Guidelines for the Clinical Evaluation of Drugs to Prevent Dental Caries* (1979)
- *Guidelines for the Clinical Evaluation of Analgesic Drugs* (Revised 1992)
- *Guidelines for the Clinical Evaluation of Drugs Used in the Treatment of Osteoporosis*
- *Guidelines for the Clinical Evaluation of Lipid-Altering Agents in Adults and Children* (1980)
- *Guidelines for the Clinical Evaluation of Antiepileptic Drugs (Adults and Children)* (1981)
- *Guidelines for the Clinical Evaluation of Radiopharmaceutical Drugs* (1981)
- *Guidelines for the Clinical Evaluation of Anti-Inflammatory and Antirheumatic Drugs (Adults and Children)* (Revised April 1988)
- *Guidelines for the Clinical Evaluation of General Anesthetics* (1982)

–continued–

**FDA Clinical Guidelines, Points to Consider,
and Related Guidelines** *(continued)*

- *Guidelines for the Clinical Evaluation of Local Anesthetics* (1982)
- *Proposed Guidelines for the Clinical Evaluation of Drugs for the Treatment of Congestive Heart Failure* (December 1987)
- *Proposed Guidelines for the Clinical Evaluation of Antihypertensive Drugs* (May 1988)
- *Guidelines for the Study of Drugs Likely to be Used in the Elderly* (November 1989)
- *Guidelines for the Clinical Evaluation of Drugs for Ulcerative Colitis* (Third Draft)
- *Draft Guidelines for the Development and Evaluation of Drugs for the Treatment of Psychoactive Substance Use Disorders* (February 1992)
- *Draft Guideline for Abuse Liability Assessment* (July 1990)
- *Draft Guidance for the Clinical Evaluation of Weight-Control Drugs* (November 1994)
- *FDA Requirements for Approval of Drugs to Treat Non-Small Cell Lung Cancer* (January 1991)
- *FDA Requirements for Approval of Drugs to Treat Superficial Bladder Cancer* (June 1989)
- *Oncologic Drugs Advisory Committee Discussion on FDA Requirements for Approval of New Drugs for Treatment of Colon and Rectal Cancers*
- *Points to Consider in the Clinical Development and Labeling of Anti-Infective Drug Products* (October 1992)
- *Points to Consider: Clinical Development Programs for MDI and DPI Drug Products* (September 1994)
- *Draft Points to Consider for OTC Actual Use Studies* (July 1994)
- *Providing Clinical Evidence of Effectiveness for Human Drug and Biological Products* (March 1997)
- *FDA Approval of New Cancer Treatment Uses for Marketed Drug and Biological Products* (March 1997)
- *Draft Guidance for Industry on Computerized Systems Used in Clinical Trials* (June 1997)

(GRP) initiative, which is designed to further standardize the application review process, is likely to provide new insights into the center's expectations regarding clinical trials and the resultant data. In November 1996, CDER released its first GRP draft guidance entitled *Conducting a Clinical Safety Review of a New Product Application and Preparing a Report on the Review.*

In recent years, FDA guidelines have been supplemented by several ICH guidelines directly relevant to the design and conduct of clinical trials, including:

- *Final Guideline on Dose-Response Information to Support Drug Registration* (November 1994);

- *Final Guideline on the Extent of Population Exposure Required to Assess Clinical Safety for Drugs Intended for Long-Term Treatment of Non-Life-Threatening Conditions* (March 1995);

- *Final Guideline on Good Clinical Practice: Consolidated Guideline* (May 1997);

- *Draft Guideline on General Considerations for Clinical Trials* (May 1997);

- *Draft Guideline on Statistical Principles for Clinical Trials* (May 1997);

- *Final Guideline on Studies in Support of Special Populations: Geriatrics* (August 1994);

- *Draft Guideline on Data Elements for [Electronic] Transmission of Individual Case Safety Reports* (October 1996);

- *Final Guideline on Clinical Safety Data Management: Definitions and Standards for Expedited Reporting* (March 1995); and

- *Final Guideline on the Structure and Content of Clinical Study Reports* (July 1996).

The ICH parties are also developing initial drafts of other clinical trial-related guidelines, including *Ethnic Factors in the Acceptability of Foreign Clinical Data* and *Choice of Control Group in Clinical Trials.*

The Structure of Clinical Trials

The design of a clinical trial will differ significantly from one drug and disease state to another. The nature of a drug, the product's proposed use, the results of the preclinical testing, and other pertinent factors are all considered when designing a clinical trial.

Although clinical trials for different drugs can vary greatly in design, they are often similar in structure. Since researchers may know little about a new compound prior to its use in humans, testing the drug through serially conducted investigations permits each phase of clinical development to be carefully designed to use and build upon the information obtained from the research stage preceding it.

Clinical programs for most new drugs begin with the cautious use of the investigational compound in small, carefully selected population groups, and proceed into larger, more clinically relevant, and increasingly diverse patient pools. In its October 1988 *Plan for Accelerated Approval of Drugs to Treat Life-Threatening and Severely Debilitating Illnesses*, the FDA discussed the structure of clinical trials and the basis for this structure:

> *"[The clinical] drug development process is generally thought of, in simplified terms, as consisting of three phases of human testing to determine if a drug is safe and effective: Phase 1 with 10 to 50 patients to study how the drug is tolerated, metabolized, and excreted; Phase 2 with 50 to 200 patients in which the safety and efficacy of the drug are first evaluated in controlled trials; and Phase 3 with 200 to 1,000 or more patients to confirm and expand upon the safety and efficacy data obtained from the first two phases... The three phases describe the usual process of drug development, but they are not statutory requirements. The basis for marketing approval is the adequacy of the data available; progression through the particular phases is simply the usual means the sponsor uses to collect the data needed for approval. The statute itself focuses on the standard of evidence needed for approval, as derived from adequate and well-controlled clinical investigations, with no mention of phases 1, 2, and 3."*

While acknowledging that clinical testing is often classified into these primary "temporal phases," the ICH's *Draft Guideline on General Considerations for Clinical Trials* (May 1997) also points out that the phases are descriptive rather than prescriptive. For some drugs, this "typical sequence" may be inappropriate or unnecessary, the guidance states (see exhibit below).

120

Phase 1 Clinical Trials

The earliest Phase 1 clinical trials, sometimes called "clinical pharmacology studies," represent the first introduction of a new drug into human subjects. The focus at this stage is the assessment of clinical safety. Except for extrapolations based on the safety profile obtained from animal studies, investigators may know little about the drug's possible clinical effects prior to these studies.

Phase 1 clinical trials provide an initial clinical indication of whether a drug is sufficiently safe to be used in further human testing. According to FDA regulations, "Phase 1 includes the initial introduction of an investigational new drug into humans... These studies are designed to determine the metabolism and pharmacologic actions of the drug in humans, the side effects associated with increasing doses, and, if possible, to gain early evidence on effectiveness. During Phase 1, sufficient information about the drug's pharmacokinetics and pharmacological effects should be obtained to permit the design of well-controlled, scientifically valid Phase 2 studies. The total number of subjects and patients included in Phase 1 studies varies with the drug, but is generally in the range of 20 to 80.

"Phase 1 studies also include studies of drug metabolism, structure-activity relationships, and mechanism of action in humans, as well as studies in which investigational drugs are used as research tools to explore biological phenomena or disease processes." These studies can also provide basic pharmacokinetic information, which allows for the comparison of human drug disposition to that of animals so that nonclinical findings can be correlated and verified.

It is worth noting that the term Phase 1 can refer not only to a stage of development (i.e., earliest human exposure), but also to a type of study (i.e., generally any clinical pharmacology study). This type of study may occur at various times throughout a drug's clinical development.

Phase 1 testing of a new drug is considered highly exploratory because there are often no human safety data available. For this reason, these studies are entered into very cautiously, with the drug being used in small numbers of subjects, each of whom must submit to close clinical observation for drug effects. Healthy adults whose schedules permit short-term confinement are ideal subjects.

Testing certain drugs in healthy adults is not considered ethical, however. Because of the known toxicities of certain classes of drugs, such as those used in treating AIDS and cancer, some Phase 1 studies are conducted with patients who have the condition for which the drug is being studied. Because healthy volunteers have no opportunity to benefit from the treatment, the administration of highly toxic compounds to such individuals is considered an unacceptable risk. Regardless of the patient population involved, however, these studies are focused on safety issues.

In the guideline entitled *General Considerations for the Clinical Evaluation of Drugs*, the FDA makes several recommendations for Phase 1 subject selection, including the following:

- in most cases, Phase 1 tests should involve "normal" volunteers (i.e., individuals free from abnormalities that would complicate the interpretation of the experiment or that might increase the subjects' sensitivity to the drug's toxic potential);

- individuals with mild but stable illnesses may be considered for inclusion in the initial study of a drug (e.g., patients with mild, uncomplicated hypertension or arthritis);

- it is permissible and is sometimes desirable to include subjects with certain abnormalities for which the drug is indicated;

- in most cases, children and patients with a serious primary disease and serious unrelated problems (e.g., cardiac, hepatic, renal, hematologic abnormalities) should be excluded from Phase 1 studies;

- generally, patients receiving concomitant drug therapy should be excluded, except when concomitant therapy is considered mandatory or routine;

- even when concomitant therapy is considered routine, every effort should be made to design and execute trials excluding concomitant therapy, provided this is consistent with ethical principles of patient care;

- generally, outpatients should not be utilized as initial recipients of an investigational drug;

- pretreatment physical exams and the following laboratory tests should be performed to screen out individuals with medically significant abnormalities: complete blood count (including platelet estimate); fasting blood sugar (or two-hour postprandial blood sugar); an electrocardiogram; blood urine nitrogen (or serum creatinine); liver function studies; and any other tests specifically indicated for the drug under study; and

- a glucose-6-phosphatase deficiency screen should be performed on individuals likely to be involved in repeated drug testing.

This guideline also reflects the FDA's previous policy that women of childbearing potential be excluded from Phase 1 studies. Because this policy was seen by some as paternalistic and because it denied women the right to make their own health-related decisions, the FDA revised the policy in 1993. The agency's *Guideline for the Study and Evaluation of Gender Differences in the Clinical Evaluation of Drugs* (July 1993) states that "the strict limitation on the participation of women of childbearing potential in Phase 1 and early Phase 2 trials that was imposed...has been eliminated." The guideline emphasizes the need to include both genders in clinical studies to "reflect the population that will receive the drug when it is marketed." Data should be analyzed to assess gender-based differences in individual studies and in the overall integrated analyses of safety and effectiveness. At this writing, the agency was developing a regulation that will address the inclusion of women in clinical trials.

PK/PD and Phase 1 Trials Based on the FDA's reviewing experience in the early 1990s, the selection of the starting dose for clinical trials was recognized as a weakness of many clinical programs. Traditional dose-based comparisons between animals and humans are inadequate largely because of major differences between species in the disposition and metabolism of drugs. Thus, calculations based on animal half-lives and dosing intervals often led to errors in selecting the starting dose for Phase 1 trials.

Under former CDER Director Carl Peck, M.D., the FDA advocated the greater use of pharmacokinetic/pharmacodynamic-based methods for the calculation of the starting dose. One such approach, which is supported by National Institutes of Health (NIH) studies of oncologic agents, reduces the number of dose levels required to reach a drug's maximum tolerated dose (MTD), thereby decreasing the number of patients needed for such tests. Termed "pharmacologically guided dose escalation," the technique uses target plasma levels based on preclinical studies to determine the size of doses to be administered during Phase 1 studies.

Peck also advocated the incorporation of pharmacokinetic/pharmacodynamic (PK/PD) studies in the first dose-tolerance trials. He maintained that these trials offer a unique, and possibly the only, opportunity to evaluate drug concentration-acute toxic effect relationships of poorly tolerated doses that will be avoided in subsequent trials.

The regulatory focus on early-stage PK/PD studies continued in the years following Peck's departure from CDER. In the ICH's 1994 final guideline entitled *Dose-Response Information To Support Drug Registration*, the ICH parties stated that dose-response data "are desirable for almost all new chemical entities" and that "assessment of dose-response should be an integral component of drug development with studies designed to assess dose-response an inherent part of establishing the safety and effectiveness of the drug. If development of dose-response information is built into the development process it can usually be accompanied with no loss of time and minimal extra effort compared to development plans that ignore dose-response."

Regarding the use of dose-response data in selecting an initial dose, the ICH guideline stated that "what is most helpful in choosing the starting dose of a drug is knowing the shape and location of the population (group) average dose-response curve for both desirable and undesirable effects. Selection of dose is best based on that information, together with a judgement about the relative importance of desirable and undesirable effects... Choice of a starting dose might also be affected by potential intersubject variability in pharmacodynamic response to a given blood concentration level, or by anticipated intersubject pharmacokinetic differences, such as could arise from nonlinear kinetics, metabolic polymorphism, or a high potential for pharmacokinetic drug-drug interactions.... In utilizing dose-response information, it is important to identify, to the extent possible, factors that lead to differences in pharmacokinetics of drugs among individuals, including demographic factors (e.g., age, gender, race), other diseases (e.g., renal or hepatic failure), diet, concurrent therapies, or individual characteristics (e.g., weight, body habitus, other drugs, metabolic differences)."

Because the shape of individual dose-response curves can be considerably different than the population (group) average dose-response curve, the ICH guideline notes that knowledge of the individual curves is useful in adjusting patient doses after observing the response to the initial dose. The guidance also discusses various approaches and specific study designs for deriving valid dose-response information, including parallel dose-response, cross-over dose response, forced titration, and optional titration (placebo-controlled titration to endpoint).

FDA efforts to develop additional guidelines provide further evidence of the agency's increasing interest in this area:

• Through an April 1997 guideline entitled *Drug Metabolism/Drug Interaction Studies in the Drug Development Process: Studies In Vitro,* the agency encourages sponsors to develop information on a drug's metabolic profile early in clinical trials. "An understanding of the metabolic profile of a drug *in vitro* would be useful prior to the initiation of Phase II studies and is especially important before Phase III trials," the guideline states. "Appropriately designed pharmacokinetic/Phase I studies could provide important information about drug metabolism, relevant metabolites, and actual or potential drug interactions. Blood level data obtained during Phase II and Phase III clinical trials, for example, via a pharmacokinetic screen, also could reveal interactions or marked inter-individual differences."

• A June 1997 CDER draft guideline entitled *Pharmacokinetics and Pharmacovigilance in Patients with Impaired Renal Function: Study Design, Data Analysis, and Impact on Dosing and Labeling* specifies when PK studies of patients with impaired renal function should be performed, and discusses the design and conduct of PK/PD studies in such individuals.

• In mid-1997, a CDER working group was developing a new draft guideline to provide recommendations on the PK/PD information necessary to support drug approval.

Phase 1 Investigator Selection Sponsors usually select the investigators to conduct their Phase 1 studies before the IND submission so that the names and qualifications of these physicians can be provided in the IND (additional investigators may be added at any time). The investigators responsible for conducting Phase 1 tests must meet specific qualification criteria; obviously, the scientific training and expertise of the clinical investigators must qualify them as suitable experts to investigate the safety of the drug.

The FDA advises that investigators performing Phase 1 tests involving "normal" volunteers should be skilled in the "initial evaluation of a variety of compounds for safety and pharmacological effect." In those cases in which diseased patients are studied under a Phase 1 protocol, investigators should be experts in the particular disease categories to be treated and/or experts in the evaluation of drug effects on the disease process.

Recording Phase 1 Data Phase 1 studies are relatively straightforward experiments. Before the administration of a drug, investigators obtain baseline data (e.g., information on a patient's existing medical condition). By defining the patient's condition before the study, baseline data give investigators a basis on which to measure a drug's short-term effects after administration.

Investigators monitor drug-related changes found in several measurable parameters. Factors such as the drug's proposed indication and the adverse effects found in preclinical studies will determine which clinical parameters investigators will monitor most closely during clinical trials.

Important baseline and drug effects information is recorded on case report forms throughout the clinical testing process. Designed specifically for the clinical study of a particular drug, case report forms (CRF) should allow for the collection of accurate and comprehensive data under a clinical protocol, and should promote the development of logical and usable data bases. These forms generally provide for the collection of objective data such as age and sex, measurements of important parameters such as blood pressure and white blood cell count, and depending on the nature of the study, subjective clinical assessments such as disease ratings. Most important, CRFs should facilitate the collection of information on validated clinical endpoints that are clinically relevant and meaningful.

It is the responsibility of the principal investigator (or his or her responsible staff) to record and verify the accuracy of data provided in case report

126

forms. When completed, the forms must be signed by the investigator and forwarded to the sponsor or the sponsor's agent for tabulation and analysis (copies are retained at the site). Federal regulations and FDA and ICH guidelines contain provisions regarding the storage and submission of case report forms and the source documents that support them, and specify that FDA inspectors must be given access to the forms during agency audits of key clinical studies.

International regulatory authorities have also taken steps in recent years to establish standards for the electronic collection, storage, and transmission of clinical trial data (e.g., remote data entry). In a June 1997 draft guidance entitled *Computerized Systems Used in Clinical Trials,* for example, the FDA establishes that when site staff enter clinical observations directly into a computer system (i.e., rather than on a patient record), the electronic record is considered the source data. The ICH's *Good Clinical Practice: Consolidated Guideline* (May 1997) also contains provisions relevant to computer-assisted clinical trials (see Chapter 7).

FDA-Sponsor Communication During Clinical Trials Although the clinical program becomes the primary focus of a drug's development once Phase 1 trials begin, other activities continue to support these trials. As clinical trials progress, FDA reviewers continually reassess the safety of these studies. Because the FDA wants these assessments to be based on the latest available data and information, the agency requires that sponsors submit periodic reports on completed and upcoming research. During clinical trials, at least four important types of data and information flow regularly from the sponsor to the FDA:

- *New Animal Data.* As mentioned previously, animal testing continues during clinical development. Submitted in the form of information amendments to the IND, additional toxicology and pharmacokinetic data may be needed from animal studies to support the safety of new and/or modified clinical studies. For example, longer-term toxicology studies are required as the duration of treatment in humans is extended.

- *Protocols and Protocol Amendments.* Because protocols for Phase 2 and Phase 3 trials are not normally included in the original IND, protocols for these studies must be forwarded to the FDA subsequently (see Chapter 4). Also, whenever sponsors want to make changes to previously submitted protocols, they must submit protocol amendments.

- *Annual Reports.* Current regulations require sponsors to submit brief annual reports on the progress of the investigation. These reports must include information on individual studies, provide a summary of the clinical experience with the drug, and provide information on the general investigational plan for the upcoming year, changes in the investigator's brochure, and foreign regulatory and marketing developments (see Chapter 4).

- *IND Safety Reports.* The drug sponsor must notify the FDA and all participating investigators about information that the company receives from any source indicating or suggesting significant hazards, contraindications, side effects, or precautions that are associated with the use of the drug. All significant safety findings must be reported (see Chapter 4).

Phase 2 Clinical Trials

Phase 2 clinical trials represent a shift away from testing designed almost entirely for safety to testing designed to provide a preliminary indication of a drug's effectiveness as well. In Phase 2 studies, a drug is used, often for the first time, in patients who suffer from the disease or condition that the drug is intended to prevent, diagnose, or treat.

FDA regulations state that "Phase 2 includes the controlled clinical studies conducted to evaluate the effectiveness of the drug for a particular indication or indications in patients with the disease or condition under study and to determine the common or short-term side effects and risks associated with the drug. Phase 2 studies are typically well-controlled, closely monitored, and conducted in a relatively small number of patients, usually involving no more than several hundred subjects."

In many ways, Phase 2 studies provide the foundation for several key aspects of the study design for the all-important Phase 3 trials. The observed

Phases of Clinical Investigation
(from the ICH's May 1997 *Draft Guideline on
General Considerations for Clinical Trials*)

Phase 1 (Most typical type of study: Human Pharmacology). Studies in Phase 1 typically involve one or a combination of the following assessments:

- *Estimation of initial safety and tolerability.* The initial and subsequent administration of an investigational new drug into humans is usually intended to determine the tolerability, and in particular, the highest dose with acceptable tolerability. These studies include both single and multiple-dose administration.

- *Determination of pharmacokinetics (PK).* Preliminary characterization of a drug's absorption, distribution, metabolism, and excretion is almost always an important goal of Phase 1. PK studies are undertaken to assess the presence of accumulation of parent drug or metabolites and to assess PK changes over time.

- *Assessment of pharmacodynamics (PD).* Depending on the investigational drug and the endpoint under study, PD studies and studies relating drug blood levels to response (PK/PD studies) may be conducted in healthy volunteer subjects or in patients with the target disease. In some studies involving patients, PD data can provide early estimates of drug activity and potential effectiveness and can guide the dosage and dose regimen in later studies.

- *Early measurement of activity.* Preliminary studies of activity or potential therapeutic benefit may be conducted in Phase 1 as a secondary objective. Such studies may be appropriate when effectiveness is readily measurable with a short duration of drug exposure.

Phase 2 (Most typical kind of study: Therapeutic exploratory). Generally, Phase 2 is considered to comprise studies in which the primary objective is to explore therapeutic effectiveness in patients. Initial therapeutic exploratory studies may use a variety of study designs, such as randomized controls and comparisons with baseline status. Subsequent trials are usually randomized and controlled to evaluate the efficacy of the drug and its safety for a particular therapeutic indication. The goals of Phase 2 studies include determining the dose(s) and regimen for Phase 3 studies and the evaluation of potential study endpoints, therapeutic regimens (including concomitant medications), and target populations (e.g., mild versus severe disease) for further study in Phase 2 or Phase 3 trials.

–continued–

Phases of Clinical Investigation *(continued)*

Phase 3 (Most typical kind of study: Therapeutic confirmatory). Usually, Phase 3 is considered to begin with the initiation of studies in which the primary objective is to confirm therapeutic effectiveness. Phase 3 studies are well-controlled trials designed to support marketing approval by confirming the preliminary evidence collected in Phase 2 that shows the drug to be safe and effective for use in the intended indication and population. Studies in Phase 3 may also further explore the dose-response relationship, or explore the drug's use in a broader population, in different disease stages, or in combination with another drug.

Phase 4 (Variety of studies: Therapeutic Use). Phase 4 includes all postapproval studies (other than routine surveillance) related to the approved indication. These studies, which are not considered necessary for approval but are often important for optimizing the drug's use, include additional drug-drug interaction, dose-response, or safety studies and studies designed to support an extended claim under the approved indication (e.g., mortality/morbidity studies).

---

magnitude of the treatment effect in Phase 2 trials is a critical factor in Phase 3 sample size calculations, for example.

Since Phase 2 trials also involve the first meaningful assessment of a drug's effects on key clinical endpoints (i.e., clinical events or measurements used to assess drug effectiveness), these studies can provide valuable information on the utility of a variety of clinical endpoints and markers. Sponsors and investigators can then use this information to select the most appropriate endpoints—those most reflective of the disease and responsive to therapy, for example—for Phase 3 trials (see discussion of clinical endpoints below).

Generally, Phase 2 study objectives also include the determination of the minimum dose that is maximally effective, or that is sufficiently effective without undue toxicity. Well-conducted Phase 2 studies of pharmacokinetic and pharmacodynamic parameters may provide useful insights as to whether different subpopulations (e.g., defined by gender, age, or concomitant illness) require different dosing regimens.

Phase 2 trials can also be used to study the use of, and the investigational drug's interactions with, concomitant therapies common to the relevant clinical setting. Drug interaction information may help identify which concomitant medications should be excluded from Phase 3 trials because of safety concerns, interference with the experimental treatment, or interference with the procedures used to measure treatment effects.

Because a drug's short-term side effects remain primary concerns during Phase 2 investigations, the compound is administered to a limited number of patients who are closely monitored by the investigators. The use of the drug in larger numbers of subjects (i.e., compared to Phase 1) may reveal less-frequent side effects and provide for better estimates of the dose-toxicity relationships for the more frequently observed adverse effects.

When it is both possible and useful, Phase 2 studies should be "controlled" investigations—in other words, the studies should involve the comparison of the experimental drug against a placebo and/or standard therapy. To minimize bias, the studies should employ a randomization and blinding scheme (see discussion below). Generally, the experimental drug is administered to one group of subjects, while the placebo or standard therapy is administered to a similar group. The safety and effectiveness of the two therapies can then be compared.

Some Phase 2 studies may also employ a parallel design in which study subjects are randomized to one of a limited number of dose levels or regimens. The assessment of response in each treatment group provides the basis for the selection of the optimal doses and regimens to be studied in Phase 3 trials.

Specific FDA recommendations for Phase 2 studies, as taken from the agency's *General Considerations for the Clinical Evaluation of Drugs*, include the following (many of these same recommendations apply equally to Phase 3):

- Phase 2 studies should be performed by investigators who are considered experts in the particular disease categories to be treated and/or in the evaluation of drug effects on the disease process;

- patients selected for early Phase 2 studies ordinarily should be free of hematologic, hepatic, renal, cardiac, or other serious diseases;

- to avoid possible interference with the assessment of safety and effectiveness of the investigational drug, patients should, in most cases, be receiving no concomitant therapy;

- patients with concomitant diseases and therapy may be included in late Phase 2 studies, since they are representative of certain segments of the population that would use the investigational drug if it gained marketing approval;

- the frequency of visits and of laboratory tests for Phase 2 will vary depending on the nature and safety of the drug (including its intended use);

- specialized "safety" and pharmacological laboratory tests should be performed as required by the nature of the drug;

- routine "safety" laboratory tests should be performed at frequent intervals (CBC should include platelet estimates);

- when an investigational drug or another active compound is altered significantly during manufacturing or through the use of excipients to accommodate a single- or double-blind trial, blood-level studies (or urinary excretion studies if blood levels are not feasible) should be performed to indicate that the alteration has not materially affected its absorption or excretory process;

- any significant change in the formulation or manufacture of the investigational drug during the course of late Phase 2 clinical trials will require bioavailability studies so that meaningful comparisons can be made among the clinical trials performed with the various formulations;

- for chronically administered drugs that are known to be absorbed, complete ophthalmologic examinations (pre- and post-drug) should be performed on a representative number of patients followed for six months or preferably longer on the drug; and

- for certain drugs administered for shorter periods in clinical trials, eye examinations should be performed at the end of drug administration (however, the possibility of delayed effects on the eye should be considered).

Given the comparatively small numbers of patients enrolled in Phase 2 trials, these studies generally are unable to provide the definitive evidence of efficacy and safety necessary to support approval. Under the FDA's expedited development (Subpart E) program, however, Phase 2 trials for products designed to treat life-threatening and severely debilitating diseases may be prospectively designed to support marketing approval (see Chapter 16).

End-of-Phase 2 Meetings Traditionally, the FDA has reserved end-of-Phase 2 conferences for sponsors of either new molecular entities (NME) or important new uses of already-marketed drugs. And although the agency still points out that these meetings are designed primarily for sponsors of such products, the FDA has made the conferences available to all new drug sponsors, regardless of the classification of their products. According to a March 1996 policy document entitled *Formal Meetings Between CDER and CDER's External Constituents*, the center claims that it will agree to sponsor requests for formal meetings "unless they are clearly unnecessary or premature."

FDA regulations state that the purposes of end-of-Phase 2 meetings are to determine the safety of proceeding to Phase 3, to evaluate the Phase 3 plan and protocols, and to identify any additional information necessary to support a marketing application for the uses under investigation. The ultimate goal of such a meeting is for the sponsor and the FDA to reach agreement on plans for the conduct and design of Phase 3 trials.

As its name implies, the end-of-Phase 2 meeting takes place after the completion of Phase 2 clinical trials and before the initiation of Phase 3 studies. Since agency recommendations may bring about significant revisions to a sponsor's Phase 3 trial plans, the agency suggests that these meetings be held before "major commitments of effort and resources to specific Phase 3 tests are made." The FDA adds, however, that such meetings are not intended to delay the transition from Phase 2 to Phase 3 studies.

The agency considers the sponsor's preparation for an end-of-Phase 2 conference to be of critical importance in determining the meeting's ultimate utility. According to federal regulations, "at least 1 month in advance of an end-of-Phase 2 meeting, the sponsor should submit background information on the sponsor's plan for Phase 3, including summaries of the Phase 1 and 2 investigations, the specific protocols for Phase 3 clinical studies, plans for any additional nonclinical studies, and, if available, tentative labeling for the drug." CDER staffers advise that the sponsor be prepared to discuss any remaining issues regarding manufacturing and controls, since the drug formulation used in Phase 3 should correspond closely to the product that is ultimately approved and marketed.

At the conference, to which both CDER and the sponsor may bring outside consultants, agency attendees may number a dozen or more, and may include the reviewing chemist, medical officer, and pharmacologist (and possibly their supervisors), the division director and deputy director, the reviewing biostatistician, a biopharmaceutics reviewer, and the project manager/consumer safety officer (CSO) assigned to the drug's IND. The focus "…should be directed primarily at establishing agreements between FDA and the sponsor of the overall plan for Phase 3 and the objectives and design of particular studies. The adequacy of technical information to support Phase 3 studies and/or a marketing application may also be discussed." Ideally, end-of-Phase 2 conferences result in FDA-sponsor agreements in each of these areas.

As they should in all communications with the FDA, sponsors should attempt to obtain from FDA reviewers and officials specific recommendations during the meeting. Agency staffers advise that sponsors develop highly specific questions, and that they focus these questions not only on safety issues regarding Phase 3 protocols, but on what studies and data will be necessary for the ultimate approval of the drug as well.

According to federal regulations, "agreements reached at the meetings on these matters will be recorded in minutes of the conference that will be taken by FDA…and provided to the sponsor. The minutes along with any other written material provided to the sponsor will serve as a permanent record of any agreements reached." The regulations add that, "barring a significant scientific development that requires otherwise, studies conducted in accordance with the agreement shall be presumed to be sufficient in objective and design for the purpose of obtaining marketing approval for the drug."

Despite such statements, the pharmaceutical industry remained concerned about what it perceived as an agency tendency to change trial design requirements, particularly clinical endpoints, even after agreements had been reached. These concerns were reflected in a 1997 FDA/industry request that Congress include new provisions regarding agency/sponsor agreements in the reauthorization of the Prescription Drug User Fee Act. After holding discussions on trial design issues, the proposal states, the FDA and a sponsor could enter a "written protocol agreement" specifying trial- and approval-related criteria that would be considered binding unless there were relevant changes in scientific understanding.

Phase 3 Clinical Trials

In Phase 3 investigations, a drug is tested under conditions more closely resembling those under which the drug would be used if approved for marketing. During this phase, an investigational compound is administered to a significantly larger patient population (i.e., from several hundred to several thousand subjects) to, in the FDA's words, "gather additional information about effectiveness and safety that is needed to evaluate the overall benefit-risk relationship of the drug and to provide an adequate basis for physician labeling."

The larger patient pool and the genetic, lifestyle, environmental, and physiological diversity that it brings allow the investigators to identify potential adverse drug reactions and to determine the appropriate dosage of the drug for the more diverse general population. Patient population criteria for Phase 3 trials may also be expanded to include those with concomitant therapies and conditions.

As defined by a trial's eligibility criteria, the patient population studied in Phase 3 trials will always be a subset of the overall population with a particular disease or condition. The study population in Phase 3 must be sufficiently homogeneous so that variability in response(s) is minimized and so that the study has adequate power to demonstrate an effect. At the same time, the study population must be adequately representative to enable the generalization of the results to the patient population at large.

Depending on the nature of a drug and the seriousness of the disease/condition under study, Phase 3 trials may be conducted on an outpatient basis. Since a drug's safety has already been established to some degree in smaller groups, Phase 3 subjects often are monitored less rigorously. An outpatient setting requires extensive coordination, including the screening, scheduling, treatment, and evaluation of the larger patient population.

The Pivotal Clinical Study Phase 3 testing may produce data from controlled and uncontrolled trials conducted at several hospitals, clinics, or other sites outlined in the protocol. But the clinical data that the FDA will review most closely and upon which the agency will base its approval/disapproval decision are those derived from tests specified in federal regulations as "adequate and well-controlled studies." These are sometimes called "pivotal studies."

The focus on pivotal clinical studies as the primary criterion for approving new drugs is rooted in the Federal Food, Drug and Cosmetic Act, which states that "the term 'substantial evidence' means evidence consisting of adequate and well-controlled investigations...on the basis of which it could fairly and responsibly be concluded by...experts that the drug will have the effect it purports or is represented to have under the conditions of use prescribed, recommended, or suggested in the labeling or proposed labeling thereof."

The concept of substantial evidence has a second important component. With rare exceptions, at least two adequate and well-controlled studies are necessary to obtain FDA approval for a new drug. According to the FDA's *Guideline for the Content and Format of the Clinical and Statistical Sections of an Application*, "the requirement for well-controlled clinical investigations has been interpreted to mean that the effectiveness of a drug should be supported by more than one well-controlled trial and carried out by independent investigators. This interpretation is consistent with the general scientific demand for replicability. Ordinarily, therefore, the clinical trials submitted in an application will not be regarded as adequate support of a claim unless they include studies by more than one independent investigator who maintains adequate case histories of an adequate number of subjects."

With the release of its March 1997 draft *Guidance for Industry - Providing Clinical Evidence of Effectiveness for Human Drug and Biological Products*, however, the FDA took an important step in clarifying—some might say evolving—its standards for approval, in particular its stance regarding the need for two well-controlled trials. The agency stated that it was appropriate to re-articulate its current thinking concerning the "quantitative and qualitative standards for demonstrating effectiveness of drugs" because "the science and practice of drug development and clinical evaluation have evolved significantly since the effectiveness requirement for drugs was established, and this evolution has implications for the amount and type of data needed to support effectiveness in certain cases... At the same time, progress in clinical evaluation has resulted in more rigorously designed and conducted clinical efficacy trials, which are ordinarily conducted at more than one clinical site. This added rigor and scope has implications for a study's reliability, generalizability, and capacity to substantiate effectiveness.

"The requirement for more than one adequate and well-controlled investigation reflects the need for *independent substantiation* of experimental results…, [which is] often referred to as the need for 'replication' of the finding. Replication may not be the best term, however, as it may imply that precise repetition of the same experiment in other patients by other investigators is the only means to substantiate a conclusion. Precise replication of a trial is only one of a number of possible means of obtaining independent substantiation of a clinical finding and, at times, can be less than optimal as it could leave the conclusions vulnerable to any systematic biases inherent to the particular study design. Results that are obtained from studies that are independent in both design and execution, perhaps evaluating different populations, endpoints, or dosage forms, may provide support for a conclusion of effectiveness that is as convincing as, or more convincing than, a repeat of the same study."

This important draft guidance also identifies situations in which the agency will consider approving new drugs or new uses of approved medicines without data from two adequate and well-controlled studies. To the pharmaceutical industry, the guidance's most intriguing aspect was a discussion of the situations in which a single pivotal study could provide the basis for marketing approval. Although the agency had issued a 1995 statement specifying when a single, multicenter study could support approval, the FDA points out that it had not "comprehensively described the situations" in which a single study might be used or the characteristics of a single study that would make it adequate to support approval.

While the FDA contends that none of the characteristics "is necessarily determinative," the presence of one or more of four characteristics can contribute to a conclusion that a single pivotal study would be adequate to support approval:

1. *Large Multicenter Study*: "In a large multicenter study in which (1) no single study site provided an unusually large fraction of the patients and (2) no single investigator or site was disproportionately responsible for the effect seen, concerns about lack of generalizability

of the finding or an inexplicable result involving a single investigator are lessened."

2. *Multiple "Studies" in a Single Study*: "Large multicenter studies may have prospective stratifications or identified analytic subsets based on variables such as disease severity, geographic residence, or demographic characteristics. Where the strata are randomized separately and each shows a significant effect, the study provides two or more separate estimates of the effect, albeit not by independent investigators and often not with a clear prospective intent to do so."

3. *Multiple Endpoints Involving Different Events*: "In some cases, a single study will include several important, prospectively identified primary or secondary endpoints, each of which represents a beneficial, but different effect. Where a study shows statistically persuasive evidence of an effect on more than one of such endpoints, the internal weight of evidence of the study is enhanced."

4. *Statistically Very Powerful Finding*: "In a multicenter study, an extreme p-value indicates that the result is highly inconsistent with the null hypothesis of no treatment effect. In some studies it is possible to detect nominally significant results in data from several centers, but even where that is not possible an overall extreme result and significance level means that most study centers had similar findings."

The guidance also offers several caveats regarding the use of a single pivotal trial for approval. Reliance on a single study, the agency points out, generally will be limited to situations in which a trial has demonstrated a clinically meaningful effect on mortality, irreversible morbidity, or prevention of a disease with a potentially serious outcome, such that confirmation of the result in a second trial would be ethically difficult or impossible.

Because of their central importance to the FDA's approval decision, pivotal studies must meet particularly high scientific standards: "The purpose of conducting clinical investigations of a drug is to distinguish the effect of a drug from other influences, such as spontaneous change in the course of the disease, placebo effect, or biased observation," the agency states. Therefore, adequate and well-controlled trials are designed to isolate the drug's effects from extraneous factors that might otherwise undermine the validity of the trials' results.

Generally, a study must meet four criteria to be considered pivotal:

1. A pivotal study must be a controlled trial. As previously discussed, a controlled trial, in many cases, compares a group of patients treated with a placebo or standard therapy against a group of patients treated with the investigational drug. The FDA states in federal regulations that five types of controls generally are recognized: placebo concurrent controls; dose-comparison concurrent controls; no treatment concurrent controls; active treatment concurrent controls; and historical controls.

2. A pivotal study must have a blinded design when such a design is practical and ethical. According to the ICH's draft guideline on *Statistical Principles for Clinical Trials*, "blinding is intended to limit the occurrence of conscious and unconscious bias in the conduct and interpretation of a clinical trial arising from the influence that knowledge of treatment may have on the recruitment and allocation of subjects, the assessment of end points, the handling of withdrawals, the exclusion of data from analysis, and so on. The essential aim is to prevent identification of the treatments until all such opportunities for bias have passed." Double-blind trials are those in which the subjects and the investigator and sponsor staff involved in treating and evaluating patients are kept from knowing which subjects are receiving the experimental drug and which are receiving the placebo/standard therapy. When double-blind trials are not feasible (e.g., because the pattern of administration differs), studies may employ single blinds, in which only the subjects are kept from knowing which treatment is administered. In some cases, however, only an open-label study is possible because of ethical or practical factors.

3. A pivotal study must be randomized. This means that clinical subjects are assigned randomly to the treatment and control groups.

Therefore, each subject has an equal chance of being assigned to the various treatment and control groups to be studied in a particular trial. In combination with blinding, randomization helps prevent potential bias in the selection and assignment of trial subjects.

4. A pivotal study must be of adequate size. The study must involve enough patients to provide statistically significant evidence that a new drug offers a therapeutic or safety advantage over existing therapies. According to the FDA's *General Considerations for the Clinical Evaluation of Drugs*, the size of a pivotal study is dependent upon factors such as: (1) the degree of response one wishes to detect; (2) the desired assurance against a false positive finding; and (3) the acceptable risk of failure to demonstrate the response when it is present in the population. Sample size calculations require many assumptions about the results to be obtained with the treatment and the population being studied. Because considerable clinical judgement is employed in making these assumptions, FDA officials warn that faulty presumptions frequently result in studies of inadequate statistical power.

These criteria also are included in FDA regulations, which add that the "characteristics" of adequate and well-controlled studies include the following:

- a clear statement of the objectives of the study;

- a design that permits a valid comparison with a control to provide a quantitative assessment of the drug effect;

- a method of subject selection that provides adequate assurance that subjects have the disease or condition being studied, or that they show evidence of susceptibility and exposure to the condition against which prophylaxis is directed;

- a method of assigning patients to treatment and control groups that minimizes bias and that is intended to assure comparability of the groups with respect to pertinent variables such as age, sex, severity of disease, duration of disease, and the use of drugs or therapy other than test drugs;

- adequate measures to minimize bias by the subjects, observers, and analysts of the data;

- well-defined and reliable methods of assessing subjects' responses; and

- an adequate analysis of the study results to assess the effects of the drug.

The FDA wrote in 1987 that it "has long considered [these] characteristics as the essentials of an adequate and well-controlled study... In general, the regulation on adequate and well-controlled studies has two overall objectives: (1) To allow the agency to assess methods for minimizing bias; and (2) to assure a sufficiently detailed description of the study to allow scientific assessment and interpretation of it."

It is worth noting that federal regulations do not provide a comprehensive discussion of the testing conditions necessary for pivotal trials. Mentions of other standards that the FDA sees as necessary for pivotal studies are scattered throughout a variety of agency guidelines. Although it does not address pivotal trials directly, the ICH's draft guideline on *Statistical Principles for Clinical Trials* offers a useful discussion regarding important aspects of later-phase study design issues, including study configuration (e.g., crossover and parallel group), trial comparisons (e.g., superiority, equivalence), and sample size.

There are, of course, multiple factors that influence the ultimate design of any one clinical trial, and the FDA does not apply its requirements inflexibly. The preamble to a 1987 regulation stated that "FDA recognizes...that ethical and practical considerations will play a central role in the type of study selected, a decision that will ordinarily depend upon the type and seriousness of the disease being treated, availability of alternative therapies, and the nature of the drug and the patient population. In each case, applicants must choose the particular type of study they will use based on ethical, scientific, and practical reasons. So long as these judgements are justifiable, and the studies are properly designed, the approvability of an application will not be affected."

Regardless of how closely the FDA works with sponsors on trial design issues, experienced researchers and agency staffers know that any of several

Drug Effectiveness and Clinical Endpoints

Clinical effectiveness endpoints were the focus of considerable controversy during the 1980s, and have been the subject of widespread discussion and debate throughout the 1990s. Endpoints are generally clinical events (e.g., death, loss of vision, myocardial infarction) or measurements (e.g., blood pressure or antibody count) used to help assess a drug's effectiveness. In the context of a clinical trial, the assessment of a drug's effectiveness will consist of the product's ability to prevent an adverse clinical event such as death or illness, or to otherwise modify a clinical endpoint in a manner that has clear clinical benefits for the patient.

The most recent discussion of clinical endpoints by regulatory authorities appears in the ICH's draft guideline on *Statistical Principles for Clinical Trials* (May 1997). While most such discussions tend to focus on primary and surrogate endpoints, this draft guideline identifies several types of endpoints, or "variables:"

- *Primary Endpoint.* Primary endpoints include death, serious morbidity, and other events whose presence or absence have a clear and definite clinical effect. Because primary endpoints have obvious clinical relevance and are comparatively easy to observe and measure, they are ideal for the objective study of drug efficacy. According to the draft ICH guideline, "the primary variable should be the variable capable of providing the most clinically relevant and convincing evidence directly related to the primary objective of the trial. There should generally be only one primary variable, [which] will usually be an efficacy variable... The selection of the primary variable should reflect the accepted norms and standards in the relevant field of research... There should be sufficient evidence that the primary variable can provide a valid and reliable measure of some clinically relevant and important treatment benefit in the subject population described by the inclusion and exclusion criteria."

- *Secondary Endpoints.* Secondary objectives "are either supportive measurements related to the primary objective or measurements of effects related to the secondary objectives."

- *Composite Endpoints.* "Another strategy that may be useful in some situations is to integrate or combine the multiple measurements into a single, or 'composite,' variable, using a predefined algorithm," the May 1997 ICH draft guidance states. "Indeed, the primary variable sometimes arises as a combination of multiple clinical measurements (e.g., the rating scales used in arthritis, psychiatric disorders, and elsewhere)."

- *Global Assessment Endpoints.* Global assessment variables, which integrate objective variables and the investigator's overall impression about the state or change in the state of the subject, are developed to measure a treatment's "overall safety, overall efficacy, and/or overall usefulness." Because of the subjective component of global assessment variables, the protocol should address the relevance of the global scale to the primary trial objective and the basis for the scale's validity.

- *Surrogate Endpoints.* A secondary measure, or "surrogate" endpoint, is generally an event or measure that is thought to be related to, and to be likely to predict, the drug's effect on a more clinically relevant, or primary, endpoint. According to the ICH draft guidance, "when direct assessment of the clinical benefit to the subject through observing actual clinical efficacy is not practical, indirect criteria (surrogate variables) may be considered. Commonly accepted surrogate variables are used in a number of indications where they are believed to be reliable predictors of clinical benefit." The ICH parties state that there are two primary concerns regarding the use of proposed surrogate endpoints: (1) an endpoint may not represent a true predictor of the clinical outcome of interest; and (2) the endpoint may not yield a quantitative measure of clinical benefit that can be weighed directly against adverse effects.

Because the acceptance of surrogate endpoints can lead to shorter and less expensive clinical trials, their identification, validation, and use has been a priority for industry. The FDA has a history of basing approval on surrogate endpoints when there exists substantial evidence that drug effects on the surrogate marker would lead to, or are associated with, the desired effects on morbidity and mortality. For example, the agency has approved drugs for hypertension based on their effects on blood pressure rather than on survival or stroke rate. Likewise, the FDA has approved drugs for hypercholesterolemia based on effects on serum cholesterol levels rather than on coronary artery disease (i.e., angina, heart attacks). The agency also has approved certain AIDS products based on surrogate endpoints (e.g., increases in CD4 cell counts).

In December 1992, the FDA established, for the first time, specific policies under which it would approve drugs based on surrogate endpoints that are "not so well established as the surrogates ordinarily used as bases for approval in the past." Under the Subpart H accelerated drug approval regulation, the agency stated that, when appropriate, it would base the approvals of drugs for serious and life-threatening conditions on surrogate endpoints, and that it would require that the sponsor conduct postmarketing studies to verify the relationship between the surrogate and the ultimate clinical benefit (see Chapter 16).

In discussing its plan, the FDA acknowledged both the benefits and drawbacks of surrogate endpoints. "Approval of a drug on the basis of a well-documented effect on a surrogate endpoint can allow a drug to be marketed earlier, sometimes much earlier, than it could if a demonstrated clinical benefit were required," the agency declares. "Reliance on a surrogate endpoint almost always introduces some uncertainty into the risk/benefit assessment, because clinical benefit is not measured directly and the quantitative relation of the effect on the surrogate to the clinical effect is rarely known. The expected risk/benefit relationship may fail to emerge because: (1) The identified surrogate may not in fact be causally related to clinical outcome (even though it was thought to be) or (2) the drug may have a smaller than expected benefit and a larger than expected adverse effect that could not be recognized without large-scale clinical trials of long duration. Reliance on surrogate markers therefore requires an additional measure of judgement, not only weighing benefit versus risk, as always, but also deciding what the therapeutic benefit is based upon the drug effect on the surrogate."

Ironically, it was concerns voiced by AIDS advocacy groups, which had been such a driving force in the establishment of the FDA's accelerated development and access programs, that caused the agency to reassess its use of surrogate endpoints in the mid-1990s. With CD4 counts seeming to represent a less reliable predictor of clinical outcome than at first hoped, these groups and others had begun to question the wisdom of basing approval on largely unvalidated surrogate endpoints.

Still, with 15 drugs approved under the Subpart H program from January 1994 through December 1996, the program remains one of the FDA's more active accelerated development programs (see Chapter 16). Other divisions charged with regulating drugs for life-threatening diseases have recently embraced the Subpart H program and the use of surrogate endpoints. Under its *Oncology Initiative*, for instance, the Division of Oncologic Drug Products announced in early 1996 that it "may now rely on partial response (such as measurable but incomplete shrinkage of a tumor) to a therapy, in addition to the current criteria such as a patient's survival and improved quality of life… By basing accelerated approval on surrogate markers such as tumor shrinkage for patients who have no satisfactory alternative therapy, and by allowing more definitive data on survival or other criteria to be developed after marketing approval, FDA believes that many cancer therapies will reach patients sooner." At the same time, the agency acknowledged that "the predictive value of partial response may still be a matter of discussion and study."

FDA reform proposals seemed to illustrate continuing industry support for the increased use of surrogate endpoints. For example, a Senate FDA reform bill introduced in mid-1997 proposed a new "fast track" drug development and review procedure under which the FDA would be required to "establish an ongoing program to encourage development and use of surrogate endpoints which are reasonably likely to predict clinical benefit for all serious and life-threatening conditions for which there exist significant unmet medical needs."

The complexities of assessing the true relationships between surrogate endpoints and clinical benefits has led researchers to seek alternative methods of confirmation. One of the more notable methods is the so-called "large, simple trial." By conducting extremely large studies (i.e., several thousands of patients) with a relatively straightforward design, researchers can assess the small-to-moderate, but real, drug effects on tangible endpoints, such as major morbidity and mortality, in a reasonably short time. Although many of these studies have been conducted on a postmarketing basis, the implication is that future large, simple trials could be conducted during Phase 3.

complicating factors can contribute to the possibility that a trial's design will be questioned. These include the following:

Limits on the Trial Design Issues that Can Be Resolved in Advance. Trial size is a typical example of the design issues that are difficult to resolve entirely in advance, according to FDA staffers.

Sponsor-FDA Disagreements. Meetings are not always successful in resolving different viewpoints.

Changes in Technology and Medical Knowledge. In the several years needed to test a new drug in humans, it is possible—in some situations likely—that new technology, medical knowledge, and competing therapies will somehow change the standards by which a drug will be evaluated. Such advances will sometimes undermine the scientific principles (e.g., the relevance of the clinical endpoints) on which a study's design is based.

Completing a Drug's Clinical Study

It is in the best interest of the sponsor, the clinical subjects, and, in many cases, the public that a drug's clinical study be completed as soon as sufficient safety and efficacy data are obtained. If a drug is found during the development process to be unsafe or ineffective, then continuing a trial only exposes more clinical subjects to a dangerous or useless compound, and in some cases, keeps study subjects from using better or safer therapies. On the other hand, if the drug is clearly shown to be safer or more effective than existing therapies, delaying the submission of an NDA to gain additional data needlessly prolongs the development process.

Clinical trials may be discontinued before reaching their subject accrual targets for any one of several reasons, including the following:

- the studies clearly establish a drug's safety and effectiveness;

- an unacceptable adverse effect is discovered; or

- it becomes apparent that the studies are unlikely to establish a drug's safety or effectiveness, or that a drug's apparent safety and effectiveness are less than that of a standard therapy.

When designing the trial, statisticians will establish what are called "stopping rules." These are rigorous statistical criteria or goals that, if met at some point during the study of a drug, will trigger the end of the clinical trial. To justify discontinuing the trial, the data generally must meet stringent standards to show, for example, that the drug's effects are: (1) statistically significant (i.e., that the drug was tested in a large enough patient population to ensure that observed effects were not due to chance); and (2) clinically significant (i.e., that the test results are sufficient to show that there is a perceptible difference in the clinical effect between the investigational drug and the placebo and/or a standard therapy).

The periodic analysis of accrued data—interim analysis—is undertaken during the clinical trial to determine if any of the stopping criteria have been met. Because interim analyses can affect the interpretation of the clinical trial, they must be planned and scheduled in advance and disclosed in the clinical protocol.

According to the ICH's draft guideline on *Statistical Principles for Clinical Trials*, "most clinical trials intended to support the efficacy and safety of an investigational product should proceed to full completion of planned sample size accrual; trials should be stopped early only for ethical reasons or if the power is no longer acceptable. However, it is recognized that drug development plans involve the need for sponsor access to comparative treatment data for a variety of reasons, such as planning other studies or when only a subset of trials will involve the study of serious life-threatening outcomes or mortality which may need sequential monitoring of accruing comparative treatment effects for ethical reasons. In either of these situations, plans for interim statistical analysis should be in place in the protocol or in protocol amendments prior to the unblinded access to comparative treatment data in order to deal with the potential statistical and operational bias that may be introduced."

Phase 4 Clinical Studies

In a very real sense, the clinical development process continues long after a product's approval. The further collection and analysis of adverse experience information and other data provide the sponsor and the FDA with a continuing flow of information so that a drug's safety and effectiveness can be reassessed periodically in light of the latest data.

Phase 4 clinical trials, which are studies initiated after a drug's marketing approval, have become an increasingly important and common method through which sponsors obtain new information about their marketed drugs. A drug manufacturer may undertake postmarketing clinical studies for any one of several reasons, including the following:

- To satisfy an FDA request made prior to an NDA's approval that Phase 4 trials be conducted following approval (see Chapter 12). For example, the FDA may want the sponsor to better characterize the drug's safety and/or effectiveness in patient groups that may not have been widely represented in pivotal trials (e.g., children, persons using concomitant medications).

- To develop pharmacoeconomic, or cost-effectiveness, data that can be used to support marketing claims highlighting the advantages of a drug over competing therapies. Given the emergence of managed care and the increased focus on health care costs, however, growing numbers of companies are incorporating the study of pharmacoeconomic parameters in their premarketing studies.

Aside from the fact that they are conducted after approval, Phase 4 studies may differ in a number of important respects from Phase 1, 2, and 3 trials. Phase 4 studies are often of a larger scale than are premarketing studies. Also, they may be less rigorously controlled than key preapproval studies, although the FDA is monitoring the scientific integrity of these studies, particularly those to be used in support of comparative efficacy and pharmacoeconomic claims.

Chapter 7

Good Clinical Practices (GCP)

Because the FDA's approval of a new drug is based largely on clinical data, the agency has a vested interest in these data and the conditions under which they are obtained. Through a set of regulations and guidelines collectively known as "good clinical practices" (GCP), the FDA sets minimum standards for conducting clinical trials.

By identifying and defining the responsibilities of the key personnel involved in clinical trials, the FDA's GCP regulations are designed to accomplish two primary goals: (1) to ensure the quality and integrity of the data obtained from clinical testing so that the FDA's decisions based on these data are informed and responsible; and (2) to protect the rights and, to the degree possible, the welfare of clinical subjects.

In reality, GCP is a term of convenience used by those in government and industry to identify a collection of related regulations that, when taken together, define the clinical trial-related responsibilities of the sponsor, the investigator, the monitor, and the institutional review board (IRB). Traditionally, these responsibilities have been found primarily in four documents:

- a 1981 final regulation on the informed consent of clinical subjects;

- a 1981 final regulation on the responsibilities of IRBs;

- the 1987 IND Rewrite regulations, which define the responsibilities of the investigator and the sponsor; and

- the 1988 *Guideline for the Monitoring of Clinical Investigations*, which outlines the monitor's responsibilities.

149

While these documents form the core of GCP, dozens of other FDA guidance documents have provided more detailed information. Among these is a set of what are called *Information Sheets for Institutional Review Boards and Clinical Investigators* (see exhibit below), which was updated and re-issued in October 1995, and a set of FDA compliance policy guidance manuals that specify how FDA inspectors ensure that clinical sponsors, monitors, and investigators are complying with GCP.

The most recent addition to the FDA's corpus of GCP documents is the International Conference on Harmonization's (ICH) *Good Clinical Practice: Consolidated Guideline*, which was adopted by the ICH parties in 1996 and was published in mid-1997. Designed to provide "a unified standard for designing, conducting, recording, and reporting trials that involve the participation of human subjects," this harmonized guideline provides guidance on IRB, sponsor, investigator, monitoring, and auditing requirements. Integrated into the consolidated ICH guideline are two guidelines that were issued as separate draft documents in 1994: *Guideline for the Investigator's Brochure,* which specifies the minimum information required in, and recommends a format for, the investigator's brochure; and *Guideline for Essential Documents for the Conduct of a Clinical Study,* which identifies the essential documents that "individually and collectively permit evaluation of the conduct of a clinical study and the quality of the data produced."

FDA officials emphasize that the ICH guidelines are entirely consistent with established GCP requirements, and that the harmonized documents will supplement, rather than replace, existing U.S. regulations and guidelines. Agency officials concede that, in a few areas, the ICH GCP guidelines clarify current U.S. practice and requirements better than the FDA's regulations and guidelines. Other analysts have stated that the ICH guidelines offer several recommendations that, despite not being mentioned in current FDA documents, reflect typical FDA expectations and industry practices. Several of these recommendations will be identified in the discussions below.

Responsibilities of the Sponsor

Federal regulations define "sponsor" as "a person who takes responsibility for and initiates a clinical investigation. The sponsor may be an individual or

FDA Information Sheets

- Acceptance of Foreign Clinical Studies
- Charging for Investigational Products
- Clinical Investigator Regulatory Sanctions
- Continuing Review After Study Approval
- Cooperative Research
- Drug Study Designs
- Emergency Use of an Investigational Drug or Biologic
- Evaluation of Gender Differences
- FDA Inspections of Clinical Investigations
- FDA Institutional Review Board Inspections
- Frequently Asked Questions: Institutional Review Board Regulations
- Frequently Asked Questions: Informed Consent Regulations
- Frequently Asked Questions: Clinical Investigations
- Frequently Asked Questions: Other
- Guide to Informed Consent Documents
- Informed Consent and the Clinical Investigator
- Investigational and "Off-Label" Use of Marketed Drugs and Biologics
- Investigations Which May be Reviewed Through Expedited Review
- Non-Local IRB Review
- Payment to Research Subjects
- Recruiting Study Subjects
- Screening Tests Prior to Subject Enrollment
- Self-evaluation Checklist for IRBs
- Significant Differences in HHS and FDA Regulations
- Sponsor-Clinical Investigator-IRB Interrelationship
- Treatment Use of Investigational Drugs
- Use of Investigational Products When Subjects Enter a Second Institution
- Waiver of IRB Requirements

Source: FDA

pharmaceutical company, governmental agency, academic institution, private organization, or other organization."

In general, the term "sponsor" refers to a commercial manufacturer that has developed a product in which it holds the principal financial interest. A sponsor may also be a physician, commonly called a "sponsor-investigator," which federal regulations define as "an individual who both initiates and conducts an investigation and under whose immediate direction the investigational drug is administered or dispensed."

The FDA defines sponsor responsibilities in Part 312, Subpart D in the Code of Federal Regulations (CFR), which states: "Sponsors are responsible for selecting qualified investigators, providing them with the information they need to conduct an investigation properly, ensuring proper monitoring of the investigation(s), ensuring that the investigation(s) is conducted in accordance with the general investigational plan and protocols contained in the IND, maintaining an effective IND with respect to the investigations, and ensuring that the FDA and all participating investigators are promptly informed of significant new adverse effects or risks with respect to the drug." Sponsor responsibilities can be divided into the following general areas:

- selecting investigators and monitors;

- informing investigators;

- reviewing ongoing investigations;

- recordkeeping and record retention; and

- ensuring the disposition of unused drug supplies.

Selecting Investigators and Monitors Investigator Selection. The sponsor must select investigators—physicians and other professionals contracted by the sponsor to conduct the clinical study, including supervising the administration of the drug to human subjects—qualified by training and experience as appropriate experts to investigate the drug. Sponsors may ship investigational product only to these investigators.

To ensure that a clinical investigator is qualified, the sponsor must obtain certain information from the investigator:

- A Completed and Signed Statement of Investigator Form (Form FDA-1572). This form contains information about the investigator, the site of the investigation, and the subinvestigators—research fellows and residents—who assist the investigator in the conduct of the investigation. By signing the form, the investigator also pledges: (1) to conduct the study in accordance with the clinical protocol(s) and to take proper actions should deviations become necessary; (2) to comply with all requirements regarding the obligations of clinical investigators (as described later in this chapter) and other relevant requirements; (3) to personally conduct or supervise the described investigation; (4) to inform patients, or any persons used as controls, that the drug is being used for investigational purposes and to ensure that the requirements related to obtaining informed consent and IRB review and approval (as described elsewhere in this chapter) are met; (5) to report to the sponsor adverse experiences that occur in the course of the investigation in accordance with regulatory requirements; (6) to review and understand the information in the investigator's brochure, including the drug's potential risks and side effects; and (7) to ensure that all associates, colleagues, and employees assisting in the conduct of the studies are informed about their obligations in meeting the above commitments. Through the form, the investigator also pledges that an IRB operating in compliance with regulatory requirements (described later in this chapter) will be responsible for the initial and continuing review and approval of the clinical investigation. In addition, the investigator promises to report to the IRB all changes in the research activity and all unanticipated problems involving risks to human subjects and to not implement any such changes without IRB approval, except when necessary to eliminate apparent immediate hazards to study subjects.

- Curriculum Vitae. The sponsor must obtain a curriculum vitae or other statement of qualifications of the investigator showing the education, training, and experience that qualify the investigator as an expert in the clinical investigation of the drug.

- Clinical Protocol. For Phase 1 investigations, the sponsor must obtain from the investigator a general outline of the planned investigation, including the estimated duration of the study and the maximum number of subjects that will be involved. For Phase 2 or 3 investigations, the sponsor must obtain an outline of the study protocol, including an approximation of the number and characteristics of investigational subjects and controls, the clinical uses to be investigated, the kinds of clinical observations and laboratory tests to be conducted, the estimated duration of the study, and copies or a description of case report forms to be used. According to the ICH GCP guideline, the protocol (or other protocol-referenced documents) must identify "any data to be recorded directly on the [patient case report forms] (i.e., no prior written or electronic record of data), and to be considered to be source data."

Selecting Monitors and Monitoring the Clinical Trial. Sponsors are required to monitor clinical investigations to ensure: (1) the quality and integrity of the clinical data derived from clinical trials; and (2) that the rights and welfare of human subjects involved in a clinical study are preserved. The monitoring function may be performed by the sponsor or its employees, or may be delegated to a contract research organization (CRO).

Specific FDA recommendations on proper monitoring duties and procedures are provided in the agency's *Guideline for the Monitoring of Clinical Investigations* (January 1988). In this document, the FDA identifies six different monitoring responsibilities:

- Selection of a Monitor. According to the guideline, a sponsor may designate one or more appropriately trained and qualified individuals to monitor the progress of a clinical investigation. Physicians, clinical research associates, paramedical personnel, nurses, and engineers may be acceptable monitors depending on the type of product involved in the study.

- Written Monitoring Procedures. A sponsor should establish written procedures for monitoring clinical investigations to assure the quality of the study, and to assure that each person involved in the monitoring process carries out his or her duties.

- Preinvestigation Visits. Through personal contact between the monitor and each investigator, a sponsor must assure that the investigator, among other things, clearly understands and accepts the obligations involved in undertaking a clinical study. The sponsor also must determine whether the investigator's facilities are adequate for conducting the investigation, and whether the investigator has sufficient time to honor his or her responsibilities in the trial.

- Periodic Visits. A sponsor must assure, throughout the clinical investigation, that the investigator's obligations are fulfilled and that the facilities used in the clinical investigation are acceptable. The monitor must visit the clinical site frequently enough to provide such assurances.

- Review of Subject Records. A sponsor must assure that safety and effectiveness data submitted to the FDA are accurate and complete. The FDA recommends that the monitor review individual subject records and other supporting documentation and compare these records with the reports prepared by the investigator for submission to the sponsor. The ICH's GCP document states that the monitor should check "the accuracy and completeness of the [case report form (CRF)] entries, source data/documents and other trial-related records against each other." Specifically, the guideline states that the monitor should verify that: (1) the data required by the protocol are reported accurately on the CRFs and are consistent with the source data/documents; (2) any dose and/or therapy modifications are well documented for each trial subject; (3) adverse events, concomitant medications and intercurrent illnesses are reported in accordance with the protocol on the CRFs; (4) visits that the subjects fail to make, tests that are not conducted, and examinations that are not performed are clearly reported as such on the CRFs; and (5) all withdrawals and dropouts of enrolled subjects from the trial are reported and explained on the CRFs.

- Record of On-Site Visits. The monitor or sponsor should maintain a record of the findings, conclusions, and actions taken to correct deficiencies for each on-site visit.

155

Informing Investigators The sponsor is responsible for keeping all investigators involved in the clinical testing of its drug fully informed about the investigational product and research findings. Before the investigation begins, a sponsor must supply participating clinical investigators with an investigator's brochure (see Chapter 4), which provides: a description of the product; summaries of its known pharmacological, pharmacokinetic, and biological characteristics; potential adverse effects as indicated by animal tests; and, if available, data on clinical use.

Once clinical trials begin, regulations require that sponsors "keep each participating investigator informed of new observations discovered by or reported to the sponsor on the drug, particularly with respect to adverse effects and safe use." This information may be distributed through periodically revised investigator's brochures, reprints or published studies, reports or letters to clinical investigators, or other appropriate means. Important safety information must be relayed to investigators and the FDA through written or verbal IND safety reports (see Chapter 4).

Review of Ongoing Investigations There are many reasons why the FDA requires sponsors to closely monitor the conduct and progress of their clinical trials. Investigator noncompliance and unreasonable and significant risks to research subjects are two of the most important reasons.

If a sponsor discovers that an investigator is not complying with his or her commitments in Form FDA-1572, the general investigational plan, or other relevant regulatory requirements, the firm must either secure compliance or discontinue product shipments to the investigator and terminate the investigator's participation in the investigation. If the latter course is chosen or is necessary, the sponsor must require that the investigator return or dispose of the product in accordance with applicable requirements and must report this action to the FDA.

The sponsor must review and evaluate safety and effectiveness data as they are supplied by the investigator. In addition to providing important safety information through IND safety reports, the sponsor must supply to the FDA annual reports on the progress of the investigation.

Sponsors finding that their drugs or studies present unreasonable and significant risks to subjects must: (1) discontinue the investigations that present the risks; (2) notify the FDA, all IRBs, and all investigators who have at any time participated in the investigations that the studies are being discontinued; (3) assure the disposition of all outstanding stocks of the drug; and (4) furnish the FDA with a full report of its actions.

Recordkeeping and Record Retention A sponsor must maintain adequate records showing the receipt, shipment, or other disposition of the investigational product. The records must include, as appropriate, the name of the investigator to whom the drug is shipped and the date, quantity, and batch or code mark of each shipment. Regulations call for a sponsor to retain the records and reports for two years after either its marketing application is approved or the withdrawal of its IND and its notification to the FDA that product shipment and delivery have been discontinued.

Disposition of Unused Drug Supplies The sponsor must ensure the return of all unused supplies of the drug from each investigator whose participation is discontinued or eliminated. The sponsor may authorize alternative plans, provided these do not expose humans to risks from the product. In June 1997, CDER published an updated version of Compliance Policy Guide 7132c.05, entitled *Recovery of Investigational New Drugs from Clinical Investigators.*

In this and other areas, the ICH's GCP guideline specifies sponsor requirements not addressed in FDA GCP documents, including:

- The requirement that the sponsor/monitor verify that the disposition of unused investigational product at the trial sites complies with regulatory and sponsor requirements.

- The requirement that "electronic trial data handling and/or remote electronic trial data systems" conform to the sponsor's established requirements for completeness, accuracy, reliability, and consistent intended performance (i.e., validation). The ICH requirements, however, are said to fall within what have been traditional FDA expectations for computer validation.

- The requirement that sponsors obtain "all required documentation" (e.g., IRB decision) before providing an investigator with the investigational product. Again, this is common practice but is not required under U.S. GCP standards.

- The requirement that the sponsor's designated representative document the review and follow-up of the monitoring reports.

Responsibilities of Investigators

A clinical investigator is the individual who actually conducts, or who is the responsible leader of a team that conducts, a clinical investigation. The product is administered or dispensed to a clinical subject under the immediate direction of this individual.

Federal regulations state that an "investigator is responsible for ensuring that an investigation is conducted according to the signed investigator statement, the investigational plan, and applicable regulations; for protecting the rights, safety, and welfare of subjects under the investigator's care; and for the control of drugs under investigation." As part of the investigator's role in protecting the rights of clinical subjects, he or she must obtain the informed consent of all human subjects to whom the product is administered. Specific investigator responsibilities detailed in GCP provisions include:

Control of the Product. The investigator can administer the product only to subjects under his or her personal supervision or under the supervision of a subinvestigator. Regulations do not allow the investigator to supply the drug to persons not authorized to receive it.

Recordkeeping and Record Retention. The investigator must keep adequate records regarding the disposition of the product and subject case histories recording all observations and data pertinent to the investigation. These records must be kept for two years after either a marketing application's approval or a sponsor has discontinued an IND and so notified the FDA. The FDA must be allowed access to these records.

The ICH's GCP guideline calls for the investigator to maintain a list of appropriately qualified persons to whom significant trial-related responsibilities have been delegated. This requirement is not included in FDA regulations or guidelines. The ICH document also calls for clinical sites to maintain, and sponsors to document the existence of, a confidential list of the names of all subjects allocated to trial numbers upon trial enrollment.

Investigator Reports. The investigator must provide to the sponsor: (1) annual reports on the progress of the clinical investigations; (2) safety reports on all adverse effects that may reasonably be regarded as caused by, or probably caused by, the drug; and (3) a final report shortly after the completion of the investigator's participation—FDA officials indicate that completed case report forms on all subjects will suffice.

Assurance of IRB Review. The investigator must assure that an IRB complying with regulatory standards will be responsible for the initial and continuing review and approval of the proposed clinical study. He or she must also promptly report to the IRB all changes in the research activity and all unanticipated problems involving risks to human subjects. The investigator must not make any changes in the research without IRB approval, except when necessary to eliminate apparent and immediate hazards to human subjects.

Handling of Controlled Substances. If the investigational product is subject to the Controlled Substances Act, the investigator must take adequate precautions to prevent theft or diversion of the substance.

The Institutional Review Board (IRB)

The IRB's function is to see that risks to clinical subjects are minimized and that the subjects are adequately informed about the clinical trial and its implications for their treatment. In fulfilling its responsibilities, the IRB has authorities that extend beyond just reviewing proposed clinical protocols and the ongoing trial. Although the board's main concern is not the adequacy of study design, the board can order that a trial be modified for safety or other reasons.

The IRB itself must consist of at least five persons, each of whom is chosen by the institution. Board members must be judged to have the professional competence necessary to review specific research activities and to have the ability to assess the acceptability of proposed research in terms of institutional commitments and regulations, applicable law, and standards and practices.

IRB members often are physicians, pharmacologists, and administrative managers from the parent institution. At least one board member, however, must have a primary interest in a nonscientific area. Federal regulations also include several other requirements that are designed to ensure the independence of the board and guard against conflicts of interest.

Generally, drug sponsors have limited direct contact with an IRB. The investigator heading the study at a particular institution usually serves as a liaison, and presents the study plans for IRB consideration and approval. Through past experience, the investigator is often familiar with the particular concerns and priorities of an IRB and, therefore, is better prepared to deal with its members.

Aside from safety concerns, an IRB may address several issues—including specific standards of the institution, state, and locality—in evaluating a certain study. Any research program that the board does approve, however, must meet several criteria specified in FDA regulations:

- risks to subjects must be minimized;

- risks to subjects must be reasonable in relation to the anticipated benefits and the importance of the knowledge that may be expected to be gained;

- subject selection must be equitable;

- informed consent must be sought from each prospective subject or the subject's legally authorized representative;

- informed consent must be appropriately documented (see discussion below);

- when appropriate, the research plan must make adequate provisions for monitoring the data collected to ensure the safety of subjects; and

- when appropriate, there must be adequate provisions to protect the privacy of subjects and to preserve the confidentiality of data.

As are sponsors, monitors, and investigators, IRBs are subject to reporting and recordkeeping requirements. The board must retain minutes of meetings and copies of all study proposals evaluated, sample consent documents, correspondence with investigators, board procedures, and other documents. IRB meetings and records are subject to FDA inspection, and a U.S.-based institution may be disqualified from conducting clinical studies if FDA inspectors find that its IRB has violated GCP requirements.

Informed Consent

Informed consent is a concept designed to ensure that patients do not enter a clinical trial either against their will or without an adequate understanding of their medical situation and the implications of the clinical study itself. Federal regulations dictate that, except under special circumstances, "…no investigator may involve a human being as a subject in research…unless the investigator has obtained the legally effective informed consent of the subject or the subject's legally authorized representative. An investigator shall seek such consent only under circumstances that provide the prospective subject or the representative sufficient opportunity to consider whether or not to participate and that minimize the possibility of coercion or undue influence. The information that is given to the subject or the representative shall be in language understandable to the subject or the representative."

Clearly, informed consent implies an informed subject. Any subject volunteering for the study must be fully aware of his or her medical condition, alternative treatments, and the purpose of and risks involved in the clinical study. Federal regulations regarding the protection of clinical subjects state that, at a minimum, the following "basic elements of informed consent" must be provided to clinical subjects before involving them in the trial:

- a statement that the study involves research, an explanation of the purposes of the research and the expected duration of the subject's participation, a description of the procedures to be followed, and identification of any procedures that are experimental;

- a description of any reasonably foreseeable risks or discomforts to the subject;

- a description of any benefits that the subject or others may reasonably expect from the research;

- a disclosure of appropriate alternative procedures or courses of treatment, if any, that might be advantageous to the subject;

- a statement that describes the extent, if any, to which confidentiality of records identifying the subject will be maintained and that notes the possibility that the FDA may inspect the records;

- an explanation as to whether any compensation or medical treatments are available if injury occurs during research involving more than minimal risk, and, if so, what the treatments and/or compensation consist of, or where further information may be obtained;

- the identity of the person to contact for answers to pertinent questions about the research and research subject's rights, and the person to contact if the subject suffers a research-related injury; and

- a statement that participation is voluntary, that refusal to participate will involve no penalty or loss of benefits to which the subject is otherwise entitled, and that the subject may discontinue participation at any time without penalty or loss of benefits to which the subject is otherwise entitled.

When appropriate, one or more of the following must also be provided to subjects:

- a statement that a particular treatment or procedure may involve risks to the subject (or to the embryo or fetus, if the subject is or may become pregnant) that are currently unforeseeable;

- anticipated circumstances under which the subject's participation may be terminated by the investigator without regard to the subject's consent;

- any additional costs to the subject that may result from participation in the research;

- the consequences of a subject's decision to withdraw from the research and procedures for ordering termination of participation by the subject;

- a statement that significant new research findings that may affect the subject's willingness to continue his or her participation will be provided to the subject; and

- the approximate number of subjects involved in the study.

While the investigator is directly responsible for obtaining a subject's informed consent and seeing that the subject is truly informed, the IRB and the sponsor/monitor also play roles in ensuring that informed consent requirements are met.

In most cases, informed consent must be obtained by having the subject or the subject's representative sign a written, IRB-approved consent form. Unless the IRB waives the informed consent requirements due to absence of risk, the consent form may take one of two forms: (1) a written consent document that embodies the basic elements of informed consent and that may be read to the subject or the subject's representative, who is then given adequate opportunity to read it before signing; or (2) a "short form" written consent document stating that the basic elements of informed consent have been presented orally to the subject or the subject's representative. If the short form is used, there are several other requirements: there must be a witness to the oral presentation; the IRB shall approve a written summary of what will be said to the subject or the representative; the witness must sign both the short form and a copy of the summary; the person obtaining the consent must sign a copy of the summary; and the subject must be given both the summary and a copy of the consent form.

In late 1996, the FDA issued two final rules that revised its informed consent regulations. The first of these was published in October 1996 and was designed to permit the emergency use of experimental products without prior informed consent. This exception is permitted only for research involving subjects who require emergency medical intervention, who cannot give informed consent due to a life-threatening condition, and who do not have a legally authorized person to represent them. The FDA establishes clear and significant regulatory burdens regarding this waiver of informed consent requirements, including special criteria for IRB review and a requirement for the sponsor to submit the study protocol and related materials under a separate IND, even if one is already in place for studies utilizing the conventional consent process.

In December 1996, the FDA revised its informed consent regulations to require that the informed consent form signed by the subject or the subject's legally authorized representative be dated by that individual at the time consent is given. The agency also clarified what adequate case histories must include and that the case histories must document that informed consent was obtained prior to a subject's participation in a study. The agency took this action in response to problems that the FDA has had in verifying that informed consent actually preceded participation.

Chapter 8

The New Drug Application (NDA)

The new drug application (NDA) is the vehicle through which drug sponsors formally propose that the FDA approve a new pharmaceutical for sale and marketing in the United States. To obtain this government authorization, a drug manufacturer submits in an NDA thousands of pages of nonclinical and clinical test data and analyses, drug chemistry information, and descriptions of manufacturing procedures.

An NDA is the largest and most complex premarketing application that the FDA reviews. Recently, CDER officials began to discuss ways of minimizing the size of NDAs. Given that data from clinical trials comprise an estimated 80 to 90 percent of many NDAs for new drugs, the discussions have focused largely on reducing the number of clinical trials submitted in these filings. The size of NDA filings is likely to remain an issue to CDER because large submissions can make it more difficult for the center to meet its review goals under the prescription drug user fee program.

Still, reports of massive NDA submissions were quite common in the mid-1990s. In 1996, CDER's Division of Anti-Infective Drug Products, a unit known to review particularly voluminous drug applications, reported that it had received what was likely its largest NDA filing ever. Further, in a study of 12 NDAs approved in 1994 and 1995, Georgetown University's Center for Drug Development Science (CDDS) found that the median number of clinical trials per NDA was 68, of which 27 were efficacy trials. Further, CDDS found that a quarter of the NDAs had data from 97 or more trials.

Regardless of its size, an NDA must provide sufficient information, data, and analyses to permit FDA reviewers to reach several key decisions, including:

1. Whether the drug is safe and effective in its proposed use(s), and whether the benefits of the drug outweigh its risks.

2. Whether the drug's proposed labeling is appropriate and, if not, what the drug's labeling should contain.

3. Whether the methods used in manufacturing the drug and the controls used to maintain the drug's quality are adequate to preserve the drug's identity, strength, quality, and purity.

The History of the NDA

For decades, the regulation and control of new drugs in the United States has been based on the NDA. Since 1938, each new drug must have been the subject of an NDA before it could be, for commercial purposes, sold in or imported to the United States.

The NDA has evolved considerably during its history. When the Food, Drug and Cosmetic Act (FD&C Act) was passed in 1938, NDAs were required only to contain information pertaining to the investigational drug's safety. In 1962, the Harris-Kefauver Amendments to the FD&C Act required NDAs to provide evidence that a new drug was effective in its intended use as well. These historic amendments also required, for the first time, that an NDA be approved before a drug could be marketed.

The NDA was again the subject of change in 1985, when the FDA completed a comprehensive revision of the regulations pertaining to new drug applications. While this revision, commonly called the NDA Rewrite, modified NDA content requirements, it was mainly designed to expedite FDA reviews by restructuring the ways in which information and data were organized and presented in the application.

A variety of initiatives in the late 1980s and early 1990s brought several less significant changes to the NDA, including a requirement that a sponsor certify that it did not use the services of an FDA-debarred individual, a greater FDA emphasis on the need for clinical data on gender, age, and racial subsets, and a requirement that sponsors provide a "field" copy of the NDA to their regional FDA district offices.

At this writing, there were several significant regulatory developments that had contributed or were about to contribute to the continuing evolution of the NDA:

- In mid-1997, the FDA adopted a new, streamlined version of the current NDA application form (Form FDA 356h). The new Form 356h, which is dated April 1997, will be used in premarketing applications for not only new drugs, but biologics and antibiotics as well. The updated form features a few minor changes, including a restructuring of the chemistry section, the addition of a debarment certification section, and the incorporation of elements that are applicable only to biological products.

- During the mid-1990s, computer-assisted new drug applications (CANDA) continued to be an important and potentially review-expediting alternative to paper-based NDA filings. Meanwhile, in March 1997, the FDA laid the regulatory groundwork for electronic submissions to be used in lieu of paper submissions (i.e., previously, electronic submissions could only supplement paper filings, which were required by regulation). Specifically, a March 1997 final regulation established the agency's criteria for accepting electronic records (including CANDAs) and electronic signatures as equivalent to paper records and handwritten signatures. This regulation provides the regulatory basis for what the agency ultimately hopes will be a more significant migration to the use of electronic submissions. There are other initiatives that seek to promote the use of computer submissions: In early 1997, the FDA and industry agreed to ask Congress, during the PDUFA reauthorization process, to call upon the agency to develop a paperless, electronic application submission system for all applications, including NDAs. Also, CDER published a revision of its *CANDA Guidance Manual* in October 1994.

- Several guidelines developed under the International Conference on Harmonization (ICH) initiative have influenced NDA submission requirements. For example, the ICH's final guideline on the *Structure and Content of Clinical Study Reports* has replaced some elements of the FDA's *Guideline for the Format and Content of*

Clinical and Statistical Sections of NDAs, and will shape elements of the clinical and statistical section of the NDA. In mid-1997, the ICH participants were scheduled to decide whether they would embark on the most daunting and significant harmonization initiative and the one that would affect NDAs most fundamentally—to develop a "common technical document," a set of technical information that could be presented in marketing applications uniformly in all three ICH regions.

- Various CDER initiatives undertaken to define and standardize its policies and procedures will also affect NDA submissions. For example, the center's Good Review Practices (GRP) initiative, which is designed to further standardize the review process, is likely to provide industry with greater insights into CDER's technical reviews and, therefore, insights on improving data presentations in NDAs. In November 1996, CDER released its first GRP draft guidance—*Conducting a Clinical Safety Review of a New Product Application and Preparing a Report on the Review.* Further, under its March 1997 *New Use Initiative,* the agency published a pair of draft guidelines—*Providing Clinical Evidence of Effectiveness for Human Drug and Biological Products* and *FDA Approval of New Cancer Treatment Uses for Marketed Drug and Biological Products*—that offer what is likely the center's most detailed discussion ever regarding the efficacy data necessary to support drug approval (see Chapter 6).

- CDER's need to expedite drug reviews and meet its PDUFA goals may be affecting the manner in which many NDAs are being submitted. In their 1996 review of Glaxo-Wellcome's Ultiva, for example, CDER reviewers had access to information ranging from clinical protocols to raw clinical data as they were developed during the clinical testing process. As a result of this "interactive" review process, the Division of Anesthetic, Critical Care, and Addiction Drug Products had virtually completed its review of Ultiva before the formal NDA submission was made. While the submission of sections of an NDA prior to the formal submission (often called a "rolling" NDA) is not a new phenomenon, many analysts believe that employing such practices will be one of the best—and possibly the only—way for the agency to meet its review goals. Further, the agency's 1997 final regulation on electronic records may now make such interactive reviews an even more attractive option for sponsors and the agency.

NDA Content and Format Requirements

With the possible exception of clinical testing, FDA regulations and guidelines collectively provide more guidance on NDA content and format requirements than any other aspect of the drug development process. In recent years, these have been supplemented, and in some cases replaced, by ICH guidelines relevant to new drug applications.

Although submission requirements are a function of a drug's nature, the NDA must, in each case, provide all relevant data and information that a sponsor has collected during the product's research and development. FDA regulations provide the most fundamental description of NDA content and format requirements: "Applications...are required to be submitted in the form and contain the information, as appropriate for the particular submission.... An application for a new chemical entity will generally contain an application form, an index, a summary, five or six technical sections, case report tabulations of patient data, case report forms, drug samples, and labeling. Other applications will generally contain only some of those items and information will be limited to that needed to support the particular submission.... The application is required to contain reports of all investigations of the drug product sponsored by the applicant, and all other information about the drug pertinent to an evaluation of the application that is received or otherwise obtained by the applicant from any source. The Food and Drug Administration will maintain guidelines on the format and content of applications to assist applicants in their preparation."

Currently, the agency has more than a dozen guidelines that relate to NDA content and formatting issues, including the following:

Guideline for the Format and Content of the Summary for New Drug and Antibiotic Applications (February 1987);

Guideline for the Format and Content of the Nonclinical Pharmacology/ Toxicology Section of an Application (February 1987);

Guideline for the Format and Content of the Clinical and Statistical Sections of New Drug Applications (July 1988);

Guideline for the Format and Content of the Chemistry, Manufacturing, and Controls Section of an Application (February 1987);

Guideline for the Format and Content of the Human Pharmacokinetics and Bioavailability Section of an Application (February 1987);

Guideline for the Format and Content of the Microbiology Section of an Application (February 1987);

Guideline for the Submission in Microfiche of the Archival Copy of an Application (February 1987);

Guideline on Formatting, Assembling, and Submitting New Drug and Antibiotic Applications (February 1987);

Guideline for Submitting Supporting Documentation in Drug Applications for the Manufacture of Drug Substances (February 1987);

Guideline for Submitting Documentation for the Manufacture of and Controls for Drug Products (February 1987);

Guideline for Submitting Documentation for Packaging for Human Drugs and Biologics (February 1987);

Guideline for Submitting Documentation for the Stability of Human Drugs and Biologics (February 1987);

Guideline for Submitting Samples and Analytical Data for Methods Validation (February 1987);

Guideline for Submitting Documentation for Packaging for Human Drugs and Biologics (February 1987);

Draft Guideline for Submitting Supporting Chemistry Documentation in Radiopharmaceutical Drug Applications (November 1991);

CANDA (Computer Assisted New Drug Application) Guidance Manual (October 1994);

Guidance for Industry for the Submission of Chemistry, Manufacturing, and Controls for Synthetic Peptide Drug Substances (November 1994);

Guidance for Industry for the Submission of Documentation for Sterilization Process Validation in Applications for Human and Veterinary Drug Products (November 1994); and

Guideline for the Submission of an Environmental Assessment in Human Drug Applications and Supplements (November 1995).

Further, a growing number of more recent ICH guidelines are now relevant to NDA submissions. Among these is the ICH's *Guideline on Impurities in New Drug Substances* (January 1996), the *Guideline on Dose-Response Information to Support Drug Registration* (November 1994), and the final guideline on the *Structure and Content of Clinical Study Reports* (June 1996), which replaces some elements of the FDA's *Guideline on the Format and Content of Clinical and Statistical Sections in New Drug Applications*. These and other ICH guidelines are cited in the discussions below.

The Fundamentals of NDA Submissions

Although the quantity of information and data submitted in NDAs can vary considerably, the component parts of drug applications are somewhat more uniform. According to Form FDA-356h, *Application To Market A New Drug, Biologic, or an Antibiotic for Human Use* (April 1997), NDAs can consist of as many as 18 different sections in addition to the form itself (*Editor's Note:* although the list below identifies 19 sections, the establishment description section is relevant only for certain biological products):

1. Index

2. Labeling

3. Summary

4. Chemistry Section
    A. Chemistry, manufacturing and controls information
    B. Samples
    C. Methods validation package

5. Nonclinical Pharmacology and Toxicology Section

6. Human Pharmacokinetics and Bioavailability Section

7. Clinical Microbiology Section

8. Clinical Data Section

9. Safety Update Report

10. Statistical Section

11. Case Report Tabulations

12. Case Report Forms

13. Patent Information on any patent that claims the drug

14. A Patent Certification with respect to any patent that claims the drug

15. Establishment Description

16. Debarment Certification

17. Field Copy Certification

18. User Fee Cover Sheet (Form FDA 3397)

19. Other Information

The components of any NDA are, in part, a function of the nature of the subject drug and the information available to the applicant at the time of submission. For example, the safety update report section is not submitted in the original NDA, but is forwarded 120 days after the NDA submission (see discussion below).

A May 1997 instruction sheet that accompanied the new Form 356h makes clear that the form's numbered listing of contents is not designed to dictate the NDA's format. "It should be noted that the numbering of the items on [Form 356h's] checklist is not intended to specify a particular order of the inclusion of those sections into the submission," the FDA states. "The applicant may include sections in any order, but the location of those sections within the submission should be clearly indicated in the index." Each NDA section is discussed further below.

The Archival, Review, and Field Copies of the NDA

Since October 8, 1993, drug sponsors have been required to submit three different copies of an NDA to the agency. The NDA's review and archival copies have been regulatory requirements for years, while the field copy of the application is the newest NDA requirement.

The FDA provides specific guidance on content requirements for the archival and review copies in its *Guideline on Formatting, Assembling, and Submitting New Drug and Antibiotic Applications* (February 1987). The role and content of these versions of the NDA differ considerably (see exhibit below). The archival copy, which is stored by the FDA as a reference document, must contain all the relevant sections identified above. It must also include cover letters confirming FDA-applicant agreements, identifying company contact persons, or providing other information relevant to the NDA review. The purpose of the archival copy is to permit individual reviewers to refer to information not included in their review copies, to give other agency personnel access to the complete application for official business, and to maintain in a single file a complete copy of the entire NDA.

The review copy is a less comprehensive version of the application. It consists of the NDA's five or six technical sections—clinical, nonclinical pharmacology/toxicology, chemistry, statistics, biopharmaceutics, and, for anti-infective drugs, microbiology as well. Each of these technical sections is packaged for distribution to, and evaluation by, reviewers in the corresponding technical disciplines. Therefore, these sections must be bound separately, and be accompanied by a table of contents and a copy of the NDA's application form, index, and summary.

Contents of the NDA's Archival and Review Copies

Elements of NDA (Color of Binder)	Archival (Blue)	Sections of the Review Copy					
		Chemistry (Red)	Pharmacology (Yellow)	Pharmacokinetics (Orange)	Microbiology (White)	Clinical (Light-Brown)	Statistics (Green)
Application Form (Form 356h)	X	X	X	X	X	X	X
-cover letter	X	X	X	X	X	X	X
-patent information	X	X	X	X	X	X	X
-letter of authorization (if applicable)	X	X	X	X	X	X	X
1. Index to application	X	X	X	X	X	X	X
index to section a	:	X	X	X	X	X	X
2. Summary	X	X	X	X	X	X	X
3. Chemistry Manufacturing Controls	X	X	:	:	:	:	:
4. Samples b	:	:	:	:	:	:	:
Methods Validation c	X	X	:	:	:	:	:
Labeling: d							
-draft labeling (4 copies) or	X	X	X	:	:	X	:
-FPL (12 copies)	X	:	:	:	:	:	:
5. Nonclinical Pharmacology Toxicology	X	:	X	:	:	:	:
6. Human Pharmacokinetics Bioavailability	X	:	:	X	:	:	:
7. Microbiology (if required)	X	:	:	:	X	:	:
8. Clinical Data	X	:	:	:	:	X	:

Contents of Application (continued)

Elements of NDA (Color of Binder)	Archival (Blue)	Sections of the Review Copy					
		Chemistry (Red)	Pharmacology (Yellow)	Pharmacokinetics (Orange)	Microbiology (White)	Clinical (Light-Brown)	Statistics (Green)
9. Safety Update	X	...	...	...	...	X	...
10. Statistical Data	X	...	...	...	...	...	X
11. Case Report Tabulations	X	...	...	...	...	...	...
12. Case Report Forms	X	...	...	...	...	...	...
13. Patent Information	[attached to application form]	X	X	X	X	X	X
14. Patent Certification	X	X	X	X	X	X	X
15. Other (if applicable)	X	X	X	X	X	X	X

a Review Sections should contain a copy of the index to the entire application in addition to the index for the specific section.

b Samples should be submitted upon request.

c One copy of methods validation should be submitted in the archival copy; three copies should be submitted in the chemistry section of the review copy.

d The applicant should submit 4 copies of draft labeling or 12 copies of FPL (if available). The archival copy should contain 1 copy of all proposed labeling for the product (draft labeling or FPL and carton labeling, if available).

175

NDA sponsors must also submit what is called a "field" copy of the NDA. To be used by FDA inspectors during preapproval manufacturing inspections, the field copy consists of an NDA's chemistry, manufacturing, and controls section, the NDA application form (Form FDA 356h), and the NDA summary. In addition, the field copy must include a certification that it includes an exact copy of the chemistry, manufacturing, and control section "contained in the archival and review copies of the application." U.S.-based applicants must submit the field copy directly to their respective "home" FDA district offices. Foreign-based applicants should submit field copies to FDA headquarters along with their archival and review copies.

In a November 1996 draft guideline, the FDA seemed to indicate that the NDA's archival copy would be among the first application components that the agency would seek to accept in electronic-only format (i.e., without a paper-based version). The agency states that its *Draft Guidance for Industry: Submitting Application Archival Copies in Electronic Format* "represents the agency's first attempt to develop a format for preparing electronic archival submissions." Although a March 1997 final regulation will permit the agency to begin accepting electronic-only drug applications, the agency indicated that it would have to approach this area cautiously, something it is likely to do by first accepting archival copies and case report forms/tabulations in electronic format.

Application Form All three versions of the NDA must contain an NDA application form, Form FDA 356h (see exhibit below). This form, which serves as the NDA's cover sheet, provides a comprehensive checklist of the elements that each application should include. The latest version of the form was implemented April 1997, although applicants will retain the option of using the previous Form FDA 356h until early 1998.

In completing the form, the sponsor also provides basic information about itself (e.g., name and address), the investigational drug (e.g., chemical name, dosage form, and proposed indication), the NDA (e.g., whether it is an original submission, amendment, or supplement), the manufacturing establishment (e.g., locations of manufacturing, packaging and control sites), and related applications referenced in the NDA.

The application form must be completed and signed by the applicant or the applicant's authorized U.S. agent. If the sponsor does not have a residence or

DEPARTMENT OF HEALTH AND HUMAN SERVICES FOOD AND DRUG ADMINISTRATION **APPLICATION TO MARKET A NEW DRUG, BIOLOGIC, OR AN ANTIBIOTIC DRUG FOR HUMAN USE** *(Title 21, Code of Federal Regulations, 314 & 601)*	*Form Approved: OMB No. 0910-0338* *Expiration Date: April 30, 2000* *See OMB Statement on last page.*
	FOR FDA USE ONLY APPLICATION NUMBER

APPLICANT INFORMATION

NAME OF APPLICANT	DATE OF SUBMISSION
TELEPHONE NO. *(Include Area Code)*	FACSIMILE (FAX) Number *(Include Area Code)*
APPLICANT ADDRESS *(Number, Street, City, State, Country, Zip Code or Mail Code, and U.S. License number if previously issued):*	AUTHORIZED U.S AGENT NAME & ADDRESS *(Number, Street, City, State, ZIP Code, telephone & FAX number)* IF APPLICABLE

PRODUCT DESCRIPTION

NEW DRUG OR ANTIBIOTIC APPLICATION NUMBER, OR BIOLOGICS LICENSE APPLICATION NUMBER (if previously issued)

ESTABLISHED NAME *(e.g., Proper Name, USP/USAN name)*	PROPRIETARY NAME *(trade name)* IF ANY
CHEMICAL/BIOCHEMICAL/BLOOD PRODUCT NAME *(if any)*	CODE NAME *(If any)*

DOSAGE FORM	STRENGTHS:	ROUTE OF ADMINISTRATION

(PROPOSED) INDICATION(S) FOR USE:

APPLICATION INFORMATION

APPLICATION TYPE (check one) ☐ NEW DRUG APPLICATION (21 CFR 314.5) ☐ ABBREVIATED APPLICATION (ANDA, AADA, 21 CFR 314.94) ☐ BIOLOGICS LICENSE APPLICATION (21 CFR part 601)

IF AN NDA, IDENTIFY THE APPROPRIATE TYPE	☐ 505 (b) (1)	☐ 505 (b) (2)	☐ 507

IF AN ANDA, OR AADA, IDENTIFY THE REFERENCE LISTED DRUG PRODUCT THAT IS THE BASIS FOR THE SUBMISSION
Name of Drug — Holder of Approved Application

TYPE OF SUBMISSION (check one) ☐ ORIGINAL APPLICATION ☐ AMENDMENT TO A PENDING APPLICATION ☐ RESUBMISSION ☐ PRESUBMISSION ☐ ANNUAL REPORT ☐ ESTABLISHMENT DESCRIPTION SUPPLEMENT ☐ SUPAC SUPPLEMENT ☐ EFFICACY SUPPLEMENT ☐ LABELING SUPPLEMENT ☐ CHEMISTRY MANUFACTURING AND CONTROLS SUPPLEMENT ☐ OTHER

REASON FOR SUBMISSION

PROPOSED MARKETING STATUS (check one)

NUMBER OF VOLUMES SUBMITTED	THIS APPLICATION IS ☐ PAPER ☐ PAPER AND ELECTRONIC ☐ ELECTRONIC
ESTABLISHMENT INFORMATION ☐ PRESCRIPTION (Rx)	☐ OVER THE COUNTER PRODUCT (OTC)

Provide locations of all manufacturing, packing and control sites for drug substance and drug product (continuation sheets may be used if necessary). Include name, address, contact, telephone number, registration number (CFN), DMF number, and manufacturing steps and/or type of testing (e.g., Final dosage form Stability testing) conducted at the site. Please indicate whether the site is ready for inspection or, if not, when it will be ready.

Cross References (list related License Applications, INDs, NDAs, PMAs, 510(k)s, IDEs, BMFs, and DMFs referenced in the current application)

FORM 356h (4/97)

177

	This application contains the following items: *(Check all that apply)*
	1. Index
	2. Labeling (check one) ☐ Draft Labeling ☐ Final Printing Labeling
	3. Summary (21 CFR 314.50 (c))
	4. Chemistry section
	A. Chemistry, manufacturing, and controls information (e.g. 21 CFR 314.50 (d) (1), 21 CFR 601.2)
	B. Samples (21 CFR 314.50 (e) (1), 21 CFR 601.2 (a)) (Submit only upon FDA's request)
	C. Methods validation package (e.g. 21 CFR 314.50 (e) (2) (i), 21 CFR 601.2)
	5. Nonclinical pharmacology and toxicology section (e.g. 21 CFR 314.50 (d) (2), 21 CFR 601.2)
	6. Human pharmacokinetics and bioavailability section (e.g. 21 CFR 314.50 (d) (3), 21 CFR 601.2)
	7. Clinical Microbiology (e.g. 21 CFR 314.50 (d) (4))
	8. Clinical data section (e.g. 21 CFR 314.50 (d) (5), 21 CFR 601.2)
	9. Safety update report (e.g 21 CFR 314.50 (d) (5) (vi) (b), 21 CFR 601.2)
	10. Statistical section (e.g. 21 CFR 314.50 (d) (6), 21 CFR 601.2)
	11. Case report tabulations (e.g 21 CFR 314.50 (f) (1), 21 CFR 601.2)
	12. Case report forms (e.g. 21 CFR 314.50 (f) (2), 21 CFR 601.2)
	13. Patent information on any patent which claims the drug (21 U.S.C. 355 (b) or (c))
	14. A patent certification with respect to any patent which claims the drug (21 U.S.C. 355 (b) (2) or (j) (2) (A))
	15. Establishment description (21 VFR Part 600, if applicable)
	16. Debarment certification (FD&C Act 306 (k)(1))
	17. Field copy certification (21 CFR 314.5 (k) (3))
	18. User Fee Cover Sheet (Form FDA 3397)
	19. OTHER (Specify)

CERTIFICATION

I agree to update this application with new safety information about the drug that may reasonably affect the statement of contraindications, warnings, precautions, or adverse reactions in the draft labeling. I agree to submit these safety update reports as provided for by regulation or as requested by FDA. If this application is approved, I agree to comply with all laws and regulations that apply to approved applications, including, but not limited to the following:

  1. Good manufacturing practice regulations in 21 CFR 210 and 211, 606, and/or 820.
  2. Biological establishment standards in 21 CFR Part 600.
  3. Labeling regulations in 21 CFR 201, 606, 610, 660 and/or 809.
  4. In the case of a prescription drug product or biological product, prescription drug advertising regulations in 21 CFR 202.
  5. Regulations on making changes in application in 21 CFR 314.70, 314.71, 314.72, 314.97, 314.99, and 601.12.
  6. Regulations on reports in 21 CFR 314.80, 314.81 600.80 and 600.81.
  7. Local, state, and Federal environmental impact laws.

If this application applies to a drug product that FDA has proposed for scheduling under the Controlled Substances Act I agree not to market the product until the Drug Enforcement Administration makes a final scheduling decision.

The data and information in this submission have been reviewed and, to the best of my knowledge are certified to be true and accurate.

Warning: a willfully false statement is a criminal offense, U.S. Code, title 18, section 1001.

SIGNATURE OF RESPONSIBLE OFFICIAL OR AGENT	TYPED NAME AND TITLE		DATE
ADDRESS (Street, City, State, and ZIP Code)		Telephone Number ( )	

Public reporting burden for this collection of information is estimated to average 40 hours per response, including the time for reviewing instructions, searching existing data sources, gathering and maintaining the data needed, and completing and reviewing the collection of information. Send comments regarding this burden estimate or any other aspect of this collection of information, including suggestions for reducing this burden to:

DHHS, Reports Clearance Officer
Paperwork Reduction Project (0910-0338)
Hubert H. Humphrey Building, Room 531-H
200 Independence Avenue, S.W.
Washington, DC 20201

An agency may not conduct or sponsor, and a person is not required to respond to, a collection of information unless it displays a currently valid OMB control number.

Please **DO NOT RETURN** this form to this address

FORM FDA 356h (4/97)

place of business within the United States, the application form must provide the name and address of, and be countersigned by, an authorized agent who resides or maintains a place of business in the United States.

By signing this form, the sponsor agrees to comply with a variety of legal and regulatory requirements, including current good manufacturing practice (CGMP) standards, advertising and labeling regulations, safety update reporting requirements, and local, state, and federal environmental impact laws.

The Index Perhaps the most critical factor in an NDA's user-friendliness is the speed and ease with which a reviewer can locate specific information during the review process. Since it is the reviewer's "roadmap" to an application that can be hundreds of volumes long and because it can influence the speed and efficiency of the review as well, the NDA's index is an important element of the application.

While the FDA states that the various NDA components may be submitted in any order, the agency emphasizes that the index should clearly indicate the location of each section within the application. Therefore, the agency recommends that, particularly for large submissions, the index "be the first item following the Form FDA 356h."

The archival copy of the NDA must provide a comprehensive index by volume number and page number to the NDA summary, each of the five or six technical sections, and the case report forms and tabulations section. FDA guidelines state that the index should serve as a detailed table of contents for the entire archival NDA.

Each of the separately bound technical sections comprising the review copies must include a copy of the NDA index as well. In addition, each section should include its own individual table of contents based upon the portions of the larger NDA index relevant to that technical section.

Labeling The NDA's archival copy must contain copies of the label and all labeling proposed for the drug product. In the NDA, applicants must submit either 4 copies of a product's draft labeling or 12 copies of the final printed labeling (FPL).

If a sponsor submits draft labeling, one copy should be bound in the archival copy, with single copies placed in the review copies of the clinical, chemistry, and pharmacology sections (labeling in the review sections may be bound separately in the appropriate colored jacket for the respective review sections).

When a sponsor provides FPL and carton labeling, one copy should be mounted, bound, and inserted in the archival copy. The remaining 11 copies should be mounted, bound, and submitted in a separate jacket clearly marked "Final Printed Labeling."

The NDA Summary In many respects, the NDA summary is an abridged version of the entire application. The summary is designed to provide an overview of the NDA, explaining its intent—to establish the drug's safety and effectiveness for a specific use—and highlighting the studies and analyses that support the product's use.

Given that the summary is one of the few elements of the application that all reviewers receive, its importance cannot be overstated. A well-prepared summary, which should include a balanced, unbiased presentation and analysis of a drug's beneficial and adverse effects, can build a reviewer's confidence in the applicant, the drug, and the validity and completeness of the information in the NDA.

As evidence of the importance that is placed on the NDA summary, the FDA dedicated an entire guideline to the topic—*Guideline for the Format and Content of the Summary for New Drug and Antibiotic Applications* (February 1987). According to this document, "each full application is required...to contain a summary, ordinarily 50 to 200 pages in length, that integrates all of the information in the application and provides reviewers in each review area, and other agency officials, with a good general understanding of the drug product and of the application. The summary should discuss all aspects of the application and should be written in approximately the same level of detail required for publication in, and meet the editorial standards generally applied by, refereed scientific and medical journals...To the extent possible, data in the summary should be presented in tabular and graphic forms....The summary should comprehensively present the most important information about the drug product and the conclusions to be drawn from this information. The summary should avoid any editorial promotion of the drug product, i.e., it should be a factual summary of safety and effectiveness data and a neutral analysis of these data. The summary should include an annotated copy of the proposed labeling, a discussion of the product's benefits and risks, a description of the foreign marketing history of the drug (if any), and a summary of each technical section."

Specifically, federal regulations require the NDA summary to provide the following:

- the proposed text of the labeling for the drug, with annotations to the information in the summary and technical sections of the application that support the inclusion of each statement in the labeling, and, if the application is for a prescription drug, statements describing the reasons for omitting a section or subsection of the labeling format;

- a statement identifying the pharmacologic class of the drug and a discussion of the scientific rationale for the drug, its intended use, and the potential clinical benefits of the drug product;

- a brief description of the marketing history, if any, of the drug outside the United States, including a list of the countries in which the drug has been marketed, a list of any countries in which the drug has been withdrawn from marketing for any reason related to safety or effectiveness, and a list of countries in which applications for marketing are pending (the section must describe marketing by the applicant and, if known, the marketing history of other persons);

- a summary of the chemistry, manufacturing, and controls section of the application;

- a summary of the nonclinical pharmacology and toxicology section of the application;

- a summary of the human pharmacokinetics and bioavailability section of the application;

- a summary of the microbiology section of the application (for anti-infectives only);

181

- a summary of the clinical data section of the application, including the results of statistical analyses of the clinical trials; and

- a concluding discussion that presents the benefit and risk considerations related to the drug, including a discussion of any proposed additional studies or surveillance the applicant intends to conduct following approval.

Chemistry Section In the NDA's first technical component, the chemistry section, the sponsor describes, and provides data regarding, the composition, manufacture, and specifications of both the drug substance (i.e., the active ingredient) and the final drug product, including their physical and chemical characteristics and stability.

The implementation of the new Form 356h has restructured this NDA section to some degree. Essentially, the outline provided in Form 356h folds the NDA's samples and methods validation package sections into the new chemistry section. Under the previous iteration of the form, these components were independent from the chemistry section.

Historically, deficiencies have been more common in the NDA's chemistry, manufacturing, and controls section than in other aspects of the application. This is probably due to several factors, including the fact that sponsors cannot develop final product formulations and commercial-scale manufacturing processes until late in the drug development process.

Recognizing this, the FDA released, in the mid-1980s, a spate of guidelines that provide agency advice on preparing chemistry, manufacturing, and controls sections for NDAs and other applications, including the following: *Guideline for the Format and Content of the Chemistry, Manufacturing, and Controls Section of an Application* (February 1987); *Guideline for Submitting Documentation for the Manufacture of and Controls for Drug Products* (February 1987); *Guideline for Submitting Documentation for Packaging for Human Drugs and Biologics* (February 1987); *Guideline for Submitting Documentation for the Stability of Human Drugs and Biologics* (February 1987); and *Guideline for Submitting Supporting Documentation in Drug Applications for the Manufacture of Drug Substances* (February 1987). A few years later, these were supplemented by the agency's *Draft Guideline for Submitting Supporting Chemistry Documentation in Radiopharmaceutical*

Drug Applications (November 1991), *Guidance for the Submission of Chemistry, Manufacturing, and Controls for Synthetic Peptide Drug Substances* (November 1994) and *Guideline for Drug Master Files* (September 1989).

In February 1996, CDER released a draft guidance for industry entitled *Content and Format for Submission of Drug Products for Investigational New Drug Applications (INDs), New Drug Applications (NDAs), Abbreviated New Drug Applications (ANDAs), and Abbreviated Antibiotic New Drug Applications (AANDAs).* Although the document remains a draft, CDER reviewers have in some cases suggested that applicants refer to the guidance. Center officials caution, however, that the contents of a final guidance in this area will be a function of several factors, including ICH developments and CDER efforts to harmonize new and generic drug chemistry requirements.

The ICH initiative has produced several guidelines relevant to the NDA's chemistry section. These documents are cited in the discussions below.

Form 356h's listing of the NDA contents indicates that the chemistry section should be comprised of three elements: A. Chemistry, manufacturing and control information; B. Samples; and C. Methods validation package.

A. Chemistry, Manufacturing, and Control Information. According to FDA regulations, an NDA's chemistry, manufacturing, and control section should comprise four principal elements: (1) a description of the drug substance; (2) a description of the drug product; (3) an environmental impact analysis report (or request for a waiver); and (4) a field copy certification.

A Description of the Drug Substance. The sponsor's description of the drug substance should include the following:

The Substance's Stability and Physical and Chemical Characteristics. Provide the substance's chemical name and related names (if available and appropriate), structural formula, physicochemical characteristics, the physical and chemical data necessary to elucidate and confirm the substance's chemical structure, and a description of the studies (including results) on the substance's stability. Regarding drug substance stability requirements for NDAs, applicants should refer to the ICH's final guideline entitled *Stability Testing of New Drug Substances and Products* (1994), and, if applicable, to a pair of draft annexes to this guideline, *Guideline for the Photostability Testing of*

New Drug Substances and Products (March 1996) and *Stability Testing for New Dosage Forms* (May 1997). Applicants should also refer to the FDA's *Guideline for Submitting Documentation for the Stability of Human Drugs and Biologics* (1987), which the agency has stated that it will update to be consistent with the ICH's 1994 final stability guideline.

The Name and Address of the Manufacturer. Provide the name and address of each facility (i.e., besides those of the applicant) that participates in manufacturing the drug substance (e.g., performs the synthesis, isolation, purification, testing, packaging, or labeling), and describe the operation(s) that each facility performs.

Method(s) of Manufacture and Packaging. Provide a full description of the materials and method(s) used in the synthesis, isolation, and purification of the drug substance, including a list of starting materials, reagents, solvents, and auxiliary materials. Also, describe the process controls used at various stages of the manufacturing, processing, and packaging of the drug substance, and information on the characteristics of, and the test methods used for, the container-closure system. In addition, the original application should provide a full description of the preparation of any reference standard substance used, including a description of the purification steps.

Specifications and Analytical Methods for the Drug Substance. Provide a full description of the acceptance specifications and test methods used to assure the identity, strength, quality, and purity of the drug substance and the bioavailability of drug products made from the drug substance, including specifications relating to stability, sterility, particle size, and crystalline form. It is also typical to include data from the validation of these studies in this section as well. For additional guidance, applicants can refer to the following ICH final guidelines: *Impurities in New Drug Substances* (1996), *Text on Validation of Analytical Procedures: Definitions and Terminology* (1995), and *Validation of Analytical Procedures: Methodology* (1997).

Solid State Drug Substance Forms and Their Relationship to Bioavailability. Provide appropriate specifications characterizing the drug substance (e.g., particle size) to assure the bioavailability of the drug product.

The sponsor may provide for the use of alternatives in meeting any of the applicable requirements, including alternative sources, process controls, methods, and specifications. In some cases, reference to the current editions of the *U.S. Pharmacopeia* and the *National Formulary* may satisfy the content requirements outlined above.

Often, applicants utilize components (e.g., drug substances, nonstandard excipients, containers) manufactured by other firms. In such cases, the contract manufacturer may want to preserve the confidentiality of its manufacturing processes. Since an NDA must provide information on these processes, contract manufacturers will often submit this information directly to the FDA in a drug master file (DMF). This allows drug sponsors using the company's products to meet submission requirements by incorporating by reference information provided in the DMF. Because the drug sponsor never sees the information in the DMF, the confidentiality of the contract facility's manufacturing processes is maintained.

An incorporation by reference should be made in the section of the NDA in which the referenced information would normally appear. The reference must identify specifically where the agency can find the information in the DMF (or other referenced document), and must identify the file by name, reference number, volume, and page number (i.e., the FDA stores DMFs and reviews the information in the file only when referenced in a pending drug application). When the applicant cross-references a DMF submitted by another firm (e.g., a bulk drug manufacturer), the NDA must include a letter of authorization from the DMF's owner in addition to the information specified above. For more information on DMFs, sponsors should refer to CDER's *Guideline for Drug Master Files* (September 1989).

A Description of the Drug Product. In many ways similar to the drug substance section, this part of the NDA should include the following:

A List of Components. Provide a list of all components used in the manufacture of the drug product (regardless of whether they appear in the final product).

A Statement of Drug Product Composition. Provide a statement of the product's quantitative composition, indicating the weight or measure for each substance used in the manufacture of the dosage form. Also, provide the batch formula to be used in the product's manufacture.

Specifications and Analytical Methods for Inactive Components. Provide a full description of the acceptance specifications and test methods used to assure the identity, quality, and purity of each inactive ingredient.

Name and Address of Manufacturer(s). Provide the name and address of each facility involved in manufacturing the drug product (e.g., the drug processing, packaging, labeling, or control applications), and describe the operations that each will perform.

Method(s) of Manufacture and Packaging. Provide a copy of the master/batch production and control records or a comparably detailed description of the production process (a schematic diagram of the production process is often helpful). Also, provide complete information on the characteristics of, and test methods used for, the container-closure system or other component parts of the drug product package to assure their suitability for packaging the drug product. For further guidance on specific issues relevant to this subsection, applicants can refer to a draft ICH guideline entitled *Impurities: Residual Solvents* (May 1997) and CDER's *Guidance for Industry for the Submission of Documentation for Sterilization Process Validation in Applications for Human and Veterinary Drug Products* (November 1994).

Specifications and Analytical Methods for the Drug Product. Provide a full description of the specifications and analytical methods necessary to assure the product's identity, strength, quality, purity, homogeneity, and bioavailability throughout its shelf life. The methods and standards of acceptance should be sufficiently detailed to permit FDA laboratories to duplicate them. Typically, applicants include data on the validation of the analytical methods in this section as well. Regarding submission requirements for impurities, applicants can refer to a final ICH guideline entitled *Impurities in New Drug Products* (1997).

Stability. Provide a complete description of, and data derived from, studies of product stability, including information establishing the suitability of the analytical method(s) used.

In this section as well, the sponsor may provide alternatives for meeting relevant requirements, including alternative components, manufacturing and packaging procedures, in-process controls, methods, and specifications. Reference to the current editions of the *U.S. Pharmacopeia* and the *National Formulary* may satisfy relevant requirements. Regarding drug product stability requirements for NDAs, applicants can refer to the ICH's final guideline entitled *Stability Testing of New Drug Substances and Products* (1994) and, if applicable, to a pair of draft annexes to this guideline, *Guideline for the Photostability Testing of New Drug Substances and Products* (March 1996) and *Stability Testing for New Dosage Forms* (May 1997). Applicants can also refer to the FDA's *Guideline for Submitting Documentation for the Stability of Human Drugs and Biologics* (1987), which the agency has stated that it will update to be consistent with the ICH's 1994 final stability guideline

A September 1993 final regulation modified content requirements for this portion of the chemistry, manufacturing, and controls section. The regulation mandates that applicants provide certain information about the batches of the drug product used to conduct the "pivotal" bioavailability and bioequivalence studies and the "primary" stability studies: (1) the batch production record; (2) the specifications and test procedures for each component and for the drug product itself; (3) the names and addresses of the sources of the active and noncompendial inactive components and of the container and closure system for the drug product; (4) the name and address of each contract facility involved in the manufacture, processing, packaging, or testing of the drug product, and identification of the operation performed by each contract facility; and (5) the results of tests performed on the drug product and on the components used in the product's manufacture.

In addition, the 1993 regulation requires that this section provide the "proposed or actual master production record, including a description of the equipment, to be used for the manufacture of a commercial lot of the drug product or a comparably detailed description of the production process for a representative batch of the drug product."

It is worth noting that CDER chemists often find it helpful when applicants submit developmental pharmaceutics information beyond that called for in current regulations and guidelines. Reviewers claim that the information can give CDER chemists a greater "comfort level" with the application because it describes the product's formulation development history and the company's rationale on formulation-related issues (e.g., methods, ranges, inactive ingredients). FDA officials strongly recommend, however, that sponsors ask CDER chemists about the utility of such information on a case-by-case basis, and about where the information should be located in the NDA if it is to be provided. Although CDER does not have a formal policy on the submission of additional developmental pharmaceutics information, agency officials claim that the issue is being addressed in ICH discussions regarding a "core technical document" (see discussion above).

Environmental Impact Analysis Report. Although the FDA had been placing increased emphasis on environmental assessments (EA) in the early 1990s, the agency seemed to shift its policy in the mid-1990s. Under a 1995 Clinton Administration regulatory reform initiative, the agency proposed to "exempt from environmental assessments virtually all applications for human drugs...[so] industry will be spared the expense of an analysis that FDA has found not to be needed." The agency claimed at the time that it would grant categorical exclusions, or exemptions, from EA requirements to all but a "fairly narrow category" of drugs and biologics.

While the agency had not proposed a new regulation to implement this change by mid-1997, it did issue a new guideline entitled *Guidance for Industry for the Submission of an Environmental Assessment in Human Drug Applications and Supplements* in November 1995. The new guideline identifies the requirements for environmental assessments, which describe the environmental implications of releasing a drug substance and drug product into the air, water, and soil. Under current regulations, an NDA must include either an environmental assessment, an abbreviated environmental assessment (AEA), or a claim for a categorical exclusion from the regulations requiring the EA submission.

Field Copy Certification. U.S.-based applicants must include in this section a statement "certifying that the field copy of the application has been provided to the applicant's home district office." Since foreign applicants must provide the field copy with the archival and review copies, no such certification is needed in their applications.

Given the nature and detail of the chemistry, manufacturing, and control section, the FDA permits sponsors to submit the completed section 90 to 120 days before the anticipated filing of the entire NDA. In some cases, the agency claims, this may speed the NDA review process.

For such early submissions, both the archival and review copies of the section are required, while the field copy may be forwarded when the full NDA is submitted. The early submission should provide a cover letter, the application form, an index to facilitate the location of the information within the section, and the identification of a sponsor contact person with whom the FDA may discuss the data. If any information required for the section is unavailable at the time of the advance submission, this should be noted in the cover letter.

B. Samples. Drug samples should not accompany the NDA submission, but should be submitted only in response to an FDA request. The FDA may request these samples to validate the adequacy of the analytical methods that the sponsor uses to identify the drug product and drug substance. Typically, the FDA requests that applicants submit samples directly to "two or more" agency laboratories that will perform the validation work.

Upon such a request, the applicant must submit "four representative samples of the following, with each sample in sufficient quantity to permit FDA to perform three times each test described in the application to determine whether the drug substance and the drug product meet the specifications given in the application:"

- the drug product proposed for marketing;

- the drug substance used in the drug product from which the samples of the drug product were taken; and

- reference standards and blanks (except that reference standards recognized in an official compendium need not be submitted).

Upon an FDA request, sponsors must also provide samples of the product's "finished market package." The FDA may ask for two copies of the package, although one generally suffices.

C. Methods Validation Package. The archival copy of the NDA must include a methods validation package, which provides information that allows FDA laboratories to validate all of the analytical methods for both the drug substance and drug product. It should provide a listing of all samples to be submitted, including lot number, identity, package type and size, and quantity. In addition, the package usually includes descriptive information copied from pertinent sections of the NDA. FDA regulations state that "related descriptive information includes a description of each sample; the proposed regulatory specifications for the drug; a detailed description of the methods of analysis; supporting data for accuracy, specificity, precision and ruggedness; and complete results of the applicant's tests on each sample." To aid the reviewing chemist, these copies should retain the original pagination of the NDA sections from which they were copied.

The FDA provides specific advice on the development of this section in its *Guideline for Submitting Samples and Analytical Data for Methods Validation* (February 1987). In March 1995, the ICH published a final guideline entitled *Text on Validation of Analytical Procedures*, which discusses "the characteristics that should be considered during the validation of the analytical procedures included as part of registration applications." More recently, the ICH parties published a final guideline entitled *Validation of Analytical Procedures: Methodology* (May 1997), which provides recommendations on how manufacturers should consider the various validation characteristics for each analytical procedure, as well as guidance on the data that should be presented in a marketing application.

Four copies of the methods validation package should be included with the initial submission. Although FDA regulations state that three of the copies should be submitted in the archival copy, agency guidelines recommend submitting one copy with the archival copy and three additional copies with the chemistry, manufacturing, and controls section of the review copy. If the applicant does the latter, the submission should include a statement indicating that this option was selected.

Nonclinical Pharmacology and Toxicology Section Federal regulations state that this section should "describe, with the aid of graphs and tables, animal and *in vitro* studies with [the] drug." The section should provide all nonclinical animal and laboratory studies involving the drug, including data from preclinical studies originally submitted in the IND; data compiled and submitted during clinical investigations (e.g., long-term testing such as carcinogenicity and reproductive testing); and, in some cases, non-clinical studies not submitted previously.

The FDA reviews these studies to evaluate their adequacy and comprehensiveness, and to ensure that there are no inconsistent or inadequately characterized toxic effects. According to federal regulations, the principal content requirements for this section are:

1. Studies of the pharmacological actions of the drug in relation to its proposed therapeutic indication, and studies that otherwise define the pharmacologic properties of the drug or that are pertinent to possible adverse side effects.

2. Studies of the toxicological effects of the drug as they relate to the drug's intended clinical use(s), including, as appropriate, studies assessing the drug's acute, subacute, and chronic toxicity, carcinogenicity, and studies of toxicities related to the drug's particular mode of administration or conditions of use.

3. Studies, as appropriate, of the effects of the drug on reproduction and on the developing fetus.

4. Any studies of the absorption, distribution, metabolism, and excretion of the drug in animals.

5. For each nonclinical laboratory study, a statement that it was conducted in compliance with good laboratory practice (GLP) regulations, or if the study was not conducted in compliance with those regulations, a brief statement of the reason for the noncompliance.

The FDA is sensitive to organizational problems regarding the presentation of toxicological, pharmacological, and other data from nonclinical studies. Therefore, drug sponsors should refer to specific recommendations in the FDA's *Guideline for the Format and Content of the Nonclinical Pharmacology/Toxicology Section of an Application* (February 1987). Although it concedes that nonclinical data are collected over several years and are submitted in varying formats, the guideline recommends that the data be reorganized for the NDA submission: "The agency recognizes that most or all of the nonclinical data submitted to an application will have been developed over several years and submitted intermittently to an investigational drug application (IND). We recommend the reorganization of the studies to…the extent feasible for submission to an application even though the formats of all individual studies cannot always easily be made to conform in all details to these guideline recommendations. We anticipate that this guideline will also shape future IND submissions so that relatively little revision will be needed for the application other than to rearrange study order."

Human Pharmacokinetics and Bioavailability Section The NDA must include a section providing data and analyses from all human pharmacokinetic and bioavailability studies (or information supporting a waiver of *in vivo* bioavailability data). The section should include data from and descriptions of any of the five general types of biopharmaceutic studies that were relevant for the investigational drug:

1. Pilot and background studies, which are conducted to provide a preliminary assessment of absorption, distribution, metabolism and/or elimination (ADME) of a drug as a guide in the design of early clinical trials and definitive kinetic studies.

2. Bioavailability/bioequivalence studies, including bioavailability, bioequivalence, and dosage form proportionality studies (this discussion should include a description of the analytical and statistical methods used in each study).

3. Pharmacokinetic studies, descriptions of which must include a discussion of the analytical and statistical methods used in each study.

4. Other *in vivo* studies using pharmacological or clinical endpoints.

5. *In vitro* studies designed to define the release rate of a drug substance from the dosage form (obviously, such dissolution tests are not relevant for drug forms such as injectables and some others).

According to FDA regulations, this section should consist of as many as three elements:

- "A description of each of the bioavailability and pharmacokinetic studies of the drug in humans performed by or on behalf of the applicant that includes a description of the analytical and statistical methods used in each study and a statement [that it was conducted according to relevant federal regulations]."

- "If the application describes in the chemistry, manufacturing, and controls section specifications or analytical methods needed to assure the bioavailability of the drug product or drug substance, or both, a statement in this section of the rationale for establishing the specification or analytical methods, including data and information supporting this rationale."

- "A summarizing discussion and analysis of the pharmacokinetics and metabolism of the active ingredients and the bioavailability or bioequivalence, or both, of the drug product."

The FDA provides its most detailed recommendations on the development and presentation of this section in its *Guideline for the Format and Content of the Human Pharmacokinetics and Bioavailability Section of an Application* (February 1987). In November 1994, the ICH published a final guideline entitled *Dose-Response Information to Support Drug Registration*, which describes the importance of dose-response information and the types of studies that sponsors can use to obtain such information (i.e., parallel-dose response, cross-over dose response, forced titration, and optional titration). More recently, the FDA has published *Guidance for Industry—Drug Metabolism/Drug Interaction Studies in the Drug Development Process: Studies In Vitro* (April 1997), which provides recommendations on current approaches to *in vitro* studies of drug metabolism and interactions.

Microbiology Section This section is required only in NDAs for anti-infective drugs. Since these drugs affect microbial, rather than clinical, physiology, reports on the drug's *in vivo* and *in vitro* effects on the target microorganisms are critical for establishing product effectiveness.

Current regulations require that an NDA's anti-infective drug section include microbiology data describing: (1) the biochemical basis of the drug's action on microbial physiology; (2) the drug's antimicrobial spectra, including results of *in vitro* preclinical studies demonstrating concentrations of the drug required for effective use; (3) any known mechanisms of resistance to the drug, including results of any known epidemiologic studies demonstrating prevalence of resistance factors; and (4) clinical microbiology laboratory methods needed to evaluate the effective use of the drug. Full reports of the studies, summary tables, and a summary narrative should be included for each portion of this section.

More specific guidance on developing the microbiology component of the NDA is available from the FDA's *Guideline for the Format and Content of the Microbiology Section of an Application* (February 1987).

Clinical Data Section Since the FDA's conclusions regarding a new drug's safety and effectiveness are based largely on the data and analyses provided in the clinical data section, it is clearly the single most important element of the NDA. When taken together with the NDA's statistical component (see discussion below), the clinical section is also the application's most complex and voluminous. As discussed above, a recent study by Georgetown University's Center for Drug Development Science found that the median number of clinical trials submitted in 12 NDAs approved in 1994 and 1995 was 68 (25 percent had 97 or more trials). Past FDA studies of NME NDAs have indicated that an average of 87 percent of the information submitted in new drug applications is clinical in nature.

In a variety of ways, the NDA's clinical data section is being reshaped by several international and FDA initiatives:

- In releasing two draft guidelines under its *New Use Initiative - Primary and Supplemental Approvals*, the FDA has provided perhaps its most detailed discussion of the clinical efficacy data necessary to support drug approval (see Chapter 6). These guidances outline specific requirements not only for the quantity of data necessary, but documentation of the quality of the data supporting an efficacy claim as well.

- In July 1996, the ICH participants published a final guideline— *Structure and Content of Clinical Study Reports*—that specified new requirements for clinical study reports provided in NDAs.

- The FDA's Good Review Practices (GRP) initiative, which in part seeks to provide "some level of standardization in clinical reviews of NDAs," is likely to affect the manner in which certain aspects of both clinical safety and efficacy data are presented in new drug applications.

Given the complexity and importance of the two sections, it is not surprising that the FDA's most detailed NDA-related guideline addresses the NDA's clinical and statistical sections. The agency's 125-page *Guideline for the Format and Content of the Clinical and Statistical Sections of an Application* (July 1988) provides recommendations on formatting and organizing these sections and on presenting the clinical and statistical information and accompanying documentation. The guideline also describes a fully integrated clinical and statistical report for documenting the results of individual studies. An ICH final guideline entitled *Structure and Content of Clinical Study Reports* (July 1996) supersedes Section III of the FDA guideline, and provides format and content standards for "an integrated full report of an individual study."

As specified in the FDA's 1988 guideline, the first two elements in the clinical data section are: (1) a list of investigators supplied with the drug or known to have studied the drug, INDs under which the drug has been studied, and NDAs submitted for the same drug substance; and (2) a background/overview of the clinical investigations (i.e., the general approach and rationale used in developing clinical data). According to FDA regulations and the guideline referenced above, the NDA's clinical data section should consist of as many as 11 additional elements:

1. A description and analysis of each clinical pharmacology study of the drug, including a brief comparison of the results of the human studies with the animal pharmacology and toxicology data.

2. A description and analysis of each controlled clinical study pertinent to a proposed use of the drug, including the protocol and a description of the statistical analyses used to evaluate the study. If

the study report is an interim analysis, this must be noted and a projected completion date provided. Controlled clinical studies that have not been analyzed in detail should be provided, along with a copy of the protocol and a brief description of the results and status of the study.

3. A description of each uncontrolled study, a summary of the results, and a brief statement explaining why the study is classified as uncontrolled.

4. A description and analysis of any other data or information relevant to an evaluation of the safety and effectiveness of the drug product obtained or otherwise received by the applicant from any foreign or domestic source. This might include information derived from commercial marketing experience, reports in scientific literature, unpublished scientific papers, and controlled and uncontrolled studies of uses of the drug other than those proposed in the application.

5. An integrated summary of the data demonstrating substantial evidence of effectiveness for the claimed indications. Evidence is also required to support the dosage and administration section of the labeling, including support for the dosage and dose interval recommended, and modifications for specific subgroups of patients (e.g., pediatrics, geriatrics, patients with renal failure).

6. An integrated summary of all available information about the safety of the drug product, including pertinent animal data, demonstrated or potential adverse effects of the drug, clinically significant drug/drug interactions, and other safety considerations, such as data from epidemiological studies of related drugs. Unless provided under section (2) above, the integrated safety summary should also describe any statistical analyses used in analyzing the safety data.

7. For drugs that might be abused, a description and analysis of studies or information related to abuse of the drug, including a proposal for scheduling and a description of any studies related to overdosage.

196

8. An integrated summary of the benefits and risks of the drug, including a discussion of why the benefits exceed the risks under the conditions stated in the labeling.

9. A statement noting that each human clinical study was conducted in compliance with the IRB regulations and with the informed consent regulations. If the study was not subject to IRB regulations, the applicant must state this fact.

10. If the sponsor transferred any of its regulatory obligations regarding the conduct of a clinical study (e.g., monitoring) to a contract research organization (CRO), a statement providing the name and address of the CRO, the identity of the clinical study, and a listing of the responsibilities transferred. When a sponsor transfers all of its obligations, the NDA may provide a "general statement of this transfer" in lieu of an itemized listing.

11. If the sponsor reviewed or audited original subject records during the course of monitoring any clinical study to verify the accuracy of the case report forms submitted by the investigator, the NDA must provide a list identifying each clinical study audited or reviewed.

Because it is designed, in part, to assist companies in assessing clinical data and preparing clinical summaries for marketing applications, the ICH's May 1997 *Draft Guideline on Statistical Principles for Clinical Trials* should also be consulted by applicants.

During the early 1990s, the FDA became increasingly concerned with gender-, age-, and race-related drug response differences, particularly following a study showing that many NDAs lacked such information, even though it is requested in the agency's 1988 *Guideline for the Format and Content of the Clinical and Statistical Sections of New Drug Applications*. In March 1993, then-CDER Director Carl Peck, M.D., wrote to industry to emphasize the importance of this information and to announce that NDAs would no longer be accepted for review without it.

This emphasis on the inclusion of key demographic subset information has continued both in the U.S. and internationally. The ICH, for example, has published *Guideline on Studies in Support of Special Populations: Geriatrics* (August 1994). In September 1995, the FDA proposed to explicitly require gender, age, and racial subgroup data in NDAs. The agency made clear in the proposal that it would not require new studies, only the analysis of data that were already being collected by drug sponsors. The FDA hoped to finalize this regulation, which was in the final clearance phase as of this writing, before year-end 1997.

Safety Update Report Section As implied by its title, the safety update report is not filed with the original NDA, but is submitted in the form of updates at specific points in the application review process. Applicants must submit safety update reports four months after the NDA's submission, following the receipt of an approvable letter, and at other times requested by CDER.

In these reports, the applicant must update its pending NDA "with new safety information learned about the drug that may reasonably affect the statement of contraindications, warnings, precautions, and adverse reactions in the draft labeling." The updates must include the same types of information (from clinical studies, animal studies, and other sources), and must be submitted in the same format, as the NDA's integrated safety summary. They must also include case report forms for each patient who died during a clinical study or who did not complete the study because of an adverse event (unless this requirement is waived).

Federal regulations encourage applicants to consult with the FDA on the form and content of these reports prior to the submission of the first report.

Statistical Section As evidenced by the fact that the FDA addressed the NDA's clinical and statistical sections in a single guideline, the two components are closely related. In fact, the core of the statistical section comprises data and analyses taken directly from the application's clinical data section.

According to the agency's *Guideline for the Format and Content of the Clinical and Statistical Sections of New Drug Applications* (July 1988), the core of the statistical section should include the following sections taken verbatim from the NDA's clinical section:

- a list of investigators supplied with the drug or known to have investigated the drug, INDs under which the drug has been studied, and NDAs submitted for the same drug substance;

- a background/overview of clinical investigations;

- the controlled clinical studies section;

- the integrated summary of effectiveness data;

- the integrated summary of safety data; and

- the integrated summary of benefits and risks.

Although it is not yet finalized, the ICH's draft guideline entitled *Statistical Principles for Clinical Trials* (May 1997) is the latest guidance addressing issues related to the statistical component of marketing applications. According to the FDA, "the draft guideline provides recommendations to sponsors in the design, conduct, analysis, and evaluation of clinical trials of an investigational product in the context of its overall clinical development. The draft guideline also provides guidance to scientific experts in preparing application summaries or assessing evidence of efficacy and safety, principally from late Phase II and Phase III clinical trials." For additional guidance, applicants should also consult the ICH guideline entitled *Structure and Content of Clinical Study Reports* (July 1996).

The FDA encourages applicants to meet with CDER—specifically, with the assigned biostatistical reviewer(s) within CDER's Division of Pharmacovigilance and Epidemiology—before an NDA's submission to discuss the section's format, tabulations, statistical analyses, and other important issues. In some cases, the agency permits applicants to submit for review and comment the preliminary tabulation of patient data and the materials on the statistical analyses of controlled clinical studies and/or safety data (see discussion of pre-NDA meetings below).

Case Report Tabulations Section During the FDA's most recent overhaul of its NDA regulations, the agency declared that "an efficient agency review of individual patient data should be based primarily on well-organized, concise, data tabulations...." Reviews of the "more lengthy patient case report forms" should be reserved for those instances in which a more detailed review is necessary, the agency stated (see discussion below).

In its *Guideline on Formatting, Assembling, and Submitting New Drug and Antibiotic Applications* (February 1987), however, the agency advises sponsors to "meet with FDA to discuss the extent to which tabulations of patient data in clinical studies, data elements within tables, and case report forms are needed. Such discussions can also cover alternative modes of data presentation and the need for special supporting information (for example, electrocardiograms, x-rays, or pathology slides)."

According to agency regulations and guidelines, the NDA must provide data tabulations on individual patients from each of the following:

- the initial clinical pharmacology studies (Phase 1 studies);

- effectiveness data from each adequate and well-controlled study (Phase 2 and Phase 3 studies); and

- safety data from all studies.

Under current regulations, these tabulations should include "the data on each patient in each study, except that the applicant may delete those tabulations that the agency agrees, in advance, are not pertinent to a review of the drug's safety or effectiveness." The FDA is willing to discuss appropriate deletions from these tabulations at a "pre-NDA" conference.

Given that case report tabulation (CRT) and case report form (see discussion below) submissions can be voluminous, it is not surprising that CRTs and CRFs were the first elements of the NDA to be accepted in electronic form without their paper-based versions. In May 1996, CDER published a policy formally establishing a waiver process through which applicants could obtain permission to do so.

In reality, however, this waiver process was a stopgap measure to be used until the FDA could finalize its proposed rule on electronic records and signatures, something that the agency did in March 1997. Under this regulation, all sections of an NDA can be submitted electronically without a paper-based submission.

Related FDA actions indicated that the agency planned to ease into the era of electronic-only filings, and that some of its early steps would be taken with electronic CRT and CRF filings. In November 1996, the agency released a draft guidance document entitled *Electronic Submission of Case Report Forms and Case Report Tabulations*. The draft guideline proposed that NDA applicants be given five options for submitting CRFs (i.e., paper-based CRFs, electronically imaged CRFs, electronically searchable CRFs, electronically captured CRFs and multi-format CRFs) and three options for submitting CRTs (i.e., paper-based CRTs, electronically imaged CRTs, electronically functional or electronically analyzable CRTs).

Case Report Forms Section As stated above, the FDA does not require the routine submission of patient case report forms. Rather, an NDA must include CRFs for: (1) patients who died during a clinical study; and (2) patients who did not complete a study because of any adverse event, regardless of whether the adverse event is considered drug-related by the investigator or sponsor.

The FDA may request that the sponsor submit additional case report forms (and tabulations) that the agency views as important to the drug's review. Typically, the agency requests all case report forms for the pivotal studies. In doing so, the review division attempts to designate the critical studies for which case report forms are required approximately 30 days after the NDA's receipt. If a sponsor fails to submit the CRFs within 30 days of the FDA's request, the agency may view the eventual submission as a major amendment and extend the review period as appropriate.

Patent Information Applicants must provide information on any patent(s) on the drug for which approval is sought, or on a method of using the drug.

Patent Certification Applicants must provide a patent certification or statement regarding "any relevant patents that claim the listed drug or that claim any other drugs on which investigations relied on by the applicant for approval of the application were conducted, or that claim a use for the listed or other drug."

According to the FDA's *Guideline on Formatting, Assembling, and Submitting New Drug and Antibiotic Applications* (February 1987), the patent certification and patent information sections (see above) should be attached to the application form (Form 356h) in the NDA submission.

Establishment Description The establishment description section is relevant for certain biological products only. Its incorporation in Form 356h is a function of the FDA's effort to develop a harmonized application form for both drugs and biologics.

Debarment Certification Since mid-1992, the FDA has required that all NDAs include a certification that the applicant did not and will not use the services of individuals or firms that have been debarred by the FDA. Under the Generic Drug Enforcement Act of 1992, the FDA is authorized to debar individuals convicted of crimes relating to the development, approval, or regulation of drugs or biologics from providing any services to applicants. The statute requires that applications for drug products include "a certification that the applicant did not and will not use in any capacity the services of any person debarred...in connection with such application."

In mid-1997, CDER was planning to release a new guidance document to assist companies in meeting the debarment certification requirement in NDAs.

Field Copy Certification As stated earlier, U.S.-based NDA sponsors must submit a "field" copy of the NDA's chemistry, manufacturing, and controls section, application form, and summary directly to the relevant FDA district office for use during the pre-approval manufacturing inspection (see Chapter 9). The applicant is also required to certify in its NDA that an exact copy of the application's chemistry, manufacturing, and controls section has been forwarded to the district office.

User Fee Cover Sheet (Form FDA 3397) Since January 1994, the FDA has required every new drug application to include a copy of the User Fee Cover Sheet. This form provides information that allows the FDA to determine whether the application is subject to user fees and, if so, whether the appropriate fee for the application has been submitted.

Other Information If necessary, the sponsor may use this portion of the application to incorporate by reference any information submitted previous to the NDA filing. The sponsor must also provide an accurate and complete English translation of any foreign language document for any information originally written in a foreign language.

Pre-NDA Meetings

Because of the NDA's complexity and because the FDA wants to avoid investing scarce resources reviewing deficient NDAs, the agency offers conferences called pre-NDA meetings to all drug sponsors. Federal regulations state that the primary purpose of pre-NDA meetings "...is to uncover any major unresolved problems, to identify those studies that the sponsor is relying on as adequate and well-controlled to establish the drug's effectiveness, to acquaint FDA reviewers with the general information to be submitted in the marketing application (including technical information), to discuss appropriate methods for statistical analysis of the data, and to discuss the best approach to the presentation and formatting of data in the marketing application."

As is true for end-of-Phase 2 conferences, a sponsor must request a pre-NDA meeting with the division responsible for a drug's review. Although federal regulations establish that all drug sponsors have access to such conferences, the importance of the drug, the time constraints facing the relevant drug review division, and the significance of the scientific and regulatory issues at hand will do much to determine whether the FDA grants a pre-NDA meeting. The meeting can take place anytime before an NDA submission, but should not be held before Phase 3 studies near completion.

In 1996, CDER published a new policy entitled *Formal Meetings Between CDER and CDER's External Constituents* (MaPP 4512.1). The policy is CDER's attempt to provide a consistent approach to sponsor meetings and to establish a time frame for CDER responses to meeting requests. According to the policy, written requests for meetings should include at least six elements: a brief statement of the purpose of the meeting; a listing of the specific objectives/outcomes the requestor expects from the meeting; a proposed agenda, including the estimated time needed for each agenda item; a listing of planned external attendees; a listing of requested participants from CDER; and the approximate time at which supporting documentation for the meeting will be sent to CDER (i.e., "x" weeks prior to the meeting, but should be received by CDER at least 2 weeks in advance of the scheduled meeting).

Within 14 days of receiving the request, the reviewing division must notify the requestor in writing (either by letter or fax) of the date, time, and place at which the meeting will be held, as well as the likely CDER participants. Under CDER policy, the meeting date should not exceed 75 days from the date of the sponsor's initial dated meeting request. If such a wait would stall its commercial development program, a sponsor can request an earlier, "special considerations meeting."

The success of a pre-NDA meeting depends largely on sponsor preparation. To help FDA staffers prepare, sponsors "...should submit to FDA's reviewing division at least 1 month in advance of the meeting the following information: (i) a brief summary of the clinical studies to be submitted in the application; (ii) a proposed format for organizing the submission, including methods for presenting the data; and (iii) any other information for discussion at the meeting."

FDA staffers stress that a particularly important element of pre-NDA meetings is that devoted to the statistical review. To make optimal use of the meeting, the sponsor should send, or have present at the meeting, sample mock-ups or computer printouts of data to provide FDA statisticians the opportunity to offer advice on data organization and presentation.

Assembling and Submitting the NDA

The FDA has extremely specific requirements for the NDA's assembly, many of which are provided in the agency's *Guideline on Formatting, Assembling, and Submitting New Drug and Antibiotic Applications* (February 1987). This 32-page document offers general guidance on such issues as content requirements, and more detailed specifications on such issues as paper size, maximum volume size, volume identification, and pagination.

Amending the NDA

Either at its own initiative or in response to an FDA request, an applicant may seek to clarify or augment the information provided in the original NDA during the review process. For example, the applicant may submit a new analysis of previously submitted data, new data not available at the time of the NDA submission, or information needed to address a deficiency in the drug application.

Any such information provided for an unapproved application is considered an NDA amendment. Depending on its timing, the submission of a significant amendment—a major reanalysis of clinical data, for example—may trigger an extension in the FDA's timeline for the application's review (see Chapter 9).

Chapter 9

The NDA Review Process

No other aspect of the U.S. drug development and approval system has evolved as significantly in recent years as the FDA's new drug application (NDA) review process. So fundamental were these changes—and the improvements in drug review times that resulted from them—that CDER's NDA review performance was transformed from one of the most harshly criticized of FDA activities into what was perhaps the agency's best defense against regulatory reform proposals advanced in 1995 and 1996.

The driving force behind this evolution, of course, was the Prescription Drug User Fee Act of 1992 (PDUFA), and the changes that CDER implemented to meet the new review timelines associated with the legislation. In the early and mid-1990s, CDER management instituted tight controls for managing and tracking drug reviews, and reorganized the center's drug review divisions into smaller, more therapeutically focused units (see Chapter 5).

By early 1997, as Congress began to consider reauthorizing PDUFA, there seemed little question that the prescription drug user fee program had brought much of the change that industry had long sought. In a February 1997 report to industry, CDER Director Janet Woodcock, M.D., wrote, "[In 1996], CDER approved 53 new molecular entities (NME) for U.S. marketing. Over the last three decades, the previous high was only 30 NMEs. In addition, the median total time to approval for these 53 NMEs was 14.3 months—the most rapid time ever. So this year, we approved the most NMEs in the shortest time ever. Contrast this performance with 1993, the beginning of the Prescription Drug User Fee Act (PDUFA) program, when CDER approved only 25 NMEs and the median time to approval for those 25 NMEs was approximately 23 months."

Despite these successes, CDER was facing its most difficult PDUFA-related challenge as of this writing: The center was called upon to review 90 percent of priority NDAs submitted in fiscal year 1997 within six months of their submission. For the first four years of the user-fee program, the review goal for both standard and priority submissions was 12 months.

In addition, several factors were rapidly pushing the NDA review process into its next evolutionary phase:

PDUFA Reauthorization. Since PDUFA was to expire in September 1997, industry and the FDA agreed in early 1997 to ask Congress to evaluate several changes in PDUFA when the legislative body considered reauthorizing the law. If implemented, these revisions will bring important changes to the NDA review process, including the following: (1) they will reduce review time frames for standard NDAs from 12 to 10 months; (2) they will replace "approvable" and "not-approvable" letters with "complete response" letters; and (3) they will require the agency to notify applicants of NDA deficiencies as these problems are identified in the review process.

New Experimental Paradigm for Drug Reviews. At this writing, CDER's Office of Drug Evaluation IV (ODE IV) was implementing a new model for managing certain aspects of the drug review process. Under the plan, ODE IV established three office-level teams responsible for "overseeing and coordinating" certain activities, including pre-IND efforts and line-extension application reviews (see Chapter 5). CDER officials characterized the ODE IV reorganization as a "forum for innovation" within the center.

Good Review Practices. Under CDER's Good Review Practices (GRP) initiative, the center is in the process of developing a series of reviewer guidelines that will seek to provide "some level of standardization in clinical reviews of NDAs." This effort is expected to provide applicants with useful insights on how CDER reviewers will conduct NDA evaluations. The first product of this effort was a draft reviewer guidance entitled *Conducting a Clinical Safety Review of a New Product Application and Preparing a Report on the Review.*

Computer-Assisted NDA (CANDA) Reviews. In March 1997, CDER laid the regulatory groundwork for computer-based NDA submissions to replace their paper-based counterparts. Specifically, a final regulation established the regulatory basis under which the agency can accept CANDAs in lieu of paper submissions. Previously, FDA regulations had required that complete paper-based applications be provided, even if a CANDA was submitted. To start in August 1997, CDER's transition to the electronic age will be cautious and gradual. This transition will begin with the center's identification of IND and NDA components that its various divisions and offices are willing and able to accept in electronic form. This listing will be maintained on CDER's new publicly available electronic submissions docket (Docket #9250251).

New Review Scheme for OTC Switch NDAs. In early 1997, CDER defined a new process for NDAs proposing prescription-to-OTC switches. Although CDER's new drug review division will continue to lead such reviews, the center's Division of Over-the-Counter Drug Products (DODP) will assume a more significant and formalized role in switch application reviews. Specifically, the new CDER policy solidifies DOPD's roles on IND and NDA review teams, in early stage "bi-divisional" meetings, and in the final approval of switch applications. This new process is defined in CDER's Manual of Policies and Procedures 6020.5.

Such changes are unlikely to affect the nature of drug reviews, however. In several ways, the NDA review is similar to the IND review. The NDA is forwarded to the same division and, most likely, many of the same reviewers who evaluated the IND for the drug. And like the IND evaluation, the NDA review involves an evaluation of key medical/clinical, nonclinical pharmacology/toxicology, and manufacturing issues.

There are several fundamental differences between IND and NDA reviews, however:

- The NDA is a significantly larger and more complex document than the IND. Therefore, the NDA review absorbs far greater resources. Whereas INDs often comprise a few dozen volumes, NDAs for new molecular entities average over 200 volumes.

- The FDA's evaluation of the NDA involves a detailed assessment of the drug's clinical safety and effectiveness, while the IND review, in many cases, involves only an assessment of the drug's likely clinical effects based on preclinical animal data.

• The implications of the actions proposed in an NDA are much greater than those proposed in an IND. Under a newly activated IND, a drug is used in patient pools of limited size and under carefully monitored conditions. When an NDA is approved, however, a drug may be prescribed for thousands of patients who comprise a group much larger and less homogeneous than the subjects who participated in the clinical trials. In addition, a marketed drug is often used under significantly less carefully monitored conditions than during the clinical testing phase.

A Profile of the NDA Review Process

Several factors make efforts to profile the FDA's NDA review process somewhat challenging. While CDER traditionally has maintained guidelines on various activities, the center has offered few analyses of the NDA review process. That may be changing, however, as the agency recently has made several policy guidances available on various aspects of the drug review process. In addition, CDER's GRP initiative is expected to provide important insights into the clinical review component of new drug reviews.

Secondly, the various approaches to the NDA review by CDER's 14 drug review divisions are likely to differ in some ways. Although these units function under the same umbrella of laws and regulations, such differences are inevitable. As discussed above, one of the center's five drug evaluation offices is implementing a new drug review model.

Still, the NDA review process is sufficiently uniform across the 14 divisions to permit a general analysis, such as that provided in the following sections.

Initial Processing of the NDA

As it does for INDs, CDER's Central Document Room (CDR) handles the initial processing of NDAs. This processing is largely administrative in nature — staffers record information on the filing, including the sponsor's name, the drug, and the application's identification number, which is assigned by the CDR. Staffers also stamp the application with a receipt date, which starts the review timeline applicable to the filing under the Prescription Drug User Fee Act of 1992 (see Chapter 10).

CDER's Central Document Room also disassembles the various copies of the NDA for distribution to the divisions that will evaluate the application. Although the bulk of the NDA review will take place within the drug review division responsible for the product, other divisions—such as the Division of Pharmaceutical Evaluation (i.e., biopharmaceutics) and Division of Biometrics—also receive the technical sections relevant to their reviews.

Processing Within the Drug Review Division

After initial processing of the NDA, CDER's Central Document Room forwards the application to a similar document control center within the review division responsible for the application's review. After the NDA is logged in, a division staffer prepares an acknowledgement letter for the applicant. This letter informs the sponsor of the application's NDA number and date of receipt, and identifies the project manager/consumer safety officer (CSO) who will be the company's FDA contact person—in most cases, the project manager assigned to a drug's IND will be assigned to the NDA as well. The project manager functions, in part, as a coordinator for the entire NDA review, ensuring that the application is distributed and is evaluated within milestones set for the NDA.

Upon receiving the NDA, the project manager performs an initial screening to ensure that the application is complete. If the submission is found to be seriously incomplete, the division will refuse to file the NDA, and return the submission to the applicant with a letter describing the deficiencies.

If the NDA passes this initial screening, the application's technical sections are distributed to reviewers in the primary technical review disciplines— medical/clinical, pharmacology/toxicology, chemistry, and microbiology (i.e., for anti-infective drugs). These individuals, along with consultancy reviewers (e.g., statistical and biopharmaceutics reviewers) within other divisions, form the NDA's review team. For NDAs proposing prescription-to-OTC switches, a reviewer from CDER's Division of Over-the-Counter Drug Products also participates on the review team.

Each reviewer then undertakes a more thorough, or technical, screening of the NDA, called a "completeness review" within some divisions. This evaluation ensures that sufficient data and information have been submitted in each area to justify "filing" the application—that is, initiating the formal review of the NDA.

Generally, the review team then convenes with division management in what is called a "45-Day Meeting" (so named because it takes place within 45 days of the NDA's submission) to determine whether the application should be filed or refused. If the team determines that the application should be filed, the meeting may then be used as a review planning session.

At this planning session, the review team will assign a review priority to the application (i.e., a standard or priority). In addition, it will often set several internal review milestones that are deemed necessary for the division to meet the 6- or 12-month review goal applicable to the NDA. Some divisions will share these mid-review goals with the NDA's sponsor. In such cases, however, CDER officials have warned that the division-established milestones are internal goals, and that applicants should not use the timelines to pressure FDA reviewers.

The FDA's Refuse-to-File Authorities

NDAs that the review team agrees are incomplete or deficient become the subject of a formal refuse-to-file (RTF) action. In such cases, the review division prepares a letter advising the applicant of the RTF decision and the deficiencies upon which it is based. The division will attempt to forward this letter within 60 days after the NDA receipt date.

For several reasons, the agency's RTF policies gained a significantly higher profile in the early 1990s. First, beginning in 1993, RTF decisions began to carry a direct financial penalty for NDA sponsors—under the user-fee program, companies have to surrender 25 percent of the full application fee when an NDA is refused.

In addition, with new pressures to take action on NDAs within the aggressive user-fee timelines, CDER officials warned industry that the application of the RTF policy would become more stringent. In a July 1993 RTF guidance document, CDER pointed out that, "in the past, decisions to refuse to file an application generally were based on extreme deficiencies, e.g., the total omission of a needed section or the absence of any study that was even arguably an adequate and well-controlled study. More recently, applications have been refused when less extreme deficiencies existed, but when it was clear that the deficiencies were severe enough to make the application not approvable without major modification."

Several years into the prescription drug user-fee program, the agency proclaimed that industry had responded to the clarion call for better submissions, and that the increased quality of NDA filings was one of the program's most significant successes. In the first four years of the user-fee program, CDER's RTF rate dropped from 26% to 4% of original NDAs submitted to the center (see table below).

CDER Refuse-to-File Actions on NDAs			
(fiscal year 1993 to fiscal year 1996)			
Fiscal Year	*NDAs Submitted*	*# Refused to File*	*%*
1993	113	29	26%
1994	111	19	17%
1995	117	6	5%
1996	120	5	4%
Source: CDER			

Another contributing factor to lower RTF rates may be CDER's establishment of an RTF Peer Review Committee, which meets quarterly to evaluate all of the center's RTF decisions. Divisions that issue RTFs must now present and defend these decisions to the committee, which is comprised largely of senior CDER officials. In addition, applicants are given the opportunity to appear before the committee to discuss RTFs placed on their NDAs.

CDER's July 1993 RTF guidance document was, in most respects, almost a verbatim restatement of a revised draft statement released in 1992. The guidance states that CDER will exercise RTF authority under three circumstances: (1) omission of a section of the NDA required under federal regulations, or presentation of a section in so haphazard a manner as to render it incomplete on its face; (2) clear failure to include evidence of effectiveness compatible with the statute and regulations; and (3) omission of critical data, information, or analyses needed to evaluate effectiveness and safety or provide adequate directions for use. Most importantly, the document instructs CDER to continue basing RTF decisions "on omissions or inadequacies so severe as to render the application incomplete on its face. To be a basis for RTF, the omissions or inadequacies should be obvious, at least once identified, and not a matter of interpretation or judgement about the meaning of data submitted. The RTF is not an appropriate vehicle for dealing with complex and close judgments on such matters as balancing risks and benefits, magnitude of drug effect, acceptability of a plausible surrogate marker, or nuances of study design (although designs that are obviously inadequate may lead to RTF...)."

Still, CDER's review divisions have considerable discretion regarding RTF decisions. For example, the document states that "minor defects or omissions that could be repaired after the review commenced and that would not materially interfere with or delay review of the remainder of the application should not lead to RTF." Further, the RTF policy provides review divisions with the following discretionary powers:

- "The agency may, for particularly critical drugs, not use the RTF procedure, even where it could be invoked, or might review parts of a refused application if it believes that initiating the full review at the earliest possible time will better advance the public health."

- "Where an application contains more than one indication, it may be complete and potentially approvable for one indication, but inadequate for one or more additional indications. The agency may accept for filing those parts of an NDA that refer to the complete submissions for particular indications but refuse to file those parts that are obviously incomplete for other indications."

- "Each division may wish to develop its own checklist of points to consider regarding the fileability of an NDA in a particular drug class... If any aspects of these checklists did more than clarify the general list, a means of conveying the additional points to pertinent sponsors should be developed." Several review divisions have developed their own RTF checklists.

Although certain CDER divisions have accepted incomplete applications, sometimes called "rolling NDAs," in an effort to expedite the review of high-priority products, a mid-1997 Senate FDA reform bill proposed to require the agency to do so in specific cases. Under the legislation's "fast track" review procedure, the FDA would be required to "accept for filing and commence review of an incomplete application for the drug's approval if the application includes a schedule for submission of information necessary to make the application complete..." This process would apply only to drugs that demonstrated the potential to address unmet medical needs for serious and life-threatening conditions.

The Preapproval Inspection A division's decision to file an NDA triggers a few actions, including the beginning of the primary review process (see discussion below). It also triggers a division request for a preapproval inspection of the sponsor's manufacturing facilities. During such inspections, FDA investigators audit manufacturing-related statements and commitments made in the NDA against the sponsor's actual manufacturing practices. Specifically, the FDA has several goals in conducting these inspections:

1. To verify the accuracy and completeness of the manufacturing-related information submitted in the NDA.

2. To evaluate the manufacturing controls for the preapproval batches upon which information provided in the NDA is based.

3. To evaluate the manufacturer's capabilities to comply with CGMPs and manufacturing-related commitments made in the NDA. In doing so, the FDA investigator will determine whether the necessary facilities, equipment, systems, and controls are functioning.

4. To collect a variety of drug samples for analysis by FDA field and CDER laboratories. These samples may be subjected to several analyses, including methods validation, methods verification, and forensic screening for substitution.

According to CDER policy, product-specific preapproval inspections generally are conducted for products: (1) that are new chemical or molecular entities; (2) that have narrow therapeutic ranges; (3) that represent the first approval for the applicant; or (4) that are sponsored by a company with a history of CGMP problems or that are manufactured in a facility that has not been the subject of a CGMP inspection over a considerable period. While the agency hopes to initiate preapproval inspections within 45 days of a filing decision, as of this writing, preapproval inspections were, on average, being conducted six or seven months after that decision is reached. For priority user-fee applications, which CDER now must review within six months, these time frames can be compressed, however. More specific guidance on CDER's preapproval inspection program is available from the center's Compliance Program Guide 7346.832.

At the conclusion of the preapproval inspection, the field office that conducted the inspection will recommend that the application be approved or that approval be withheld because of the inspection results. Based on preapproval inspections made from March 1996 through March 1997, the most common reasons for recommendations to withhold approval were plants' unpreparedness to commercially manufacture the drugs and CGMP problems (see graph below).

The Primary Review Process

Once the review team determines that an NDA is "fileable," the "primary" review begins. During this process, the members of the review team sift through volumes of research data, analyses, and information applicable to their reviewing expertise:

Clinical Reviewer: Evaluates the clinical data to determine if the drug is safe and effective in its proposed use(s). In determining the product's risk/benefit ratio, the clinical reviewer(s) assesses the clinical significance of the drug's therapeutic effects in relation to the possible adverse effects of the drug. In the mid-1990s, CDER undertook a Good Review Practices (GRP) initiative designed to provide "some level of standardization in clinical reviews of NDAs." The center is in the process of developing a series of reviewer guidelines that will seek to outline both the safety and efficacy components of the clinical review. The first product of this effort was a draft reviewer guidance entitled *Conducting a Clinical Safety Review of a New Product Application and Preparing a Report on the Review*, which stated that "the goals of a safety review are (1) to identify important adverse events that are causally related to the use of the drug, (2) to estimate incidence for those events, and (3) to

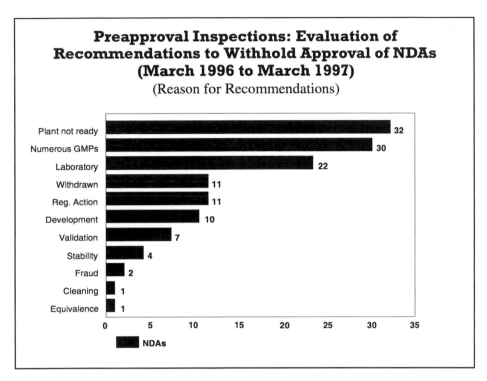

Preapproval Inspections: Evaluation of Recommendations to Withhold Approval of NDAs (March 1996 to March 1997)
(Reason for Recommendations)

Reason	NDAs
Plant not ready	32
Numerous GMPs	30
Laboratory	22
Withdrawn	11
Reg. Action	11
Development	10
Validation	7
Stability	4
Fraud	2
Cleaning	1
Equivalence	1

identify factors that predict the occurrence of those events. If there is one principle that underlies this guidance it would be the inadequacy of an approach involving only the review of individual studies in an NDA without any attempt to integrate the findings. Consequently, this guidance focuses on approaches to organizing and integrating the findings across studies in a manner that facilitates the regulatory tasks."

Pharmacology/Toxicology Reviewer: Evaluates the entire body of nonclinical data and analyses, with a focus on the newly submitted long-term test data, to identify relevant implications for the drug's clinical safety.

Chemistry Reviewer: Evaluates commercial-stage manufacturing procedures (e.g., method of synthesis or isolation, purification process, and process controls), and the specifications and analytical methods used to assure the identity, strength, purity, and bioavailability of the drug product.

Statistical Reviewer: Evaluates the pivotal clinical data to determine if there exists statistically significant evidence of the drug's safety and effectiveness; the appropriateness of the sponsor's clinical data analyses and the assumptions under which these analyses were performed; the statistical significance of newly submitted nonclinical data; and the implications of stability data for establishing appropriate expiration dating for the product.

Biopharmaceutics Reviewer: Evaluates pharmacokinetic and bioavailability data to establish appropriate drug dosing.

Microbiology Reviewer (for anti-infectives): Evaluates the drug's effects on target viruses or other microorganisms.

Much of the primary review process involves reviewers' attempts to confirm and validate the sponsor's conclusion that a drug is safe and effective in its proposed use. However, it is also likely to involve a reanalysis or an extension of the analyses conducted and presented by the sponsor in the NDA. For example, the medical reviewer may seek to reanalyze a drug's effectiveness in a particular patient subpopulation not analyzed in the original submission. Similarly, the reviewer may disagree with the sponsor's assessment of evaluable patients, and seek to retest effectiveness claims based on the reviewer-defined patient populations.

There is also likely to be considerable communication between review team members. If a medical reviewer's reanalysis of clinical data produces results different from those of the sponsor, for example, the reviewer is likely to forward this information to the statistical reviewer with a request for a reanalysis of the data. Likewise, the pharmacology reviewer may work closely with the statistical reviewer in evaluating the statistical significance of adverse drug effects in long-term animal studies (e.g., tumor rates).

Invariably, the primary review produces the need for agency communication with, and the clarification of some issues or data by, the NDA sponsor. With the shortening of drug reviews, it is likely that all FDA/sponsor communication, including mid-review dialogue, has increased in recent years. In one recent case, a company reported logging "hundreds" of FDA communications during the development process.

As part of Congress's reauthorization process for the Prescription Drug User Fee Act, industry has supported a move to formalize some aspects of mid-review communications. Specifically, industry has asked that the agency be required to communicate NDA deficiencies to the applicant as reviewers discover them rather than just in action letters forwarded at the completion of a review cycle. While some firms believe that such notifications will allow them to address NDA deficiencies earlier, many agency reviewers maintain that applicants are alerted to most NDA deficiencies during the review process.

Sponsors must continue forwarding to the FDA new safety information during the entire NDA review. Through "safety update reports," sponsors must provide periodic updates on any new safety-related information obtained from clinical studies, animal studies, or other sources. Sponsors must submit these reports four months after the original NDA submission, following the receipt of an "approvable" letter, and after an FDA request.

When the technical reviews are completed, each reviewer must develop a written evaluation of the NDA that presents his or her conclusions on, and recommendations regarding, the application. In most cases, the medical reviewer is responsible for evaluating and reconciling the conclusions of reviewers in all other scientific disciplines. The result is an action letter (see discussion below), which provides an approval/disapproval decision and the basis for that recommendation.

In reality, the reconciling of all reviewer conclusions and the development of what CDER calls an "institutional decision" on an NDA's approvability is likely to involve considerable dialogue between the medical reviewer and reviewers in the other disciplines. Since the ultimate decision hinges most directly on clinical safety, effectiveness, and risk/benefit issues, however, the medical reviewer is said to have the most influence in this process. To address those cases in which a review team is not able to reach a consensus, CDER developed MaPP 4151.1 entitled *Resolution of Disputes: Roles of Reviewers, Supervisors, and Management Documenting Views and Findings and Resolving Differences* (August 1996).

The results of the preapproval inspection may also figure into the final approval decision. When such inspections discover significant CGMP problems or other issues, the reviewing division may withhold approval until these are addressed and corrected (see discussion above). The division's response to such deficiencies is likely to depend on several factors, including the nature of the problem, the prognosis for the problem's correction, and the status of the NDA review.

The Final Approval of the NDA

The final channels through which an NDA must pass to obtain FDA approval will depend on issues such as the drug's novelty and importance. NDAs for NMEs, for example, need the approval of higher levels of FDA management than do marketing applications for less innovative products. Although federal regulations specify authority delegations for NDA "sign-off" powers (i.e., final approval authority), the regulations do give the FDA some flexibility to delegate these powers.

Once a single approval or disapproval recommendation is reached by the reviewers and their supervisors, the decision must then be evaluated and approved by the director of the applicable drug review division. For the director's review, the project manager/CSO assembles a "decision package" containing the action letter and any data, FDA memos, or other information supporting the reviewers' recommendation. Reviewers, their supervisors, and the division's director and deputy director then have an opportunity to examine the decision package.

After conducting what is sometimes called a "secondary review," the division director may begin a dialogue with the chemistry, medical, or pharmacology reviewers or their supervisors. Most often, the director will support the decision of the review group. For those drugs that are not considered particularly innovative or that are not seen as offering significant therapeutic advantages, the director's decision generally serves as the final FDA ruling. In this respect, the division director is said to have "sign-off" authority for such drugs.

Other drugs, however, require an additional level of review to be considered approved. According to federal regulations, applications for new molecular entities require either CDER-level or office-level (i.e., ODE I, II, III, IV, or V) concurrence. In most instances, however, sign-off authorities for such products have been delegated to the office-level. This office-level review is sometimes called the "tertiary review."

Average NME Review Times by CDER Division in Months, 1991-1996

(number of NME approvals in parentheses)

	1991	1992	1993	1994	1995	1996
Division of Cardio-Renal Drug Products	39.5 (6)	42.6 (4)	30.0 (2)	36.0 (1)	21.4 (6)	14.1 (3)
Division of Oncology Drug Products[1]	14.2 (3)	32.3 (3)	45.7 (2)	19.2 (4)	14.0 (4)	12.0 (4)
Division of Neuropharmacological Drug Products	44.6 (1)	37.9 (3)	20.9 (5)	35.6 (3)	5.5 (1)	15.2 (7)
Division of Anesthetic, Critical Care, and Addiction Drug Products	*	*	*	*	11.3 (2)	13.9 (2)
Division of Gastrointestinal and Coagulation Drug Products	18.5 (3)	*	16.9 (4)	16.2 (2)	17.8 (1)	23.8 (1)
Division of Pulmonary Drug Products	*	*	*	*	89.3 (1)	30.7 (4)
Division of Antiviral Drug Products	9.2 (2)	13.3 (4)	36.1 (2)	8.7 (3)	4.4 (3)	5.5 (5)
Division of Medical Imaging and Radiopharmaceutical Drug Products	*	*	*	*	37.5 (2)	29.8 (5)
Division of Anti-Infective Drug Products	27.4 (5)	21.1 (6)	24.9 (4)	*	25.6 (2)	14.3 (8)
Division of Anti-Inflammatory, Analgesic and Ophthalmic Drug Products[2]	*	*	*	*	15.5 (1)	11.5 (3)
Division of Metabolic and Endocrine Drug Products[3]	28.4 (6)	18.8 (2)	48.8 (2)	13.6 (2)	11.4 (4)	19.2 (7)
Division of Dermatologic and Dental Drug Products[2]	*	*	*	*	18.5 (1)	27.0 (3)
Division of Reproductive and Urologic Drug Products	*	*	*	*	*	30.5 (1)

* no NME approvals during that year or division not in existence at that time

[1] Data from 1991-1994 include pulmonary drug reviews as well.

[2] In January 1996, the Division of Anti-Inflammatory, Analgesic and Dental Drug Products and the Division of Dermatologic and Ophthalmic Drug Products swapped responsibilities for dental and ophthalmic drugs. The 1996 data reflect this reorganization.

[3] In 1996, the division's responsibilities for urologic and reproductive drugs were shifted to the new Division of Reproductive and Urologic Drug Products. While the 1996 data reflect this change, divisional statistics for 1991 through 1995 include these products.

Note: Table does not include Division of Special Pathogens and Immunologic Drug Products.

Source: PAREXEL's Pharmaceutical R&D Statistical Sourcebook 1997

Non-NME NDAs that raise clinical issues beyond those presented by the previously approved versions of the subject drugs also revert to the office level for final approval. For example, an NDA proposing a major new indication or the first controlled-release dosage form of a previously approved drug would require office-level approval.

FDA Action Letters

The FDA communicates its official decision on an NDA through what is called an "action letter." Action letters are an important element in the agency's efforts to meet its review performance goals under the user-fee program—that is, the agency must "act on" NDAs within specific time frames. CDER fulfills this requirement by issuing an action letter, which constitutes a complete action on the application and which stops the review clock for the filing.

Three types of action letters—approval, approvable, and not-approvable—detail CDER's decisions on NDAs. In some cases, knowing how and when to respond to an action letter can affect the ultimate approval decision on an application and how quickly that decision is made.

Approval Letter When CDER sends an approval letter, the subject drug is considered approved as of the date of the letter. Generally, an applicant must submit final printed labeling before a drug is approved. However, if CDER finds that the draft labeling is acceptable or if the agency requires only minor editorial changes, the NDA may be approved based on the draft labeling. In such cases, the agency reminds the firm that marketing of the product with labeling other than that agreed to by the agency would cause the product to be viewed as an unapproved product.

Rarely, if ever, do drug sponsors receive an approval letter for an original NDA without first receiving a request for more data, a clarification of existing data or analyses, or modification of the application in its originally submitted form (e.g., product labeling). In many cases, such requests are made through mid-review communications that do not comprise a formal agency action on the NDAs.

Under the user-fee program, greater numbers of NDAs are being approved in CDER's first formal actions on the applications. Of the 58 FY1995 NDAs acted on as of December 1996, for example, 38 were approved in CDER's first action on the applications (i.e., as opposed to an approvable or not approvable letter).

Prior to granting approval, the review division may also ask for an applicant's commitment to conduct certain drug studies following approval. Although the agency states that such postmarketing studies are not considered essential for a drug's approval, the studies provide "additional information or data that could, for example, change the prescribing information or use of the drug or provide additional assurance or verification of product quality and consistency." Under a new policy guide on such "Phase 4 commitments," the FDA and drug sponsor must agree to the specific commitments and a schedule for fulfilling these commitments prior to approval (see Chapter 12). Either prior to, or at the time of, drug approval, the applicant must submit a letter describing the Phase 4 commitments and a schedule for initiating and completing the Phase 4 studies. The approval letter should list all Phase 4 commitments and the schedule for their completion.

Approvable Letter According to federal regulations, the FDA will send the applicant "an approvable letter if the application…substantially meets the requirements [for marketing approval] and the agency believes that it can approve the application…if specific additional information or material is submitted or specific conditions (for example, certain changes in labeling) are agreed to by the applicant." Often, the FDA will use an approvable letter to request changes to the product's proposed labeling and to require the submission of safety update reports and the product's final printed labeling.

Unless otherwise specified by the FDA, the sponsor has ten days after the date of the approvable letter to do one of the following:

- Amend, or acknowledge its intent to amend, the NDA.

- Withdraw the application. The FDA will consider the applicant's failure to respond to an approvable letter within ten days to represent the applicant's request to withdraw the application.

- For applications involving new drugs (not including antibiotics), ask the FDA to provide the applicant an opportunity for a hearing on whether grounds exist for denying the application's approval. Sponsors would make such a request when the FDA issues an approvable letter, but specifies in the letter marketing conditions that are unacceptable to the applicant. For example, the FDA may state in the letter that it considers only one of two indications proposed in an NDA to be "approvable" at that time. Should the FDA then refuse to approve the application under terms agreeable to the sponsor, the agency must give the applicant an opportunity for a hearing.

- For an antibiotic, file a petition or notify the FDA of an intent to file a petition proposing the issuance, amendment, or repeal of a regulation.

- Notify the FDA that the applicant agrees to a review period extension of a specified length so the applicant may give further consideration as to which of the previous four options it will pursue. The FDA will grant any reasonable request for an extension, and will consider the applicant's failure to respond during the extended review period to represent a request to withdraw the application.

CDER credits faster drug approval times in part to more timely industry responses to action letters and quick division reviews of these so-called "resubmissions." For fiscal year 1995 NDAs approved as of December 1996, for example, it took applicants an average of only 1.1 months to respond to CDER approvable letters. In turn, the center took an average of only 2.0 months to review these resubmissions and approve the applications.

Not-Approvable Letter A not-approvable letter is forwarded to the applicant if the FDA believes that the drug application is insufficient to justify approval. The letter describes the deficiencies in the application that were the basis for the not-approvable action. Unless otherwise indicated by the FDA, the sponsor must do one of the following within ten days:

- Amend, or notify the FDA of an intent to amend, the NDA.

- Withdraw the application. The FDA will consider the applicant's failure to respond within ten days to represent the applicant's request to withdraw the application.

- For applications involving new drugs (not including antibiotics), ask the FDA to provide the applicant an opportunity for a hearing on whether grounds exist for denying the application's approval. Should the FDA then refuse to approve the application, the agency will give the applicant an opportunity for a hearing.

- For an antibiotic, file a petition or notify the FDA of an intent to file a petition proposing the issuance, amendment, or repeal of a regulation.

- Notify the FDA that the applicant agrees to a review period extension of a specified length so the applicant may give further consideration to which of the previous four options the company will pursue. The FDA will grant any reasonable request for an extension, and will consider the applicant's failure to respond during the extended review period as a request to withdraw the application.

Under the user-fee program, fewer NDAs are receiving not-approvable letters. After issuing not-approvable letters to 48 percent of FY1994 NDAs, for instance, CDER took such actions for only 24 percent of FY1995 applications.

The FDA has pointed to industry's response time to not-approvable letters and its own ability to review these resubmissions quickly as another reason for faster drug review times. For those FY1995 NDAs that received not-approvable letters and that were approved as of December 1996, the applicant responded to the letters in an average of 1.5 months. The agency then reviewed those resubmissions in an average of 3.3 months.

Final Printed Labeling

Labeling is usually the final major consideration in a drug's approval. Not until an NDA is virtually approved, or is judged to be "approvable," does labeling become the focus of FDA reviewers.

There are several practical reasons why labeling concerns are left until late in the drug review process. First, it is impossible to develop labeling with accurate accounts of indications, warnings, contraindications, and specific use instructions without conclusions drawn from pivotal clinical study data. Also,

FDA reviewers will not invest significant time in evaluating proposed labeling until they are reasonably convinced that a drug is safe and effective, and that the drug's NDA is nearing approval.

Labeling often becomes a principal concern once the agency issues an approvable letter, which, among other things, requests that the applicant forward its final printed labeling (i.e., all the labeling to appear on or to accompany a drug's package or container). At this point, only the labeling and possibly some minor deficiencies in an NDA stand between a drug and its approval.

Perhaps because of this, CDER officials hoped to implement a pilot program for the electronic submission of final printed labeling during 1997. Ultimately, the center hopes to permit labeling submissions to be made, and related negotiations to be conducted through, the Internet.

Draft Package Labeling Drug sponsors first propose labeling for a new pharmaceutical through what is called draft package labeling. Generally, draft labeling is submitted as part of the original NDA (see Chapter 8).

The specific labeling requirements facing a drug in its finished package form will depend on whether it is proposed for use as a prescription or as an over-the-counter (OTC) medicine. Principally because of dispensing differences, FDA labeling requirements for OTC and prescription drugs differ significantly.

Prescription Drug Labeling According to federal regulations, prescription drug labeling must be "informative and accurate..., contain a summary of the essential scientific information needed for the safe and effective use of the drug...," and "be based, whenever possible, on data derived from human experience." In enforcing these and other requirements, the FDA has authority over the format and types of information that appear: (1) on the immediate drug container (i.e., manufacturer name, general brand name, lot number, etc.); and (2) on the outer carton in which the drug is shipped to physicians, hospitals, pharmacies, and other prescription drug dispensers.

A primary element in prescription drug labeling is the package insert. Drug manufacturers use prescription drug package inserts to meet the requirement that the physician or pharmacist be provided with the essential information needed to ensure the safe and effective use of the drug. Since the large body of information needed to satisfy this requirement cannot reasonably be placed on a prescription product's immediate container or package, manufacturers include it on a package insert. Such inserts generally consist of:

- a product description section describing the drug's dosage form, route of administration, ingredients, and therapeutic/pharmacologic effect;

- a clinical pharmacology section describing the action of the drug in humans and, if pertinent, its activity and effectiveness in animal and *in vitro* tests;

- an indications and usage section describing specific safety conditions and identifying indications supported by evidence of clinical effectiveness;

- a contraindications section;

- a warnings section describing potential safety hazards and steps to be taken if reactions occur;

- a precautions section discussing drug interactions and possible side effects in specific population groups such as pregnant women;

- an adverse reactions section;

- a drug abuse and dependence section, including a discussion of possible abuses and physical or psychological dependencies;

- an overdose section identifying specific signs, symptoms, complications, and laboratory findings that are associated with overdosage (this section might also specify the amount of the drug in a single dosage likely to cause overdosage symptoms and/or a life-threatening situation);

- a dosage and administration section identifying the recommended usual dose, safe upper dosage limit, and dosage modifications for children and the elderly; and

- a section describing how the drug is supplied (i.e., the drug's dosage form, strength, and unit availability).

Although the information on many inserts is reprinted in publications such as the *Physician's Desk Reference for Prescription Drugs*, consumers are generally not given this information directly when the prescription drug is dispensed. Under a cooperative public/private program launched in January 1997, however, industry and pharmacists and other health-care professionals will work to provide consumers with more prescription drug information. The plan calls for "useful drug information" to reach 75 percent of patients by the year 2000 and 95 percent of patients by 2006.

OTC Drug Labeling OTC labeling requirements are, with regard to content at least, similar to those for prescription pharmaceuticals. Information regarding active ingredients, dosage and administration, indication, drug action, warnings, precautions, drug interaction, and overdosage must be provided.

However, because OTC products are self-prescribed, and because their use usually does not involve the guidance of a physician or pharmacist, OTC drug labeling must be structured differently. Much of the essential information provided to a pharmacist or physician through the package insert of a prescription drug must be detailed on the outer package of the container of the OTC product. In fact, all of the information that will allow the consumer to select and use the OTC product safely and effectively must appear on the outer package. This information must be presented in a manner suitable for the comprehension of the lay public.

Due to what it perceived as consumer difficulties in understanding OTC product labeling information, the FDA proposed in early 1997 to establish a standardized format for such labeling. The proposal would require that OTC drug labeling include standardized headings, be presented in a specified order, and meet minimum type size, type style, and graphics requirements.

The FDA's Review of Draft Labeling

When it becomes apparent that an NDA will be approved, agency reviewers evaluate the draft package labeling on at least two levels. First, the draft labeling is reviewed for its consistency with the regulatory requirements for applicable prescription or OTC drugs. Each important element of the proposed labeling (i.e., indications, use instructions, warnings, etc.) is then evaluated in view of conclusions drawn from nonclinical and clinical testing. All claims, instructions, and precautions must be based upon and accurately reflect the findings of the key test results, preferably from clinical studies.

If the FDA has major reservations about the draft labeling, the agency will usually forward to the sponsor a letter detailing its suggestions for revised labeling. In some cases, FDA reviewers themselves may revise a portion of the labeling, and instruct the sponsor to include the revision in the final printed labeling. Agency comments can relate to virtually any aspect of the proposed drug labeling, including:

- Drug Indications. The FDA and the applicant may disagree on the indications for which a drug was shown to be safe and effective in clinical trials.

- General Wording. FDA reviewers may believe that the proposed labeling is promotional or suggestive in nature and, therefore, may mislead physicians, pharmacists, or consumers.

- Labeling Format. The format must meet regulatory requirements, and must give proper emphasis to important elements of the labeling, such as warnings and precautions.

- Warnings/Precautions. The warnings and precautions must directly reflect potential problem areas identified during human and/or animal testing.

The labeling "negotiation process," through which a drug's final approved labeling is agreed upon, can consume several weeks or several months. The length and complexity of the process will depend upon the nature and number of the FDA's comments, the degree to which the applicant is agreeable to making recommended revisions, and, of course, the applicant's desire to put the subject drug on the market.

In some cases, the sponsor will have to submit several revisions of its labeling before the FDA finds an acceptable version. Disagreements over labeling content, wording, and design are generally resolvable through either mail and telephone correspondence or through FDA-sponsor meetings.

Sponsor Rights During the NDA Review Process

In the early 1990s, legislative and regulatory initiatives affected several aspects of NDA sponsors' rights during the review of their applications. Companies should be aware of these rights and the courses of action available to them should these rights be violated. Sponsor rights during the NDA review process fall into roughly four categories:

- the right to a timely review;

- the right to confidentiality;

- the right to request meetings or conferences with the FDA; and

- the right to protest if the sponsor believes its rights are violated.

The Right to a Timely Review Under the provisions of the Prescription Drug User Fee Act of 1992, the federal government has redefined the time frames for NDA reviews. For years previous to this law, CDER had operated under legal requirements mandating that the agency review and act on NDAs within 180 days of their submission. Most often, however, the 180-day time frame has been called a "phantom" requirement that CDER used as a goal or target, but seldom as a strictly enforced rule.

The Prescription Drug User Fee Act of 1992 established a new series of drug review targets for the FDA, and provided the means—specifically, revenues derived from user fees—through which the agency could restaff and retool itself to meet these deadlines. The review goals, which the FDA began to phase in during FY1994 (October 1, 1993 - September 30, 1994), were to reach a full implementation level for drug applications submitted in FY1997, to which the following agency goals apply:

1. To review and act on 90 percent of "standard" original and supplemental NDAs within 12 months of submission, and to review and act on 90 percent of "priority" original and supplemental NDAs within 6 months of submission.

2. To review and act on 90 percent of manufacturing supplements within 6 months.

3. To review and act on 90 percent of resubmitted applications (i.e., after the applicant receives a not-approvable letter) within six months.

Under the provisions of the law, the FDA was to fulfill the "act on" requirement by issuing an action letter—approval, approvable, or not-approvable letter (see discussion above).

Because of the different time frames applicable to standard and priority applications (i.e., beginning in FY1997), the agency has introduced the following criteria for classifying original and supplemental submissions:

Priority Application. A priority application is for a product that, if approved, "would be a significant improvement compared to marketed products [approved (if such is required), including non-'drug' products/therapies] in the treatment, diagnosis, or prevention of a disease. Improvement can be demonstrated by, for example: (1) evidence of increased effectiveness in the treatment, prevention, or diagnosis of disease; (2) elimination or substantial reduction of a treatment-limiting drug reaction; (3) documented enhancement of patient compliance; or (4) evidence of safety and effectiveness of a new subpopulation."

Standard Application. All applications not qualifying as priority are classified as standard submissions.

The applicable review timelines can be extended if the sponsor submits a "major" amendment to the original application during the review process. A major amendment involves the submission of a large amount of new, previously unreviewed data (e.g., new clinical or animal studies) or any submission that significantly affects the review process (e.g., a reanalysis involving multiple reviewing disciplines). When major amendments are submitted within three months of the action due date, the FDA can extend the review time frames by three months.

In each of the first several years of the prescription drug user fee program, the FDA reported that it exceeded its review performance goals. Through a December 1996 performance report to Congress, for example, the agency

Key Drug Submission and Approval Statistics, 1989-1996

	1989	1990	1991	1992	1993	1994	1995	1996
NDA Submissions	118	98	112	100	86	133*	142*+	128*+
NDA Approvals	87	64	63	91	70	62	82	131
Mean Review Time for All Original NDAs (in months)	24.1	25.0	25.7	26.3	24.1	26.0	22.7	21.6
Median Review Time for All Original NDAs (in months)	19.2	22.6	21.4	20.0	20.8	19.0	16.5	15.4
NME Approvals	23	23	30	26	25	22	28	53
Mean Review Time for NMEs (in months)	32.4	27.7	30.3	29.9	26.5	19.7	19.2	17.8
Median Review Time for NMEs (in Months)	23.6	23.8	22.2	22.6	21.0	17.5	15.9	14.3

* includes resubmission after refusal to file, withdrawn before filing and unacceptable for filing
+ fiscal year data

Source: U.S. Regulatory Reporter

revealed that it had met the review target for 95% of the FY1995 original NDA and product license applications (for biologics) submissions, surpassing the goal of 70%.

In fulfilling its user-fee goals, CDER has produced significant reductions in average and median NDA review times. In 1996, for example, the center improved its average NME approval time for the fifth consecutive year, approving 53 NMEs in an average of 17.8 months (see table above).

In their efforts to support the reauthorization of the Prescription Drug User Fee Act of 1992, which expires in September 1997, the FDA and industry agreed to ask Congress to further refine the agency's review performance goals. If implemented by Congress, the plan would lower the agency's review targets for standard therapies to 10 months, and for standard supplements to 4 months. Also, the agency would be encouraged to explore ways to complete the reviews of priority products in less than 6 months. The 6-month target would remain the stated review goal for priority NDAs, however.

The Right To Confidentiality Given the quantity of competitively sensitive data and information submitted in NDAs, confidentiality issues are of great importance to drug sponsors. Both the FDA and the federal government have policies and procedures designed to protect from public disclosure certain types of information submitted in NDAs. The FDA does have limited rights to disclose certain NDA information to foreign drug regulatory agencies, however.

The agency may not disclose or release any information or test data that qualify as trade secret or commercial or financial information. A trade secret is defined as "any formula, pattern, device, or compilation of information which is used in one's business and which gives him an opportunity to obtain an advantage over competitors who do not know or use it." This information, says the agency, has been defined by the courts as information relating to the making, preparing, compounding, or processing of trade commodities. In requiring a direct relationship between the trade secret and the production process, this definition applies to a more narrow category of information than the current definition.

Commercial or financial information is "valuable data or information which is used in one's business and is of a type customarily held in strict confidence or regarded as privileged and not disclosed to any member of the public" by the company to which it belongs. Chemistry information and marketing assessments are included in this definition.

Non-confidential information (i.e., information not falling within one of the two definitions detailed above) may, at some point in the review process, be released by the FDA. However, the agency is restricted as to when it can publicly release such details as the NDA's existence, the name of the subject drug and its active ingredients, and other non-confidential information.

Non-confidential information is carefully guarded during the NDA review. However, the extent of protection afforded by the FDA depends on whether or not the existence of the NDA and any of its information have been previously disclosed or acknowledged publicly by the sponsor or another source. The FDA cannot announce the submission of an NDA or release any of the application's data if this information has not been previously disclosed.

When the NDA's existence and submission have been announced by the sponsor or discussed in a medical journal or other publication, a different set of confidentiality rules apply. In such cases, federal regulations state that the FDA may "disclose a summary of selected portions of the safety and effectiveness data that are appropriate for public consideration of a specific pending issue, for example, for consideration of an issue at an open session of an FDA advisory committee." The agency, however, is restricted in that it cannot make the sponsor's data or information directly available for public disclosure.

Many of the provisions restricting the FDA's public release of NDA-related non-confidential information apply only during the NDA review. More information is made publicly available once the FDA issues an approval letter to the applicant:

- a "disclosable review package," sometimes called an "approval package," that provides information on the results of each aspect of the NDA review (e.g., medical, pharmacology, and chemistry review);

- a non-confidential protocol for a test or study;

- a list of all active ingredients and any inactive ingredients previously disclosed to the public; and

- a non-confidential assay method or other analytical method.

FDA regulations implemented in late 1993 provided the agency with greater powers to disclose nonpublic drug safety, effectiveness, and quality information to foreign regulatory agencies. At the time, the FDA sought to revise its regulations because previous standards for information disclosure were severely complicating its efforts to conduct cooperative drug reviews with foreign drug regulators—principally the Canadian Health Protection Branch (HPB).

The specific issue of concern was the requirement that, if the FDA shared confidential commercial information with foreign regulatory officials, the agency was required to make the information publicly available as well. Because of this, the FDA and HPB had to develop special and time-consuming agreements and contracts—including the FDA's hiring of HPB reviewers as special U.S. government employees—to avoid the disclosure requirement. The need for such agreements, FDA officials contended, undermined the value of international drug reviews, which were intended to expedite the process.

In response, the FDA published a November 1993 final rule that established conditions under which such information can be released to foreign regulatory officials without triggering public disclosure requirements. The regulation establishes separate standards for the release of confidential commercial information and trade secret information.

According to the regulation, the FDA "may authorize the disclosure of confidential commercial information submitted to the Food and Drug Administration, or incorporated into agency-prepared records, to foreign government officials who perform counterpart functions to the Food and Drug Administration as part of cooperative law enforcement or regulatory efforts, provided that:

(i) The foreign government agency has provided both a written statement establishing its authority to protect confidential commercial information from public disclosure and a written commitment not to disclose any such information provided without the written permission of the sponsor or written confirmation by the Food and Drug Administration that the information no longer has confidential status; and

(ii) The Commissioner of Food and Drugs or the Commissioner's designee makes one or more of the following determinations: (A) The sponsor of the product application has provided written authorization for the disclosure; (B) Disclosure would be in the interest of public health by reason of the foreign government's possessing information concerning the safety, efficacy, or quality of a product or information concerning an investigation; or (C) The disclosure is to a foreign scientist visiting the Food and Drug Administration on the agency's premises as part of a joint review or long-term cooperative training effort authorized under [existing statutes], the review is in the interest of public health, the [FDA] retains physical control over the information, the [FDA] requires the visiting foreign scientist to sign a written commitment to protect the confidentiality of the information, and the scientist provides a written assurance that he or she has no financial interest in the regulated industry of the type that would preclude participation in the review of the matter if the individual were subject to the conflict of interest rules applicable to the Food and Drug Administration advisory committee members...."

With only two exceptions, the FDA will not authorize the disclosure to "government officials of other countries of trade secret information concerning manufacturing methods and processes...." First, the FDA will release trade secret information if the submitter has provided its "express written consent." Also, foreign scientists visiting the FDA will be given access to trade secret information "when such disclosures would be a necessary part of the joint review or training." These disclosures would be subject to the identical conditions as the FDA's sharing of confidential commercial information with visiting foreign scientists.

Despite industry criticism of this provision, the FDA granted itself the authority to disclose confidential commercial information to foreign regulators without sponsor consent. In discussing its motivations, the FDA stated that, "there are situations in which it might be inappropriate to seek a sponsor's consent. For example, if communications and consultation with the submitters of the information have not resolved agency concerns, there may be circumstances in which FDA reviewers and investigators will want to consult with foreign government counterparts who are in the possession of similar submissions by the sponsor. It may even be that, during the course of an application review, FDA employees may discover problems with studies that raise the possibility that a sponsor or his employee had engaged in deliberate fraud or misrepresentation. Similarly, there are circumstances in which FDA investigators may wish to share with foreign counterparts confidential commercial information obtained through an FDA investigation for the foreign counterparts' use in their own regulatory efforts. This could include, for example, information in an open investigation concerning customer-supplier relationships or marketing plans. This type of information is customarily held in close confidence by businesses and therefore [is] usually protected from public disclosure by FDA in response to a [freedom-of-information] request. Disclosure of this information to foreign government counterparts, however, may facilitate efforts to keep unapproved, adulterated, counterfeit, or mis-branded products off world markets as well as American markets." The FDA added that it would seek sponsor authorization before most information exchanges.

The Right to Meetings Given their importance in the drug development and review process, agency/sponsor meetings were the subject of several industry and CDER initiatives in the mid-1990s. In early 1996, for example, CDER released a new policy document outlining the center's policies and procedures for scheduling and conducting formal meetings with sponsors.

CDER communicates openly with sponsors about scientific, medical, and procedural issues that arise during the NDA review process. These exchanges may take the form of telephone or video conferences, letters, or face-to-face meetings, whichever is the most appropriate to discuss and resolve the relevant issue.

All sponsors have the right to at least one, and possibly several, conferences with the FDA during and after the NDA review. While other forms of correspondence will occur routinely throughout the NDA review, the sponsor usually must make a written request before CDER will grant and schedule a conference.

The number of meetings to which a sponsor is entitled may depend upon the subject drug and the priority given to it by the FDA. Under regulations codified in 1985, the agency claimed to have made FDA-sponsor conferences more accessible to all applicants. Conferences relevant to the NDA review process include the following:

The 90-Day Conference. Approximately 90 days after it receives an NDA, CDER provides sponsors of certain drugs an opportunity to meet with officials and drug reviewers. Generally, such meetings are available only to sponsors of either NMEs or major new indications of currently marketed drugs. The purpose of the conference is to inform an applicant about the general progress and status of its NDA, and to advise the company of deficiencies that have been identified but not yet communicated. However, the 90-day conference is not mandatory, and sponsors may choose not to request such a meeting. Also, the conference may be either a telephone or face-to-face meeting.

The End-of-Review Conference. The end-of-review conference is offered to all applicants after CDER has issued either an approvable or not-approvable letter for an NDA. During this meeting, FDA officials discuss what further steps the sponsor must take before the application can be approved.

Other Meetings. Sponsors may request additional meetings to discuss scientific, medical, and other issues that arise during the review process. Because of already heavy demands for its time, however, CDER is likely to grant conferences only for more important issues. For resolving less significant issues, the agency will probably suggest communication by telephone or letter.

According to CDER MaPP 4512.1, entitled *Formal Meetings Between CDER and CDER's External Constituents* (March 1996), "the center will respond to requests for scheduling a formal meeting from external constituents consistently and promptly and will agree to such meetings unless they are clearly unnecessary or premature." The MaPP states that meeting requests should provide the following: (1) a brief statement of the purpose of the meeting; (2) a listing of the specific objectives/outcomes the requestor expects from the meeting; (3) a proposed agenda, including estimated times needed for each agenda item; (4) a listing of planned sponsor attendees, including any external consultants/participants; (5) a listing of requested participants from CDER; and (6) the approximate time at which supporting documentation for the meeting will be sent to CDER (this should not be less than 2 weeks in advance of the scheduled meeting).

Regardless of whether a meeting request is granted or refused, the review division should notify the sponsor in writing (i.e., letter or fax) within 14 days of the meeting request. The meeting date should reflect "the next available date on which all applicable center personnel are available to attend, consistent with the component's other business, but shall not exceed 75 days from the date of the [sponsor's] initial dated meeting request." If a sponsor claims —and the FDA agrees—that a commercial development program will be stalled until the meeting is held, a "special considerations meeting" will be granted within 30 days of the request.

As part of their efforts to support the reauthorization of the Prescription Drug User Fee Act, the FDA and industry have agreed to ask Congress to appropriate user fee monies to fund an FDA meetings-management system. Included under this system would be a requirement that the FDA meet with sponsors within a defined period (e.g., within 60 days for pre-IND and pre-NDA meetings) following a meetings request.

The Right to Protest Although recent regulatory initiatives have done much to make the FDA and sponsors "partners" in drug development, the NDA review process can, in some senses, make adversaries of the agency and applicants. The sponsor's goal—to obtain the most rapid approval possible for a product—is not always entirely consistent with the FDA's, which is to take the time necessary, within limits, to ensure that the drug is both safe and effective before approving it. In addition, CDER and drug sponsors may simply disagree on some scientific, procedural, or administrative issue.

Like the meetings management process, dispute resolution has become a fairly visible issue in recent years. In fact, CDER has undertaken several related initiatives on the subject:

- In 1996, CDER Director Janet Woodcock pledged to include, in all of the center's action letters, instructions on how sponsors can dispute FDA decisions.

- At this writing, CDER was also in the process of developing a new policies and procedures guide entitled *Appeals Process in Resolving Disputes Over Applications in the Office of New Drug Evaluation.*

- The FDA and industry have asked Congress to consider establishing a two-tier appeals process for resolving scientific agency/sponsor disputes as part of the reauthorization of the Prescription Drug User Fee Act of 1992.

- In 1995, CDER established the CDER Ombudsman function, which is designed to provide a mechanism through which sponsors and others can "seek solutions to problematic interactions and suggest better ways for [the center] to do its work" (see discussion below).

Currently, CDER has a fairly sophisticated process for helping sponsors settle disputes. The process through which a particular dispute is resolved depends upon whether the problem is procedural/administrative or scientific/medical in nature.

Administrative and Procedural Disputes. Administrative and procedural disputes may involve problems such as sponsor difficulties in scheduling FDA meetings and obtaining timely agency responses to inquiries. The sponsor may also believe that the agency is not following procedures consistent with current laws or regulations.

When such problems arise, the FDA recommends that a sponsor first contact the project manager/CSO who is handling its application. Most project managers/CSOs are experts in the NDA review process, and are likely to have the most complete information about the status of a pending application. Because of this and because project managers/CSOs work very closely with NDA reviewers, they can solve most procedural or administrative problems if the agency is at fault.

As of late 1995, sponsors of all FDA-regulated products have had another route to pursue their administrative/procedural disputes with the agency. In October 1995, the FDA created the position of FDA ombudsman, which the agency says is a position "designed to facilitate the investigation and resolution of complaints and disagreements that arise about the application of agency policy and procedures." With the exception of scientific and technical issues, sponsors can refer to the ombudsman problems for which there are "no other legal or established means of redress."

Scientific and Medical Disputes. The FDA believes that the 90-day and end-of-review conferences as well as various other FDA-sponsor communications provide adequate vehicles for addressing and resolving scientific and medical disputes. The agency recognizes, however, that there are exceptions.

When the sponsor believes that conferences have proven inadequate, it may request a meeting with the management of the appropriate reviewing division. At that time, the applicant may suggest that the FDA seek the advice of outside experts, such as consultants and other agency advisors. The sponsor may also invite its own consultant when such a meeting is granted.

If a specially scheduled meeting fails to resolve a dispute, the FDA may refer the matter to one of its standing advisory committees, which consist of non-FDA medical experts among others (see Chapter 11). The committee will review the issue and make recommendations. The FDA can then follow these recommendations or take its own course of action.

Chapter 10

The FDA's Drug Classification System

Traditionally, the FDA has used a relatively straightforward drug classification system to assist its reviewers in prioritizing NDA reviews. Although the system has been revamped in recent years, its goal has always been to permit the agency to channel its resources to the reviews of potentially important new drugs, independent of such factors as the chronological order of NDA submissions.

Although some have argued that CDER's drug classification system has not been particularly significant in the past, the FDA's prescription drug user fee program has placed greater emphasis on FDA-assigned "therapeutic ratings." For the first several years of the user-fee program, a drug's therapeutic rating—either priority or standard—meant very little, at least according to agency policy. Regardless of whether a drug was rated a priority or standard product, for instance, the agency faced the same 12-month review timeline for products submitted from fiscal year (FY) 1993 (October 1, 1992 to September 30, 1993) through fiscal year 1996. Beginning with drugs submitted in FY1997, however, the agency implemented a new 6-month review goal for priority drugs.

Given the practical need to review priority drugs rapidly and the fact that the agency has been tracking its performance against both the 12- and 6-month goals, it is not surprising that a priority-versus-standard drug review gap pre-dated the FY1997 submissions. In 1995, for instance, priority new molecular entities (NME) were approved in an average of 10.1 months, compared to 23.6 months for standard NMEs. This gap was narrowed in 1996, when priority NMEs were approved in an average of 13.7 months compared to 19.7 months for standard NMEs.

Data on 1995 and 1996 drug approvals may also indicate that the agency is conferring priority status on fewer new drugs (see exhibit below). Only 32 percent of the NMEs approved during these two years were classified as priority products. In contrast, fully half of the NMEs approved from 1990 to 1994 were priority drugs.

Although CDER's priority review policy and the user-fee review goals are designed to focus resources on important new drugs, the user fee timelines also offer important assurances for non-priority products. While CDER must concentrate reviewing resources on priority products, for example, it cannot do so to the point that it is unable to meet the 12-month review goal for standard applications.

NMEs Approved Based on Therapeutic Potential, 1984-1996

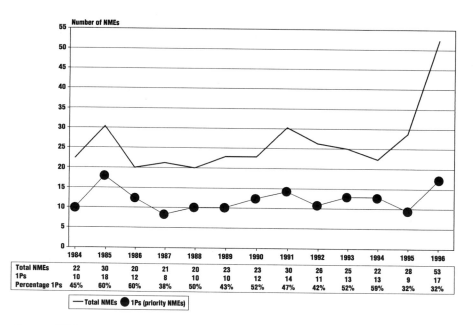

	1984	1985	1986	1987	1988	1989	1990	1991	1992	1993	1994	1995	1996
Total NMEs	22	30	20	21	20	23	23	30	26	25	22	28	53
1Ps	10	18	12	8	10	10	12	14	11	13	13	9	17
Percentage 1Ps	45%	60%	60%	38%	50%	43%	52%	47%	42%	52%	59%	32%	32%

—— Total NMEs ● 1Ps (priority NMEs)

Source: FDA

In the mid-1990s, CDER decided to replace its existing policy guide on the drug classification system—1992's Staff Manual Guide 4820.3—with a pair of policy documents. The first of these, an April 1996 guidance entitled *Priority Review Policy* (MaPP 6020.3), addresses the assignment of a drug's therapeutic rating. Still under development as of this writing, the second policy document will discuss issues relating to a drug's chemical rating.

Therapeutic Rating

While the existing alphanumeric classification system generally consists of two primary elements—a chemical rating and a therapeutic rating (e.g., 1P)—it is the therapeutic rating that determines a drug's review priority. According to MaPP 6020.3, all original NDAs and effectiveness supplements are to be given a therapeutic rating "based on an estimate of [the drug's] therapeutic, preventative or diagnostic value." The document adds that "the priority determination does not take into consideration any information or estimate of price and is based on conditions and information available at the time the application is filed. It is not intended to predict a drug's ultimate value or its eventual place in the market."

This estimate of therapeutic, preventative or diagnostic value must be considered in the context of CDER's definition of a "priority" product.

Priority Drugs Under CDER policy, a priority drug is one that "if approved, would be a significant improvement compared to marketed products [approved (if such is required), including non-'drug' products/therapies] in the treatment, diagnosis, or prevention of a disease. Improvement can be demonstrated by, for example: (1) evidence of increased effectiveness in treatment, prevention, or diagnosis of disease; (2) elimination or substantial reduction of a treatment-limiting drug reaction; (3) documented enhancement of patient compliance; or (4) evidence of safety and effectiveness of a new subpopulation."

Standard Drugs Under the FDA's user-fee program, drugs that do not qualify as priority products (P) are classified as standard therapies (S).

Special Situation Drugs The FDA may consider the conventional priority or standard rating code to be inadequate to properly identify a product's defining characteristics. In such cases, a review division may assign a drug one or more "special situation" ratings in addition to the "P" or "S" rating:

Type AA-AIDS Drug: "The drug is indicated for the treatment of AIDS or HIV-related disease."

Type E-Subpart E Drug: "The drug was developed and/or evaluated under the special procedures for drugs intended to treat life-threatening and severely debilitating illnesses" (see Chapter 16).

Type F-Fraud Policy Applies: "Substantive review of the application is deferred pending the outcome of a validity assessment of the submitted data as provided for by Compliance Policy Guide 7150.09. This code remains in the system throughout the audit and after when (a) the data are found to be not valid and a not approvable letter is issued or (b) the applicant withdraws the application before the audit is completed or after the audit is completed (data found to be not valid) but before a not approvable letter is issued."

Type G-Data Validated: "A validity assessment was performed on the application as provided for by CPG 7150.09, and the questions regarding the reliability of the data were satisfactorily resolved."

Type N-Non-Prescription Drug: "The drug has product labeling that provides for non-prescription (over-the-counter [OTC]) marketing. Applications will be labeled with an N designator whether all indications, or only some, are non-prescription."

Type V-Designated Orphan Drug: "The drug has officially received orphan designation...at the request of its sponsor/applicant" (see Chapter 14).

Assigning the Therapeutic Rating CDER's *Priority Review Policy* (MaPP 6020.3) puts the responsibility for assigning a drug's priority classification on the relevant medical team leader within the division evaluating the product. The team leader is to make the decision "after consulting, as needed, with the reviewing medical officer, supervisory chemist, pharmacologist, microbiologist and new drug division director."

Since the priority classification determines the review timeline applicable to an NDA, MaPP 6020.3 states that "the review priority should be determined and assigned at the 45-day meeting if the application is to be filed." The document is clear in establishing that, although a drug may be classified down from a priority to a standard product during the NDA review, the initial classification is locked in during the initial 6- or 12-month review cycle.

"The final review classification of a new drug may change from [priority] to [standard] during the course of the review of a marketing application (NDA), either because of the approval of other agents or because of availability of new data; however, the review priority classification assigned at the time of filing will not change during the first review cycle and the user fee time frame of the original review cycle will be that based on the original priority." If the reviewing medical officer or team leader wishes to change a drug's classification following the first review cycle, he or she must recommend the change "justified on the basis of, for example, new information in an IND or NDA, medical literature, advisory committee opinions or approval of a pharmacologically similar drug." The division director is responsible for approving the recommended change. MaPP 6020.3 makes no reference to the possibility of applications being upgraded from standard to priority during the initial review cycle.

Chemical Novelty Rating

The numeric element in CDER's priority classification code represents the chemical novelty of a drug product's active ingredient. This rating indicates to FDA chemistry reviewers whether the active ingredient is new or is related to compounds already on the market.

Until CDER releases a new MaPP for assigning chemical novelty ratings, policy guide 4820.3 will remain in effect. According to this document, a drug is to be assigned one of the following seven chemical ratings:

Type 1-New Molecular Entity: "A drug for which the active moiety (present as the unmodified base [parent] compound, or an ester or a salt, clathrate, or other noncovalent derivative of the base [parent] compound) has not been previously approved or marketed in the United States for use in a drug product, either as a single ingredient or as part of a combination product or as part of a mixture of stereoisomers.

"The active moiety in a drug is the molecule or ion, excluding those appended portions of the molecule that cause the drug to be an ester, salt (including a salt with hydrogen or coordination bonds) or other noncovalent derivative (such as a complex, chelate, or clathrate) of the molecule, responsible for the physiological or [pharmacological] action of the drug substance. The active moiety is the entire molecule or ion, not the 'active site.'

"Ordinarily, an ester is not considered an active moiety as most ester linkages are rapidly broken, with the de-esterified molecule circulating in the blood. However, there can be exceptions to this where a stable ester is the active moiety, the de-esterified molecule being inert; an example of this is organic nitrates, where the nitrate esters are the active moieties. The organic base molecules (glycerol, isosorbide) are inert."

Type 2-New Ester, New Salt, or Other Noncovalent Derivative: "A drug for which the active moiety has been previously approved or marketed in the United States but for which the particular ester, or salt, clathrate, or other noncovalent derivative, [of] the unmodified base (parent) compound has not yet been approved or marketed in the United States, either as a single ingredient, part of a combination product, or part of a mixture of stereoisomers."

Type 3-New Formulation: "A new dosage form or formulation, including a new strength, where the drug has already been approved or marketed in the United States by the same or another manufacturer. The indication may be the same as that of the already marketed drug product or may be new.

"A drug with changes in its inactive ingredients such that clinical studies (as opposed to bioequivalence studies) are required is considered to be a Type 3 drug. A drug previously approved or marketed only as a part of a combination (either a manufactured combination or a naturally occurring mixture) or a mixture of stereoisomers will also be considered a Type 3 drug. A combination product all of whose components have previously been approved or marketed together in combination with another drug will also be considered to be a Type 3 drug.

"A change in the strength of one or more drugs in a previously approved or marketed combination is considered to be a new formulation, not a new combination."

Type 4-New Combination: "A drug product containing two or more active moieties that have not been previously approved or marketed together in a drug product by any manufacturer in the United States. The new product may be a physical or a chemical (ester or non-covalent) combination of two or more active moieties. A new physical combination containing one or more active moieties that have not been previously approved or marketed is considered to be a Type 1,4 drug.

"A chemical combination of two or more active moieties previously approved or marketed as a physical combination is considered to be a Type 1 drug if the chemical bond is a non-ester covalent bond. If the two moieties are linked by an ester bond, the drug is considered a Type 4 drug if the moieties have not been previously marketed or approved as a physical combination, and a Type 2 drug if the combination has been previously marketed or approved."

Type 5-New Manufacturer: "A drug product that duplicates a drug product (same active moiety, same salt, same formulation [i.e., differences not sufficient to cause the product to be a Type 3; may require bioequivalency testing, including bioequivalence tests with clinical endpoints, but not clinical studies], or same combination) already approved or marketed in the United States by another firm. This category also includes NDAs for duplicate products where clinical studies were needed because of marketing exclusivity held by the original applicant."

Type 6-New Indication: "A drug product that duplicates a drug product (same active moiety, same salt, same formulation, or same combination) already approved or marketed in the U.S. by the same or another firm except that it provides for a new indication."

Type 7-Drug Already Marketed But Without An Approved NDA: "The application is the first NDA for a drug product containing one or more drugs marketed at the time of application or in the past without an approved NDA. Includes (a) first post-1962 application for products marketed prior to 1938, and (b) first application for DESI-related products first marketed between 1938 and 1962 without an NDA. The indication may be the same as, or different from, the already marketed drug product."

CDER's Prioritization Policy At Work

It is difficult to know precisely how CDER's drug review divisions implement the drug classification system. According to MaPP 6020.3, "a 'priority' designation is intended to direct overall attention and resources to the evaluation of applications for products that have the potential for providing significant preventative or diagnostic therapeutic advance as compared to 'standard' applications.

"The review priority classification determines the overall approach to setting review priorities and user fee review time frames but is not intended to preclude work on all other projects. It does not imply that staff working on a priority application cannot work on other projects, such as 30-day safety reviews of a newly submitted investigational new drug application (IND), preparation for end-of-phase 2 conferences, etc. Certain *ad hoc* special assignments may also take precedence. The supervisor is to advise the reviewer and team leader when an *ad hoc* assignment is to take precedence."

Chapter 11

Advisory Committees and the Drug Approval Process

CDER's 14 new drug review divisions do not conduct their scientific and medical reviews in a vacuum free from all outside input. Throughout the review process, these divisions have access to prescription drug advisory committees whose purpose is to provide advice on technical and medical issues related to the safety, effectiveness, testing, labeling, and use of new and approved drugs.

Today, CDER has 15 prescription drug advisory committees (see listing below) composed largely of leading scientists, most of whom are active researchers with academic appointments. In addition, CDER has two other advisory panels—the Nonprescription Drugs Advisory Committee and the Advisory Committee for Pharmaceutical Science—that can also become involved in prescription drug issues.

The advisory committees convene periodically to discuss issues that the FDA believes to be of major importance to public health. Since 1964, CDER's new drug review divisions have looked to the advisory committees for recommendations on issues such as the approvability of specific drugs, the adequacy of drug development approaches (e.g., evaluating new guidelines or study design issues), and the status of certain marketed drugs. According to the agency, committee discussions of such issues bring more diverse input to the decision-making process, provide access to technical expertise that may not be available within the agency, and open FDA decision-making procedures to broader scrutiny.

247

CDER's Prescription Drug Advisory Committees

Division of Gastrointestinal and Coagulation Drug Products
- Gastrointestinal Drugs Advisory Committee

Division of Antiviral Drug Products
- Antiviral Drugs Advisory Committee

Division of Cardio-Renal Drug Products
- Cardiovascular and Renal Drugs Advisory Committee

Division of Neuropharmacological Drug Products
- Peripheral and Central Nervous System Drugs Advisory Committee
- Psychopharmacologic Drugs Advisory Committee

Division of Oncologic Drug Products
- Oncologic Drugs Advisory Committee

Division of Pulmonary Drug Products
- Pulmonary-Allergy Drugs Advisory Committee

Division of Medical Imaging, Surgical, and Dental Drug Products
- Medical Imaging Drugs Advisory Committee

Division of Anti-Infective Drug Products
- Anti-Infective Drugs Advisory Committee

Division of Special Pathogens and Immunologic Drug Products
- Anti-Infective Drugs Advisory Committee
- Antiviral Drugs Advisory Committee

Division of Metabolism and Endocrine Drug Products
- Endocrinologic and Metabolic Drugs Advisory Committee

Division of Reproductive and Urologic Drug Products
- Advisory Committee for Reproductive Health Products

Division of Anesthetic, Critical Care, and Addiction Drug Products
- Drug Abuse Advisory Committee
- Anesthetic and Life Support Drugs Advisory Committee

Division of Anti-Inflammatory, Analgesic and Ophthalmic Drug Products
- Arthritis Advisory Committee
- Dermatologic and Ophthalmic Drugs Advisory Committee

Division of Dermatologic and Dental Drug Products
- Dermatologic and Ophthalmic Drugs Advisory Committee

Largely because advisory committee recommendations often have major medical and financial implications, the public profile of the committees has risen dramatically since the late 1980s. Although committee recommendations are not binding on the FDA, these recommendations are seen by the financial community and the pharmaceutical industry as forerunners of agency decisions on products. As a result, committee meetings receive considerable attention not just from the companies whose products are being considered, but from financial analysts and the trade press as well.

Although CDER's advisory committee program is three decades old, the significant evolution in the center's drug review process has had several implications for the advisory committee program. For example, even though advisory committee meetings have been more common in recent years, the environment for committee use is now more complex. Tight drug review timelines under the agency's user-fee program, for example, have made it difficult to schedule and hold advisory committee meetings in some cases.

One division, the Division of Neuropharmacological Drug Products, has even announced its intention to forego, whenever possible, bringing new drugs to an advisory committee. According to this new policy, which is a direct result of user fee timelines, the division will seek committee input only when a drug presents a particularly difficult issue or question. Some CDER officials claim that this is not necessarily a new policy, and point out that only 55 percent of new drugs approved in 1995 were reviewed by an advisory committee.

Another factor affecting advisory committees in recent years has been growing pressure to standardize committee processes. In response to a series of Institute of Medicine (IOM) recommendations in 1991, CDER revised its existing advisory committee procedures and detailed them in a document entitled *Policy and Guidance Handbook for FDA Advisory Committees* (1994). The handbook represented the agency's first real attempt to establish criteria for identifying intellectual bias and for granting conflict-of-interest waivers for committee members (see discussion below).

The agency has adopted many of the IOM's recommendations, including a system for advance scheduling of committee meetings and a policy that sponsors will "generally" receive questions to be posed to advisory committees prior to the meeting. The handbook, which the agency is now in the process of revising and updating, addresses virtually every aspect of the committee process, from member recruitment to seating arrangements for committee meetings.

A Look at Committee Membership

The nature of an advisory committee's membership is a function of several factors, including the panel's charter and the technical expertise needed to evaluate the issues likely to come before the panel. Membership is comprised primarily of physicians, although qualified experts in such disciplines as epidemiology, nursing, biostatistics, pharmacology, toxicology, and psychology are also included. A technically qualified, consumer-nominated member may be designated as a voting member of a committee as well. Recently, the FDA revised the charters of its scientific advisory committees to allow the agency to supplement the committee's voting membership when necessary expertise is not available from existing members.

Nominated by professional or consumer organizations, other committee members, private individuals, or FDA staffers, advisors must be judged to be broadly trained and experienced, of established professional reputation and personal integrity, and committed to the public interest. Although the agency seeks balance in terms of gender, race, and geographic location, technical competence is the overriding consideration in selecting members. Because members serve four-year terms and are likely to address a wide variety of issues during these periods, perhaps the ideal committee members are those who have recognized accomplishments and leadership within their fields and demonstrated abilities and interests in issues outside their specialties.

The FDA has several standards for ensuring the independence and objectivity of its advisory committees. First, no FDA employees may serve as voting committee members. The FDA does, however, appoint an employee as an executive secretary for each committee. Although not a panel member, the executive secretary is the agency's liaison to the committee, and is responsible for all administrative planning and preparation for meetings.

The agency's dialogue with advisors is an aspect of the committee process that has remained controversial. Some critics argue that agency staffers influence the views of advisors during such exchanges, an argument that top agency staffers openly reject. According to an internal CDER guide on policies and practices for center discussions with committee members, "it is never appropriate for either applicants or agency staff to lobby or negotiate with committee members about positions or conclusions the advisory committee should adopt on issues about to come before them. It is, however, appropriate for agency staff and corporate sponsors to provide members with background information on the issues at hand, and during meetings, to discuss the data and their own interpretation of the data with the whole committee."

In discussions for the reauthorization of the Prescription Drug User Fee Act, however, industry was pressing hard for Congress to take legislative steps to ensure the independence of FDA advisory committees from the review divisions that they serve. One proposal advanced in early 1997, for example, would remove committee-administration responsibilities from CDER and place them within the Office of the FDA Commissioner. Industry also wanted to require the agency to provide drug sponsors with all of the relevant materials sent to advisory committee members.

Finally, the agency has stringent financial conflict-of-interest standards for its members. Committee members are screened for such conflicts when they are nominated. In addition, appointed members must file a statement disclosing their financial interests prior to each meeting.

Since many leading clinicians and scientists in academia work closely with product sponsors, conflict-of-interest concerns can be a severely limiting factor in recruiting committee members. However, individuals who have affiliations or investments that might present conflict-of-interest problems may be appointed to committees based on their qualifications. On a case-by-case basis, the agency will consider waivers to allow the participation of such advisors in committee deliberations. According to the FDA's 1994 handbook, when an advisory committee is to consider issues involving a specific product or manufacturer, the FDA will not seek a waiver for a committee member or consultant who:

- has been hired by the sponsoring company to serve as a consultant on the product and for the indication in question or by the sponsor of a directly competitive product in a prominent role (e.g., principal investigator, project manager, study designer);

- has a "substantial personal financial interest in the sponsoring company or a company involved in the development of a competing product, where 'substantial' means (a) for a [committee] member, ownership of stock or other similar interest worth more than $100,000 and representing more than 25% of the member's net worth, and (b) for a [committee] consultant, $50,000 and more than 10% of the consultant's net worth;" or

- is, or is negotiating to become, the principal investigator under a grant or contract (held either by the consultant/committee member or his/her employer) for a study on a product to come before the committee or on a competing product, where the grant of contract exceeds $100,000 for a member, or $50,000 for a consultant.

In less clear-cut situations, the handbook says, the decision on whether to exclude, or seek a waiver for, a committee member will involve the weighing of the extent of the financial interest against the agency's need for the member's expertise.

To a lesser extent, the handbook also addresses the subject of intellectual bias, which the agency states should be handled through committee member training and by emphasizing to committee chairpersons their role in ensuring balanced discussions. According to the agency, intellectual bias by committee members may exist in the following situations: (1) "when the member is identified as a primary advocate or so strongly associated with a position on a [relevant matter] that reasonable persons would express concern that the member's impartiality and objectivity might be compromised;" and (2) when a member's statements of record (e.g., from judicial proceedings, press reports) suggest that a member has drawn conclusions on a relevant issue to a degree that would appear, to informed experts, to preclude an impartial and objective evaluation of information.

Committee members are paid $150 per day, and are reimbursed at the standard federal rate for travel, food, and lodging costs. Because of this cost structure, the advisory committee program is seen as a cost-efficient vehicle for obtaining input from many of the country's most knowledgeable, talented, and experienced scientists and clinicians.

When CDER Uses Advisory Committees

As stated, the advent of the prescription drug user fee program has complicated CDER's use of advisory committees in some ways. Further, given the limited number of advisory committee meetings, CDER must be careful to select for panel consideration issues with major implications for the public health.

As an internal FDA policy document points out, "advisory committees are composed of committed but busy leading scientists, most of whom are active researchers with academic appointments. Participation in FDA deliberations does not free them of their other obligations. As meetings are usually 2 days long, occur 2 to 5 times per year, and involve substantial pre-meeting preparation, it is clear that, for many committee members, current meeting schedules represent a substantial commitment. Therefore, we must select issues for discussion in ways that maximize the valuable contribution of our advisors as a public health resource, as well as make efficient use of the agency's staff's time preparing for and participating in such meetings."

Various FDA and CDER documents have attempted to identify the broad range of issues that may be considered by the committee, and general rules for selecting the most significant issues. Although this range includes general drug development issues (e.g., guidelines, study designs), emerging issues regarding marketed drugs (e.g., adverse reactions, labeling), and CDER's management of the drug evaluation process, the most important in the context of this discussion is committee deliberation on the approvability of specific drugs.

The FDA's 1994 advisory committee handbook made no important changes to the criteria that the agency uses in selecting drugs and issues. According to the handbook, CDER attempts to select topics for advisory committee presentations as follows:

- "Applications for approval of the first entity in a pharmacological class will routinely be presented as well as any other new chemical entity whose evaluation poses special problems or raises issues of broader interest."

- "New drugs that are expected to have a major therapeutic impact, whether or not they are [new chemical entities] will ordinarily be presented. Similarly, major new uses of marketed drugs will ordinarily be presented to advisory committees."

- "Applications for initial Rx to OTC switches of a drug will routinely be presented to an advisory committee..."

- Major safety concerns involving marketed drugs will "usually be presented" to advisory committees.

- Clinical guidelines "will routinely be presented" to the relevant committee for consideration before being adopted.

- At least once annually, a new drug review division will be selected to present a "program review on important and controversial drugs under development and applications for NCEs that are pending."

The process for selecting issues often involves several steps. To identify potential topics for committee meetings, the executive secretary for each advisory committee periodically meets with the director of the drug review division that the committee serves. These topics may be discussed during internal staff meetings.

It is important to note that CDER is not the only body involved in setting committee agendas. For example, a drug sponsor may request that a pending issue involving its product be brought before a committee. Likewise, committee members themselves may request that certain issues of interest be considered.

Agenda items agreed to within CDER are then discussed with the committee chairperson to obtain his or her advice on the ones that should be selected and how best to present the issues. Meeting agendas agreed to during this process are then published in the *Federal Register*.

In considering the data on a new drug or a significant new use of an already approved drug, the committee might evaluate any of several issues depending on the nature of the questions posed to it. These issues can include:

- the adequacy of the design and conduct of studies intended to provide substantial evidence of effectiveness;

- the data supporting the proposed dose and dosing schedule;

- critical studies;

- the appropriateness of surrogate endpoints for particular situations;

- the safety data base;

- the need for additional studies or special surveillance after marketing;

- the need to limit indications to a particular subset of the overall potential treatment population;

- the overall risk/benefit relationship of the new agent;

- the need for special labeling features, such as boxed warnings, limitations on use, monitoring requirements, or patient package inserts;

- the appropriateness of proposed prescription-to-OTC switches; and

- the primary review of selected portions of NDAs.

How Advisory Committees Function

CDER officials are quick to point out that each advisory committee has its own personality and its own unique relationship with the review division that it serves. The committee's personality and method of functioning is influenced largely by the committee's chairperson. As noted above, the chairperson has input on which issues are selected for committee deliberation and the presentation of these issues.

Although the product of the advisory committee process is generally a recommendation discussed and issued during a committee meeting, the process is considerably more involved. In many respects, periodic committee meetings represent the final stage of a lengthier and more complex process.

One of the fundamental principles of this process is that advisors be given sufficient information to allow them to provide informed recommendations during meetings. According to CDER's policy guide on committee discussions, "it is essential that the advisory committee collectively receive input from the agency regarding the staff's review of the data that will be presented to the committee. This provides committee members with the agency's expert analysis of the validity and organization of the data offered by sponsors, an analysis to which the agency usually brings more resources, expertise and experience than are available to the committee. It is also important that the committee have access to the agency's evaluation of the sponsor's data analyses, including the agency's evaluation of statistical techniques used, analysis of design issues, and assessment of the results of studies. Without such information, the committee may fail to address issues that will be critical to the agency's reasoning when it formulates a final decision on the issue." Sponsors often provide "additional data, sometimes with additional documentation to focus discussion or assist an identified committee member serving as a primary or secondary reviewer of the drug."

Because they often play important roles during committee meetings, sponsors must also be informed of meeting agendas. "Every effort should be made to be sure the sponsor understands the issues that will be raised for discussion by agency reviewers. There are many ways to do this, including deficiency letters to sponsors, pre-meetings between the sponsor and agency in anticipation of any advisory committee discussions (it is useful to offer the sponsor an opportunity for such a meeting), and communicating to the sponsor any questions to be posed to the committee in advance of the meeting."

A review division assembles an information package and forwards it to the committee members at least two weeks before the scheduled meeting. Rarely, if ever, do committee members review an entire NDA or IND, although some committee chairpersons are encouraged to appoint a "committee reviewer"— a committee member who would either become involved in the evaluation of an application or would receive more detailed information on an application and make a separate report to the full committee.

In mid-1997, Congress heard at least one proposal that advisory committee members be involved earlier in the drug development process. The proposal stated that the FDA and sponsor could select an outside advisor from a small cadre of relevant experts to become involved in the drug development and review process and, if necessary, to serve as a mediator in resolving disputes.

Committee meetings, during which issues are discussed and recommendations are voted upon, are attended by committee members, key personnel from the relevant drug review division(s), and often representatives from the drug firm whose product is under discussion. A meeting will generally consist of two or more of the following segments:

- *Open Public Hearing.* Every advisory committee meeting includes an open hearing (at least an hour in duration), during which any interested person may present data, information, or oral or written views that are relevant to the advisory committee's agenda or other work.

- *Open Committee Discussion.* With limited exceptions, advisory committees are required to conduct their discussions of pending matters in open sessions. Although access to open discussions is not restricted, no public participation is permitted during this segment without the consent of the committee chairperson. External consultants and the drug sponsor may be asked, or may request the opportunity, to present data to the committee. Typically, sponsor and FDA presentations consume much of the time allocated to open committee discussions.

- *Closed Presentation of Data.* Data and information that are prohibited from public disclosure are presented to the advisory committee in a closed portion of the meeting. This policy applies to discussions involving information considered to be trade secrets by the sponsor, and the disclosure of personal information about clinical subjects. Only key FDA staffers, advisory committee members, agency consultants, and drug sponsors attend this segment of a meeting. This allows the sponsor to present and discuss sensitive information such as manufacturing processes without concern that competitors will gain access to the information.

- *Closed Committee Deliberations.* Committees may also choose to discuss issues in a closed session, in which attendance is limited to agency staff, committee members, and individuals invited by the committee chairperson. Such sessions are generally reserved for the discussion of existing internal documents whose premature disclosure might significantly impede proposed agency action.

Advisory committees are asked to make their recommendations as specific as possible, and to address key questions posed by the FDA. Depending on the nature of the question being considered, the committee may vote on an issue by a show of hands or a more in-depth discussion of individual member recommendations and the rationales for them.

How Influential Are CDER's Advisory Committees?

There is no real measure of advisory committee influence in the drug review process. Although committee recommendations are not binding on the FDA, there are few instances in which agency decisions contradict these recommendations. According to FDA statistics from 1975 to mid-1978, the agency followed 98.7 percent of advisory committee recommendations.

Still, it remains difficult to gauge whether committee decisions direct or simply support FDA decisions. As stated above, some critics of the process even suggest that FDA officials direct committee recommendations during pre-meeting communications.

It is also difficult to determine whether the agency would have reached the identical decision had the division not consulted an advisory committee. In fact, CDER's advisory committee policy guide acknowledges that a division may seek committee recommendations on a drug for which the division has already reached "a strong conclusion as to approvability."

In all likelihood, the influence of committee recommendations differs from case to case. Some FDA officials claim that the degrees of committee influence are best portrayed through several scenarios:

Scenario #1: The review division is faced with a particularly complex technical issue on which it has not reached a decision. This might also include situations in which the advisory committee has expertise not available within the agency, or situations in which a drug's approval represents a "close call" given the risk/benefit profile of the product. In such situations, advisory committees are likely to have the most influence on FDA decision making.

Scenario #2: The review division has reached a preliminary decision, but wants advice on specific issues. For example, the division may have decided to approve a certain drug, but wants committee input on issues such as appropriate dosing, labeling, or the need for follow-up studies.

Scenario #3: The review division has made a decision, but would be more comfortable if an independent review supported the initial determination. For example, the FDA may have reached a not-approvable decision on an NDA, but may decide to bring the decision before an advisory committee to permit the sponsor to present its case to an outside review body. Although the division is open to reconsider its decision if so advised by the committee, recommendations offered in this context may be less likely to affect agency decision making.

What Sponsors Should Know About Advisory Committees

Given the importance of advisory committee meetings, drug sponsors have much to gain by studying a committee before making a presentation to it. This is particularly important given the dynamic nature of the advisory committee process and the fundamental differences between the panels themselves.

Today, entire seminars are dedicated to preparing firms for advisory committee meetings. Although such detailed discussions cannot be presented here, there are several essential principles worth mentioning:

- Learn as much as possible about the committee members, particularly the chairperson. Each member's particular areas of expertise and interest are also extremely important. Some experts advise obtaining each member's curriculum vitae and research papers to gain insights about their interests, and to help anticipate possible concerns and questions.

- Gain a full understanding of the relevant issues as the review division views them. Division reviewers set the committee's agenda, and frame and phrase the specific questions to which the committee must respond.

- Learn how the committee functions, how meetings are conducted, how the committee reaches its decisions, and how much it values solicited and unsolicited input from the sponsor, clinical investigators, statisticians, outside consultants, and others.

- Research what topics are on the committee's agenda. This will affect the amount of time a drug sponsor will be given to present its case. For example, the Oncology Drugs Advisory Committee is known to move quickly through agenda topics, and to address two or more products at a single meeting. CDER provides agenda-related materials to all companies scheduled to participate in an upcoming meeting.

Chapter 12

Beyond Approval: Drug Manufacturer Regulatory Responsibilities

When a new drug obtains FDA approval, it enters another stage of the product life cycle to which different regulatory standards apply. But considering the fundamental differences between general marketing and comparatively tightly controlled clinical testing, the premarketing and postapproval responsibilities facing drug companies are remarkably similar in many respects.

Just as the sponsor must ensure that its drug is produced according to accepted manufacturing standards during clinical testing, the company must provide similar assurances when the product is marketed to the general public. Similarly, as the FDA calls upon sponsors to submit important test data during a drug's development, the agency also requires sponsors to report any postmarketing data or information that might cause the FDA to reassess a drug's safety and effectiveness.

In addition to abiding by the conditions of use (e.g., labeling, manufacturing commitments) detailed in its approved application and any subsequent supplements, an NDA holder must fulfill several postapproval responsibilities in both product reporting and manufacturing. Most postmarketing requirements fall into one of three areas:

- General Reporting Requirements;

- Adverse Experience (AE) Reporting Requirements; and
- Current Good Manufacturing Practice (CGMP).

Sponsor commitments made at the time of a drug's approval may also become, in effect, postmarketing requirements. For example, a sponsor may agree, at the time of approval, to conduct additional testing on a drug to further discern a drug's safety/effectiveness or effects in specific subpopulations. Often called "Phase 4 commitments," these commitments—and sponsors' progress in fulfilling them—are actively tracked by the FDA following approval (see discussion below).

General Reporting Requirements

According to federal regulations, sponsors of approved NDAs must develop and submit to the FDA several different types of reports and materials—field alert reports, annual reports, advertising/promotional labeling specimens, and "special" reports. Taken together with AE reports, these submissions allow the FDA to monitor the distribution and effects of the drug. The reports also alert the FDA to information that might represent grounds for regulatory action (e.g., product recall).

Field Alert Reports   Federal regulations require NDA holders to report, within three days of receipt, any information:

- "…concerning any incident that causes the drug product or its labeling to be mistaken for, or applied to, another article."

- "…concerning any bacteriological contamination, or any significant chemical, physical, or other change or deterioration in the distributed drug product, or any failure of one or more distributed batches of the drug product to meet the specifications established for it in the application."

Companies may provide this information by telephone or other rapid means, provided that the initial notification is followed by a prompt written follow-up report. The written report should be plainly marked "NDA-Field Alert Report," and be submitted to the FDA district office responsible for the reporting manufacturing facility.

Annual Reports The annual report plays several important roles in the FDA's monitoring of a marketed drug's safety and quality. First, the report provides the FDA with a convenient summary of new research data, distribution information, and labeling changes. Also, the annual submission is the vehicle through which manufacturers must report certain types of information that need not be provided in any other mandatory filing.

Annual reports must be filed with the FDA drug review division responsible for evaluating and approving a subject drug's NDA. These reports must be submitted each year within 60 days of the anniversary date of the drug's approval, and must be accompanied by a *Transmittal of Periodic Reports for Drugs for Human Use* (Form FDA-2252).

Annual reports must include the following types of information "that the applicant received or otherwise obtained during the annual reporting interval which ends on the anniversary date [of the drug's approval]:"

Summary of New Information. A brief summary of the significant new information obtained during the previous year that might affect the safety, effectiveness, or labeling of the drug product. Also, the sponsor must detail any action it has taken or is planning to take in response to this new information (e.g., submitting a labeling supplement, adding a warning to the labeling, or initiating a new study).

Distribution Data. Information on the quantity of the product distributed, and the amounts forwarded to drug distributors. This section must provide the National Drug Code (NDC) number, the total number of dosage units of each strength or potency distributed (e.g., 100,000/5 milligram tablets, 50,000/10 milliliter vials), and the quantities distributed for domestic and foreign use.

Labeling. Labeling information and samples, including currently used professional labeling, patient brochures or package inserts (if any), a representative sample of the package labels, and a summary of product labeling changes implemented since the last report. If the manufacturer implemented no labeling changes, this should be stated in the report.

Chemistry, Manufacturing, and Controls Changes. Information on chemistry, manufacturing, and controls (CMC) changes, including reports of any new experiences, investigations, studies, or tests involving chemical, physical, or other properties of the drug that may affect the FDA's previous conclusions on the product. The report should also provide a full description of all implemented manufacturing and controls changes that did not require a supplemental application (see Chapter 13). Due to what the FDA viewed as the "wide variability" of CMC sections submitted in annual reports, the agency published a 1994 guideline entitled *Guidance for Industry: Format and Content for the CMC Section of an Annual Report.*

Nonclinical Laboratory Studies. Information from nonclinical laboratory studies, including copies of unpublished reports, summaries of published reports of new toxicological findings in animal studies, and *in vitro* studies conducted or otherwise obtained by the sponsor relating to the product's ingredients.

Clinical Data. Published clinical trials on the drug (or abstracts of them), including: data from trials on safety and effectiveness or new uses; biopharmaceutic, pharmacokinetic, and clinical pharmacology studies; and reports of clinical experiences pertinent to safety (e.g., epidemiologic studies) conducted or obtained by the sponsor. Also needed are summaries of completed unpublished clinical trials—a study is considered completed one year after its conclusion—or pre-publication manuscripts developed or obtained by the applicant. Supporting information should not be reported. Review articles, papers describing the use of the drug product in medical practice, papers and abstracts in which the drug is used as a research tool, promotional articles, press clippings, and papers that do not contain tabulations or summaries of original data should not be reported.

Status Reports. A statement on the current status of any postmarketing studies performed by, or on behalf of, the applicant, including those that the sponsor agreed to conduct (see section below on Phase 4 commitments).

Other Reports Federal regulations state that sponsors must be prepared to file other reports, including:

Advertisements and Promotional Labeling. NDA holders must "submit specimens of mailing pieces and any other labeling or advertising devised for promotion of the drug product at the time of initial dissemination of the labeling and at the time of initial publication of the advertisement for a prescription drug product. Mailing pieces and labeling that are designed to contain samples of a drug product are required to be complete, except the sample of the drug product may be omitted. Each submission is required to be accompanied by a completed transmittal Form FDA-2253 (Transmittal of Advertisements and Promotional Labeling for Drugs for Human Use) and is required to include a copy of the product's current professional labeling."

The agency has different standards for the submission of advertisements and promotional labeling approved under its accelerated approval program (see Chapter 16). Under this program, a sponsor must submit these materials for evaluation during the NDA review process for any advertising and labeling that the company plans to disseminate within 120 days of a drug's approval. For advertising and promotional labeling that the firm hopes to disseminate after this 120-day period, the sponsor must submit the materials at least 30 days prior to release.

Special Reports. The FDA may request that the applicant submit any of the reports profiled above at times different than those required under federal regulations.

Adverse Experience Reporting Requirements

Following a drug's approval, NDA holders must continue to collect, analyze, and submit data on adverse drug experiences (AE) so that the company and the FDA can continually reassess the product's risk/benefit relationship and the conditions under which it should be used.

During the mid-1990s, CDER's postmarketing AE reporting requirements were on the verge of being revised. In an October 1994 proposed rule, the FDA proposed wide-ranging changes to both its premarketing and postmarketing AE reporting requirements. The purposes of the proposed revisions were to codify various aspects of the agency's MedWatch Program and to modify certain definitions and reporting requirements to facilitate international harmonization of postmarketing AE reporting.

Although the FDA had intended to finalize the proposed requirements during 1995, various factors, including regulatory reform and ongoing international harmonization efforts, impeded their progress. In mid-1997, more than two years after the October 1994 proposal, the new requirements remained in the proposal stage (see discussion below). This chapter focuses on current AE reporting requirements and discusses the changes likely to be implemented when the new requirements are finalized.

A pending change in the FDA's adverse experience reporting system is also worth noting. In the fall of 1997, a new system called the Adverse Event Reporting System (AERS) will replace the FDA's current Spontaneous Reporting System (SRS) database for adverse event reports. According to the agency, "AERS will enable FDA to receive [adverse experience] reports from pharmaceutical companies by electronic submission, transmitted data base to data base through standardized pathways." Reports still received on paper will be full-text entered and scanned by the agency. In addition, a new international adverse event terminology developed by ICH—Medical Dictionary for Drug Regulatory Affairs (MEDDRA)—will be utilized; manufacturers will precode reports prior to electronic submission. Further, AERS will provide a "paperless" means for FDA postmarketing safety evaluators to screen individual reports, and will provide new tools for the enhanced surveillance of drug safety.

CDER's current postmarketing AE reporting requirements are a product of a series of revisions implemented in the mid- and late-1980s. These requirements are described in FDA regulations and CDER's *Guideline for Postmarketing Reporting of Adverse Drug Experiences* (March 1992).

Defining Adverse Experience The adverse experience reporting area has very much its own language. In fact, reporting requirements are directly linked to criteria outlined in the definitions of at least three important terms that appear in federal regulations: "adverse experience," "unexpected adverse experience," and "serious adverse experience."

An adverse experience is defined as "any adverse event associated with the use of a drug in humans, whether or not considered drug related, including the following: an adverse event occurring in the course of the use of a drug product in professional practice; an adverse event occurring from drug overdose, whether accidental or intentional; an adverse event occurring from drug abuse; an adverse event occurring from drug withdrawal; and any failure of expected pharmacological action."

An "unexpected" event is an adverse experience "that is not listed in the current labeling for the drug." This definition includes an event that may be symptomatically and pathophysiologically related to an event listed in the labeling, but that differs from the event because of greater severity or specificity.

A "serious adverse experience" is "an adverse drug experience that is fatal or life-threatening, is permanently disabling, requires in-patient hospitalization, or is a congenital anomaly, cancer, or overdose." Under the FDA's October 1994 proposed regulation, this definition would be revised so that it is compatible with international standards and with the definition outlined in the agency's MedWatch Program (see discussion below).

Adverse Experience Reporting Requirements NDA holders and any person whose name appears on the drug product's label as a manufacturer, packer, or distributor have AE reporting responsibilities. To avoid unnecessary duplication of reporting, however, federal regulations permit "nonapplicants" to meet their reporting requirements by submitting all serious AE reports directly to the applicant rather than to the FDA. The agency requires NDA holders to make three types of postmarketing AE reports when necessary:

- 15-day alert reports;

- periodic adverse experience reports; and

- increased frequency reports.

15-Day Alert Reports. All adverse experiences that are both serious and unexpected must be reported by manufacturers within 15 working days of becoming aware of the event. These 15-day alert reports, sometimes called expedited reports, should be provided on Form FDA 3500A.

Like other AE reports, 15-day alert reports submitted on Form FDA 3500A should provide an identifiable source, a patient (even if not precisely identified by name and date of birth), a suspect product, and a suspect adverse event. Sponsors must investigate each AE that is the subject of a 15-day alert report, and "submit follow-up reports within 15 working days of receipt of new information or as requested by FDA. If additional information is not obtainable, a follow-up report may be required that describes briefly the steps taken to seek additional information and the reasons why it could not be obtained. These 15-day alert reports and follow-ups to them are required to be submitted under separate cover and may not be included, except for summary or tabular purposes, in a periodic report" (see discussion below).

15-day alert reports based on information in the scientific literature must be accompanied by a copy of the published article. The alert reporting requirements for serious, unexpected AEs or therapeutic failures "apply only to reports found in scientific and medical journals either as case reports or as the result of a formal clinical trial." The alert reporting requirements for significant increases in the frequency of a serious, expected AE "apply only to reports found in scientific and medical journals either as the result of a formal clinical trial, or from epidemiologic studies or analyses of experience in a monitored series of patients" (see discussion on increased frequency reports below).

To promote international harmonization, the FDA permits serious and unexpected AE reports originating outside of the United States to be submitted on a form developed by the Council for International Organizations of Medical Sciences (CIOMS). An independent body located in the World Health Organization's headquarters in Geneva, Switzerland, CIOMS provides a forum for manufacturers and regulators to develop and test uniform approaches and formats for adverse experience reporting. The use of a CIOMS form enables a manufacturer to submit one adverse experience report form to all participating national regulatory agencies. The FDA prefers to receive foreign 15-day alert reports on Form FDA 3500A, however.

Periodic Adverse Experience Reports. Periodic reports must be submitted, in duplicate, quarterly for the first three years following a drug's approval, and annually thereafter. The quarterly reports must be submitted within 30 days of the close of each quarter (i.e., the first quarter beginning on an application's approval date). Annual reports must be filed within 60 days of the anniversary date of the application's approval.

A periodic report must contain each of the following components:

- A copy of Form FDA-3500A for each AE not reported as a 15-day alert report, with an index consisting of a line listing of the applicant's patient identification number and adverse reaction terms.

- A narrative summary and analysis of the information in the periodic report, and an analysis of the 15-day alert reports submitted during the reporting period.

- A narrative discussion of actions taken since the last report because of adverse experiences (e.g., labeling changes or studies initiated).

Increased Frequency Reports. In late 1996, the FDA proposed to eliminate the current requirement that companies submit increased frequency reports (see discussion below). Under current regulations, however, licensed manufacturers must periodically review the frequency with which serious expected adverse experiences are reported. If a manufacturer determines that a particular event is being reported with substantially increased frequency compared to previous reporting intervals, the company must submit an increased frequency report within 15 days of the periodic reporting cycle.

The report, which cannot be submitted as part of a periodic report, must be provided in narrative form and must describe the method of the analysis, the time period upon which the analysis is based, and the interpretation of the results. Licensed manufacturers should conduct periodic reviews at least as often as the periodic reporting cycle.

As stated, the FDA proposed eliminating expedited reporting requirements for increased frequency reports in an October 1996 proposed rule. The agency's proposal stated that the increased frequency of expected adverse events could be addressed in the overall safety evaluation within periodic safety reports. A final rule to implement this change was said to be moving quickly through the agency, which had hoped to publish it by mid-1997.

Likely Changes to AE Reporting Requirements As stated, the FDA proposed changing drug and biologic AE reporting requirements in several substantial ways in October 1994. Specifically, the FDA issued an omnibus AE reporting proposal that represented agency initiatives on three fronts: (1) changes in clinical trial AE reporting requirements that comprised its response to deaths in the clinical testing of fialuridine (FIAU); (2) efforts to advance the international harmonization of postmarketing AE reporting standards; and (3) initiatives to codify provisions of 1993's MedWatch Program.

In May 1995, FDA officials announced that, for practical reasons, the omnibus proposal had been broken into sections that would be implemented serially. As of this writing, the agency had not yet implemented final regulations for any of the three sections, two of which will have direct relevance for postmarketing AE reporting for drug products.

The furthest along of these final regulations is one that will implement new and harmonized definitions and conventions for expedited clinical trial and postmarketing AE reporting. In the provisions that were most relevant to postmarketing AE reporting requirements, the October 1994 proposed rule sought to redefine "serious" AE to be consistent with FDA Form 3500A (MedWatch Form) and with international standards: "an adverse drug experience occurring at any dose that is fatal or life-threatening, results in persistent or significant disability/incapacity, requires or prolongs inpatient hospitalization, necessitates medical or surgical intervention to preclude permanent impairment of a body function or permanent damage to a body structure, or is a congenital anomaly." In the expected final rule, however, the FDA is likely to adopt language that is closer to the definition of serious AE included in the ICH's March 1995 final guideline entitled *Clinical Safety Data Management: Definitions and Standards for Expedited Reporting*. This document defines a serious AE as "any untoward medical occurrence that at any dose: results in death, is life-threatening, results in persistent or significant disability/incapacity, or is a congenital anomaly/birth defect."

To help companies determine what comprises a "serious" AE, the FDA is also expected to define two terms used in the new definition as follows: disability, which "means a substantial disruption of one's ability to carry out normal life functions;" and life threatening, which "means that the patient was, in the view of the initial reporter, at immediate risk of death from the adverse experience as it occurred."

If it is implemented as proposed, the final rule would also change the reporting time frames for postmarketing alert reports from 15 working days to 15 calendar days.

At this writing, the final rule had been developed and was in the final stages of the FDA's clearance process. Agency officials hoped to implement the final rule during the second half of 1997.

The second final rule in the regulatory queue will revamp the FDA's periodic postmarketing AE reporting requirements to conform to a CIOMS II Working Group's proposal. Among its other provisions, the regulation will require a new format for periodic reports called a periodic safety update report (PSUR).

If implemented, the agency's October 1994 proposed rule would require the following:

- A six-month periodic reporting cycle throughout a product's life. Currently, the agency requires quarterly periodic reports for the first three years following approval, and then annual reports thereafter.

- Submission of the periodic report within 45 days of the date on which the product was first licensed anywhere in the world. This is referred to as the international birth date.

- An international core data sheet containing all relevant safety information. The core data sheet enables a manufacturer to produce a periodic report acceptable to all participating countries. This core data sheet differs from the FDA-approved product labeling. The U.S. labeling will remain the document of reference when determining if an event is "unlabeled" for purposes of expedited (15-day) reporting.

- A report format that is based on CIOMS II and that includes information on patient exposure and worldwide regulatory decisions concerning marketing, regulatory, or manufacturer actions taken for safety reasons.

During the mid-1990s, the content and publication of the FDA's postmarketing AE reporting final rule remained tied to the ICH's *Final Guideline on*

Clinical Safety Data Management: Periodic Update Reports for Marketed Products, which was published in May 1997. Regulatory authorities from the U.S. and European Union had agreed not to implement their formal requirements for postmarketing periodic reporting until the ICH finalized this guideline.

At this writing, there were indications that the FDA would revise what had been a controversial element of its proposal—to require six-month AE reports throughout a product's life. To remain consistent with ICH requirements, the FDA is certain to implement a reporting time frame that is based on six-month reporting intervals. As of mid-1997, however, it appeared that the agency was considering several options, including requiring PSURs every six months for the first three years of marketing and annual reports thereafter.

Having just completed work on the expedited AE reporting regulation discussed above, however, FDA officials were just turning their attention to the postmarketing AE reporting rule as of mid-1997. Given this, it seemed unlikely that the agency would meet its goal of implementing a final regulation by fall 1997.

Current Good Manufacturing Practice (CGMP)

Since 1962, federal drug law has mandated that firms producing drugs for administration to humans operate under standards called Current Good Manufacturing Practice (CGMP). The statutory requirement calls for all drugs—including drug products (i.e., finished dosage forms) and drug components (i.e., bulk ingredients)—to be made in conformance with CGMP to ensure that the substances meet legal requirements of safety, and that they have the identity, strength, quality, and purity that they purport or are represented to possess.

In the late 1970s, the FDA had envisioned several different sets of CGMPs, with separate standards for finished dosage forms, bulk ingredients, and other classes of products. To date, however, the FDA has published only one broadly applicable CGMP regulation, which is relevant to finished dosage forms. Since establishing CGMP requirements, the FDA has exhibited a preference for a "general regulatory approach," and for supplementing this approach with additional specificity when necessary. In the most recent effort to add specificity to its CGMP requirements, the agency proposed to clarify certain manufacturing, quality control and documentation requirements and to update requirements for process and methods validation (see discussion below).

The agency states that its CGMP regulations are based on "fundamental concepts of quality assurance: (1) Quality, safety, and effectiveness must be designed and built into a product; (2) quality cannot be inspected or tested into a finished product; and (3) each step of the manufacturing process must be controlled to maximize the likelihood that the finished product will be acceptable."

It is worth noting that the applicability of CGMP requirements is not restricted to approved drug products. As the FDA establishes in its *Guideline on the Preparation of Investigational New Drug Products* (Human and Animal) (March 1991), experimental drugs used in clinical testing are subject to certain CGMP requirements as well.

CGMP regulations seek to ensure the quality of drugs by setting minimum standards for all drug manufacturing facilities. The regulations establish standards in ten separate areas:

- organization and personnel;

- buildings and facilities;

- equipment;

- control of components and drug product containers and closures;

- production and process controls;

- packaging and labeling controls;

- holding and distribution;

- laboratory controls;

- records and reports; and

- returned and salvaged drug products.

Organization and Personnel One of the most important CGMP require-ments addresses a facility's quality control unit, which each manufacturing facility must have to ensure compliance with CGMP. According to federal regu-lations, the quality control unit assumes "the responsibility and authority to approve or reject all components, drug product containers, closures, in-process materials, packaging materials, labeling, and drug products and the authority to review production records to ensure that no errors have occurred or, if errors have occurred, that they have been fully investigated." In addition, the one-or-more-person quality control unit is responsible for approving or rejecting all procedures or specifications affecting the identity, strength, quality, and purity of the drug product.

Obviously, the professionals responsible for performing, supervising, or consulting on the manufacture, processing, packing, or holding of a drug must be adequate in number and sufficiently qualified by education, training, and experience to carry out their respective tasks. Facility staff must be trained not only in their specific tasks, but in CGMP as well. The facility must document this training.

Buildings and Facilities CGMP building and facility requirements are designed to ensure that any structures used to manufacture, process, pack, or hold a drug are of a suitable size, construction, and location to allow proper cleaning, maintenance, and operation. These requirements call for the separa-tion of several plant operations (e.g., control and laboratory operations, pack-aging and labeling operations) to reduce the possibility of cross-contamination and other mishaps. Specific requirements for lighting, ventilation, heating and cooling systems, plumbing, sanitation, and mainte-nance are also provided.

Equipment CGMP equipment requirements are generally concerned with equipment design, size, location, and maintenance. To ensure that drug prod-uct attributes are not adversely affected, surfaces that contact components, in-process materials, or drug products must not be reactive, additive, or absorptive. Lubricants and other substances required for equipment opera-tions must not cause product contamination.

At predetermined intervals, all utensils and equipment must be cleaned, maintained, and sanitized according to specific written procedures. Filters and automatic, mechanical, and electronic equipment (including computers) face special validation requirements.

Components and Drug Product Container and Closure Controls

A facility must maintain detailed written procedures for the receipt, identification, storage, handling, sampling, testing, and approval/rejection of components and drug product containers and closures. Upon receipt, these materials must be inspected visually for appropriate labeling and contents, container damage, broken seals, and contamination. Before use, samples from each lot of components must be drawn, and the components tested for identity and conformity with purity, strength, and quality specifications. Drug product containers and closures must be tested for conformance to applicable written requirements.

Production and Process Controls Manufacturing facilities must maintain written procedures for production and process controls designed to ensure that the drug products have the identity, strength, quality, and purity they claim or are represented to possess. Special CGMP requirements exist for the charge-in of components, yield calculations, the identification of compounding and storage containers, processing lines, and the major equipment used in the production of a drug's batch, the sampling and testing of in-process materials and drug products, and the limiting of production times.

Packaging and Labeling Controls All packaging and labeling materials must be sampled, examined, or tested before their use. Documented procedures must be established for the receipt, identification, storage, handling, sampling, examination, and testing of labeling and packaging materials. CGMP regulations also specify requirements for labeling issuances and accountability, packaging and labeling operations control and inspection, tamper-resistant packaging for OTC drugs, drug product inspection, and expiration dating.

To reduce the frequency of drug product mislabeling, the FDA revised the CGMP labeling control regulations in 1993. Specifically, the revision defined the term "gang-printed labeling," specified conditions for the use of gang-printed or cut labeling, and exempted manufacturers that employ certain automated inspection systems from labeling reconciliation requirements. To provide industry with more time to comply with these changes, the agency extended the effective date of some elements of the final rule to August 1997.

Holding and Distribution Requirements Facilities must maintain detailed written procedures describing the warehousing operations (including quarantine and special storage procedures) and distribution methods in use for a drug product. In most cases, facilities should implement the "first in, first out" (FIFO) principle in storing and distributing the product.

Laboratory Controls Each organizational unit within a firm is required to maintain procedures for control mechanisms. These procedures and mechanisms, such as specifications, standards, sampling plans, and test procedures, are designed to ensure that components, drug product containers, closures, in-process materials, labeling, and drug products conform to appropriate standards of identity, strength, quality, and purity. Laboratory controls, which must be reviewed and approved by the quality control unit, include:

- the determination, through documented sampling and testing procedures, that each shipment lot of components, drug product containers, closures, and labeling conforms to relevant specifications;

- the determination, through sampling and testing procedures, that in-process materials conform to written specifications;

- the determination that the laboratory is complying with written descriptions of drug product sampling procedures and specifications; and

- the determination that instruments, apparatus, gauges, and recording devices have been calibrated at suitable intervals according to written procedures that provide specific directions, schedules, limits for accuracy and precision, and provisions for remedial action in the event accuracy and/or precision limits are not met.

A written program must be designed for stability testing studies. The results of these tests are used to determine appropriate storage conditions and expiration dates for each drug. Reserve samples of drug substances and drug products must be retained for specific intervals.

Also included in the laboratory controls subpart of the CGMP regulations are requirements for: (1) the sampling, testing, and release for distribution of drug product batches; (2) special testing for sterile, pyrogen-free, ophthalmic, and controlled-release drugs, reserve sample retention, laboratory test animals; and (3) testing for penicillin contamination.

Records and Reports Facilities must retain records for all drug components, drug product containers, closures, and labeling for at least one year after the expiration date of the drug product for which they were used. Certain OTC drugs do not require expiration dating because they meet specific exemption criteria. For these drugs, records must be kept for three years after distribution of the last lot of drug product incorporating the component or using the container, closure, or labeling. CGMP regulations also specify requirements for master and batch production records, laboratory records, distribution records, and complaint files.

Returned and Salvaged Drug Products Any returned drug products must be identified and held. A manufacturer must destroy such products if there is any doubt about their safety, identity, strength, quality, or purity, but may reprocess the products if the resultant drug can meet applicable standards, specifications, and characteristics. Reprocessing must be conducted according to written and company-approved procedures. Drugs subjected to improper storage, including extremes in temperature, humidity, smoke, fumes, pressure, age, radiation due to natural disasters, fires, accidents, or equipment failures, may not be salvaged and returned to the marketplace.

Expected Changes to CGMP For several reasons, including rapid technological change, industry misunderstanding of certain CGMP requirements, and serious validation deficiencies at some firms, the FDA proposed to clarify and amend certain CGMP requirements in mid-1996. The proposal, which had not been finalized at this writing, would do the following:

Define and Clarify Process Validation and Methods Validation Requirements. Because the agency continues to find a few firms that have not validated and that do not revalidate their manufacturing processes when necessary, the agency proposed to specify in the CGMP regulations "the nature and extent of validation that are necessary to ensure that the resulting products have the identity, strength, quality and purity characteristics that they purport to possess."

Dedicated Production Processes for Certain Drugs. For certain substances that pose a serious threat of contamination (i.e., substances to which humans or animals show a particular sensitivity even at extremely low levels), the FDA has proposed requiring dedicated production facilities and equipment.

Clarify Requirements for Testing and Investigation of Discrepancies/Failures. After finding that some firms are not conducting adequate testing and are not adequately evaluating test discrepancies or investigating failures, the FDA has proposed to clarify related CGMP requirements, to amend procedures for component testing, calculation of yield, and blend testing, and to specify procedures for out-of-specification results.

Quality Control. The proposed rule would make the quality control unit responsible for reviewing changes in product, process, equipment, or personnel, and for determining if and when revalidation is required.

The Enforcement of CGMP While some critics have claimed that CGMP provisions are too general and difficult to enforce, the FDA has an active program designed to ensure manufacturer compliance. Enforcement responsibilities fall mainly on the FDA's district offices located throughout the United States. These offices monitor the industry by inspecting each drug manufacturing facility within their regions at least once every two years.

When a foreign or domestic inspection is completed, the manufacturer is alerted to any detected CGMP violations. Minor violations are generally handled by the FDA's district offices, which provide the manufacturer a period of time within which to address the detected violations. For major violations, the district office files a report with FDA headquarters, which reviews the case and decides on the appropriate regulatory action.

Legal sanctions available to the agency include product seizure, injunction, and prosecution. When necessary, the FDA proposes such actions to the U.S. Justice Department, which may then file cases with the appropriate U.S. district court.

CGMP inspections are conducted on an impromptu basis—that is, the facility to be inspected is generally not given advance notice by the FDA field office.

The CGMP inspector arrives at the plant and, after the presentation of credentials and a notice of inspection, must be given immediate access to the building.

This procedure, however, is not applicable to the inspection of non-U.S. drug manufacturers. For foreign manufacturing facilities, the FDA makes only CGMP inspections that are pre-arranged with the manufacturers a few months in advance. The most frequent subjects of foreign CGMP inspections are bulk active pharmaceutical ingredient manufacturers.

In recent years, the FDA's international surveillance activities have increased considerably. With greater funding targeted for foreign inspections, the FDA had significantly increased its inspectional activities targeted at foreign manufacturing facilities during the mid-1990s.

In mid-1997, the FDA and European Union (EU) regulators established a mutual recognition agreement (MRA) under which they would exchange and generally accept each other's CGMP inspections without necessitating reinspections. The MRA, which was being ratified in the United States and Europe at this writing, would begin with a three-year transitional period during which the regulators would establish the equivalence of their GCMP inspections.

Phase 4 Commitments

Prior to the approval of its drug, an applicant may agree to conduct postapproval studies either voluntarily or at the FDA's request. While it maintains that such postapproval studies are not considered essential to product approval, the agency might seek such a "Phase 4 commitment" for any of several reasons, including the need to confirm a drug's clinical effectiveness.

Although the agency can pursue Phase 4 commitments for any drug, the FDA's 1993 regulations on accelerated approval (Subpart H) codified its authority to require postapproval studies under the Subpart H program (see Chapter 16). These regulations establish that the FDA can require Phase 4 studies when it approves an application on the basis of a surrogate endpoint or on the basis of an effect on a clinical endpoint other than survival or irreversible morbidity.

Because differing policies within the center's review divisions made tracking Phase 4 commitments unmanageable, CDER used an October 1996 MaPP entitled *Procedures for Tracking and Reviewing Phase 4 Commitments*

(MaPP 6010.2) to standardize the manner in which these commitments are sought, implemented, and tracked. MaPP 6010.2 states that CDER's policy regarding Phase 4 commitments will be based on the following requirements:

- Phase 4 commitments and a schedule for fulfillment of those commitments should be agreed upon with the applicant prior to the approval of an application.

- The agency's approval letter should list all Phase 4 commitments and the schedule for completing each commitment.

- Relevant information regarding Phase 4 study commitments also should be documented in the administrative record. These might include, for example, study objectives, research designs, reporting frequency, and study report formats for clinical studies or test methodology, frequency of testing, and method of data analysis for chemistry commitments. If these details are not determined at the time of approval, this should be noted and a schedule for resolving the issues should be described in the approval letter.

- A Phase 4 tracking system linked to the Centerwide Oracle-based Management Information System (COMIS) will be used to monitor the status of Phase 4 commitments.

Just prior to, or at the time of, NDA approval, a division's project manager (i.e., consumer safety officer) will be responsible for assuring "that the applicant of the pending NDA submits a letter of commitment describing any Phase 4 studies they agree to conduct after approval of the application and the schedule for initiation and completion of those studies and submission of the study results," MaPP 6010.2 states.

For applications that receive accelerated reviews (Subpart H), the division must assure at this time that the Phase 4 study protocols are evaluated for their ability to meet the stated objectives and commitments. Phase 4 protocols for other applications may be submitted following approval, after which CDER must review the protocols "promptly (usually within 30 days)."

At least annually, a division's project manager must evaluate the status of outstanding voluntary Phase 4 commitments and, at least twice annually, must evaluate the status of outstanding Subpart H Phase 4 commitments. "For overdue outstanding commitments (some studies may be time-sensitive and need closer scrutiny), [the project manager must] generate what is called a 'Dunner Letter,'" which is a notification to the sponsor that it has failed to respond to a Phase 4 commitment.

Editor's note: "dunner" is a generic term used to refer to a letter that is not an action letter (i.e., approval, approvable, or not-approvable). MaPP 6010.2 does not address compliance actions beyond the issuance of dunner letters.

Chapter 13

The Supplemental NDA and Postapproval Changes to Marketed Drugs

Perhaps more than any other aspect of FDA drug regulation, requirements for supplemental new drug applications (SNDA) were affected by regulatory reform initiatives in the mid-1990s. While these reforms have not changed the nature or function of the supplemental NDA, they have fundamentally changed the situations in which such submissions are needed and have provided detailed clarifications regarding the data and information that they must include.

Following a drug's approval, the NDA holder can access and "supplement" the application's data to seek FDA authorization to market variations of the drug beyond those provided for in the approved NDA. SNDAs are submitted to the FDA when a firm wants to change an approved drug (e.g., dosage form, strength), its specifications, its manufacturing processes, its indication, or certain elements of its labeling. Federal regulations require that "the applicant... notify the Food and Drug Administration about each change in each condition established in an approved application beyond the variations already provided for in the application."

In practice, SNDAs are submitted to obtain regulatory authorization for a wide variety of modifications to approved drugs. These include proposed changes to an approved drug's:

- manufacturing and control methods (manufacturing supplement);

- dosage form or route of administration;

- indication (efficacy supplement);

- ingredients or strength;

- dosage schedule;

- labeling; and

- container and closure system.

Regulatory Reform and SNDAs

The most significant regulatory reforms affecting SNDAs address the review and approval of manufacturing changes. Although Congress proposed and considered legislation that would have established which manufacturing changes require preapproval through SNDAs, these initiatives ultimately failed.

In early 1995, however, the FDA promised to issue a guidance document that would "reduce the number of manufacturing changes that require preapproval by FDA." The agency fulfilled this commitment by publishing a November 1995 guideline that established submission requirements for a variety of postapproval manufacturing and drug composition changes to immediate release solid oral dosage form drugs (see discussion below). Specifically, the guideline exempted more types of manufacturing process, site, equipment, and formulation changes from the requirement for FDA approval prior to implementation.

During 1995, Congress also considered various proposals to reform the FDA's standards and processes for approving new uses of already marketed drugs. Based on the position that FDA requirements discouraged many firms from pursuing SNDAs for new uses even though many of the uses were quite common in medical practice, the legislative initiatives and related proposals sought to ease the FDA's requirements for supplemental indications. One legislative proposal, for example, would have given medical societies the ability to petition the FDA to approve new indications for new therapies, and to support the petitions with information establishing that a specific unapproved use has existed in clinical practice for a minimum of five years, that the new use is prevalent, and that the use is standard medical practice.

In March 1997, following months of industry/FDA negotiations and agency efforts to find ways to encourage drug companies to develop and submit SNDAs for new uses of approved drugs, the FDA unveiled what it called the *New Use Initiative*. The goal of this initiative was "to speed up the development of new and supplemental uses of medications by using all available data to determine the effectiveness of drugs and biological products."

Essentially, the agency's *New Use Initiative* comprises two draft guidances that clarify its efficacy data requirements for new and supplemental uses. The guidances establish that the FDA is willing to accept efficacy data from a variety of different sources (i.e., not just from two pivotal trials) as the basis for approving supplemental uses (see discussion below).

When To Submit Supplemental versus Original NDAs

In past years, sponsors often had the option of submitting either full or supplemental NDAs for drug changes that required FDA approval before implementation. Some companies maintained that SNDAs had certain advantages over full submissions, while others held that original NDAs should have been submitted whenever possible.

Under policies instituted as part of the FDA's user-fee program, however, such options no longer exist in most cases. Because different fees apply to certain original and supplemental NDAs, the agency now specifies when each type of application should be used. In a guidance document entitled *Separate Marketing Applications and Clinical Data for Purposes of Assessing User Fees Under the Prescription Drug User Fee Act of 1992*, the FDA specifies when original and supplemental NDAs are appropriate for changes to approved products:

1. Changes in the composition of an approved product to support a change in the dosage form or route of administration should be submitted in separate original NDAs. Route of administration changes in which the new product remains quantitatively and qualitatively identical to the approved product in composition (e.g., an injectable liquid dosage form intended for use by the intravenous and intraperitoneal routes) can be submitted in SNDAs, however. Also eligible for SNDAs are dosage form changes in which the new

product is identical to the approved product in quantitative and qualitative composition (e.g., a sterile liquid in a single dose vial that is intended for use as either an injectable or an inhalation solution).

2. Modifications to an approved product that are based on chemistry, manufacturing, or controls data and bioequivalence or other studies (e.g., safety and immunogenicity) and that change the strength or concentration, change the manufacturing process, equipment or facility, or change the formulation (e.g., different excipients) should be submitted as supplements to an approved application. Ordinarily, such modifications do not warrant a new original application unless they involve a change in the dosage form or route of administration.

3. Requests for approval of a new indication, or a modification of a previously approved indication, should each be submitted individually in a separate supplement to an approved NDA. According to the FDA, "each indication is considered a separate change for which a separate supplement should be submitted. The policy allows FDA to approve each indication when it is ready for approval rather than delaying approval until the last of a group of indications is ready to be approved."

The FDA's user-fee policies have several other implications for SNDAs. First, sponsors of supplements that require clinical data to support approval must pay user fees for such applications.

On the other hand, the FDA's user-fee program also provides SNDAs with a significantly higher level of review priority. Under the program, for example, the agency has the following goals for SNDAs submitted in fiscal year 1997 (October 1, 1996 - September 30, 1997): to review 90% of priority supplements within 6 months, 90% of standard supplements within 12 months, and 90% of manufacturing supplements within 6 months.

Supplemental NDA Submission Requirements

No universal SNDA data submission requirements exist. The change proposed in an SNDA directly determines the testing and submission requirements.

Federal regulations state that "the information required in the supplement is limited to that needed to support the change."

Obviously, changes to a drug's indication, ingredients, or route of administration are likely to require clinical data to prove the product's safety and effectiveness. In contrast, some modifications to a drug's manufacturing or control methods may require only that the change be described and supported by stability and bioequivalence data. Therefore, SNDAs can range from minor filings to documents longer and more complex than some NDAs. All SNDAs, however, are required to provide an archival copy and a review copy that include an application form, appropriate technical sections, samples, and labeling.

The nature of the change proposed in an SNDA also determines when the application must be submitted and whether the sponsor must await FDA approval prior to implementing the change. In its regulations and relevant guidance documents, the FDA has categorized postapproval changes into various classes. Those changes that are most likely to affect the FDA's conclusions about the approved drug's safety and effectiveness require the submission, and FDA approval, of an SNDA before being instituted. Less significant changes do not require FDA approval, but call for either the submission of an SNDA at the time of implementation or a description in the sponsor's annual report.

SUPAC and SNDAs for Manufacturing Changes

The FDA's 1995 guidance document entitled *Immediate Release Solid Oral Dosage Forms; Scale-Up and Post Approval Changes (SUPAC-IR): Chemistry, Manufacturing and Controls; In Vitro Dissolution Testing; In Vivo Bioequivalence Documentation* has revised the SNDA requirements applicable to postapproval manufacturing changes for relevant drug products. Non-manufacturing related changes for immediate release solid oral dosage form drugs and all postapproval changes for other drugs are subject to general agency requirements (see discussion below).

The November 1995 document was the first in what the FDA hopes will be a series of SUPAC guidances for various dosage forms. At this writing, the agency was developing separate SUPAC guidances for modified release, semi-solid, transdermal, and sterile solution dosage form drugs.

The published SUPAC-IR guidance classified postapproval manufacturing changes into as many as three levels—Levels 1, 2, and 3—and established postmarketing reporting requirements for changes within each of these levels (i.e., SNDA, annual report). The agency has defined these levels broadly for each type of change. The following levels apply to component, composition, and process changes, for example:

Level 1: changes that are unlikely to have any detectable impact on formulation, quality, or performance.

Level 2: changes that could have a significant impact on formulation, quality, or performance.

Level 3: changes that are likely to have a significant impact on formulation, quality, or performance.

It is worth noting that some types of changes, such as manufacturing changes, have only two levels.

For each type of postapproval manufacturing change addressed by the document—components and composition changes, manufacturing site changes, scale up/scale down of manufacture, and manufacturing process/equipment changes—the level of the change and the testing and reporting requirements (e.g., SNDA, annual report) associated with the change are established.

Generally, the less significant changes—most Level 1 changes, for example—require only a description in an annual report. The more important changes—most Level 3 changes, for instance—call for the submission and FDA approval of an SNDA prior to implementation (i.e., a "prior approval" supplement). Many Level 2 changes can be implemented simultaneously with an applicant's submission of an SNDA, called a "changes being effected" supplement.

It is worth noting, however, that the requirements differ for the various levels within each type of change. For example, in contrast to most other Level 3 changes, a Level 3 site change requires only the submission of a "changes being effected" supplement. Also, all scale up/scale down changes are categorized into Level 1 or Level 2. The examples of postapproval manufacturing

Submission Requirements for Various Postapproval Manufacturing Changes for Immediate Release Solid Oral Dosage Form Drugs

Changes Requiring an Approved SNDA Prior to Implementation

- Changes in the technical grade of the excipient (Level 2 components and composition change).

- Change in equipment to a different design and different operating principles (Level 2 equipment change).

- Change in the type of process used in the manufacture of the drug product, such as a change from wet granulation to direct compression of dry powder (Level 3 process change).

Changes Requiring a "Changes Being Effected" SNDA

- Site changes within a contiguous campus, or between facilities in adjacent city blocks, where the same equipment, standard operating procedures, environmental conditions and controls, and personnel common to both manufacturing sites are used, and where no changes are made to the manufacturing batch records, except for administrative information and the location of the facility (Level 2 site change).

- A change in manufacturing site to a different campus (Level 3 site change).

- Changes in batch size beyond a factor of 10 times the size of the pilot/biobatch, where: (1) the equipment used to produce the test batch(es) is of the same design and operating principles; (2) the batch(es) is (are) manufactured in full compliance with CGMPs; and (3) the same standard operating procedures are used on the test batch(es) and on the full-scale production batch(es) (Level 2 site change).

–continued–

289

–continued from previous page–

- Process changes, including changes such as mixing times and operating speeds outside of application/validation ranges (Level 2 process change).

Changes Requiring Only the Description of the Change in an Annual Report

- Changes in batch size, up to and including a factor of 10 times the size of the pilot/biobatch, where: (1) the equipment used to produce the test batch(es) is of the same design and operating principles; (2) the batch(es) is (are) manufactured in full compliance with CGMPs; and (3) the same standard operating procedures and controls, as well as the same formulation and manufacturing procedures, are used on the test batch(es) and on the full-scale production batch(es) (Level 1 batch size change).

- Deletion or partial deletion of an ingredient intended to affect the color or flavor of the drug product or a change in the ingredient of the printing ink to another approved ingredient (Level 1 components and composition change).

- Site changes within a single facility where the same equipment, standard operating procedures, environmental conditions (e.g., temperature and humidity) and controls, and personnel common to both manufacturing sites are used, and where no changes are made to the manufacturing batch records, except for administrative information and the location of the facility (Level 1 site change).

- Changes from nonautomated or nonmechanical equipment to automated or mechanical equipment to move ingredients and changes to alternative equipment of the same design and operating principles of the same or of a different capacity (Level 1 equipment change).

- Process changes, including changes such as mixing times and operating speeds within application/validation ranges (Level 1 process change).

changes are listed in the exhibit above according to the submission requirements facing each change (*Editor's note*: please keep in mind that the testing requirements for each change may differ even if the submission requirements are the same).

Since releasing the SUPAC-IR guidance, the agency has published two related documents: a 52-page draft manufacturing equipment addendum to the SUPAC-IR guidance and a February 1997 *Questions and Answers* letter to assist industry in interpreting the SUPAC-IR guidance's provisions.

Requirements for Non-SUPAC Postapproval Changes

To some degree, the SUPAC document has complicated any discussion attempting to characterize supplemental NDA requirements. As noted, the SUPAC document addresses just a subgroup of postapproval changes—manufacturing changes for immediate release solid oral dosage form products. Non-manufacturing-related changes (e.g., labeling, new indications) for this drug class and all postapproval changes for the remaining drug classes are still subject to existing FDA regulations.

Similar to the SUPAC-IR guidance, these regulations group postapproval changes into three classes: (1) changes requiring SNDAs that need FDA approval prior to implementation; (2) changes requiring SNDAs that do not need FDA approval prior to implementation; and (3) changes not requiring SNDAs.

Supplements Needing Prior FDA Approval Changes to an approved drug substance, drug product, or important elements of drug labeling require FDA approval before being implemented. If the sponsor believes that any delay in making the change would impose an extraordinary hardship, it can request that the FDA expedite the review of the application.

Drug Substance Changes Drug substance changes requiring FDA approval include any modifications that would:

- relax the limits for a specification;

- establish a new regulatory analytical method;

- delete a specification or regulatory analytical method;

- change the synthesis of the drug substance, including a change in solvents and a change in the route of synthesis; or

- involve a different facility or establishment in the manufacture of the drug substance, where: (a) the manufacturing process in the new facility or establishment differs materially from that in the former facility or establishment; or (b) the new facility or establishment has not received a satisfactory current good manufacturing practice (CGMP) inspection covering that manufacturing process within the previous two years.

Drug Product Changes Drug product changes requiring FDA approval include any modifications that would:

- add or delete an ingredient, or otherwise change the composition of the drug product, other than the deletion of an ingredient intended only to affect the color of the drug product;

- relax the limits for a specification;

- establish a new regulatory analytical method;

- delete a specification or regulatory analytical method;

- change the drug product's method of manufacture, including changing or relaxing an in-process control;

- change the facility or establishment, including a different contract laboratory or labeler, used to manufacture, process, or pack the drug product;

- change the container and closure system for the drug product (for example, glass to high density polyethylene-HDPE-or HDPE to polyvinyl chloride), or change a specification or regulatory analytical method for the container and closure system;

- change the size of the container, except for solid dosage forms, without a change in the container and closure system;

- extend the expiration date of the drug based on data obtained under a new or revised stability testing protocol that has not been approved in the application; or

- establish a new procedure for reprocessing a batch of the drug product that fails to meet specifications.

Significant Labeling Changes All significant drug labeling changes must be approved by the FDA before implementation. Although some labeling changes of lesser importance can be made prior to approval (see discussion below), the following modifications require FDA clearance:

- the addition of new indications;

- changes in dosage strengths;

- changes in dosage form; and

- changes in recommended dosage schedules.

Pursuing Supplemental Indications. SNDAs for new indications are more visible than most other types of supplements. Because these "efficacy supplements," as they are called, often propose therapeutically important new uses for approved drugs, they are given a higher regulatory priority than other SNDAs. For example, the FDA's review goal for priority efficacy supplements—six months for those submitted in fiscal year 1997—is identical to that for priority NDAs.

The FDA's requirements for efficacy supplements also came under fire during the regulatory reform movement in the mid-1990s. Following months of efforts to find ways to encourage companies to develop and submit SNDAs for new uses of approved drugs, the FDA unveiled its *New Use Initiative* in March 1997. This initiative is designed to give "industry clear guidance on whether the agency can determine that a drug is effective for a new use without requiring data from two new clinical trials. For example, in some cases, a drug's effectiveness can be extrapolated from existing efficacy data; it can be shown by evidence from a new single trial supported by already existing related clinical data; or it can be documented by adequate evidence from a single multi-center study."

The *New Use Initiative* comprises two draft guidelines—*Providing Clinical Evidence of Effectiveness for Human Drug and Biological Products* and *FDA Approval of New Cancer Treatment Uses for Marketed Drug and Biological Drugs.* These guidelines provide what might be the FDA's most detailed discussion to date on the agency's efficacy standards for new and supplemental indications (for a further discussion of these guidelines, see Chapter 6). Although these were both draft guidelines, FDA officials had promised in late 1996 to implement their general concepts upon publication.

Another FDA action affecting efficacy supplements was the agency's revision of its standards for the "pediatric use" section of drug labeling. In a December 1994 final rule, the agency established that NDA holders could support the inclusion of pediatric use information in drug labeling without data from controlled clinical trials in children. Under the regulation, the agency established that it would approve a drug for pediatric use "based on adequate and well-controlled studies in adults, with other information supporting pediatric use." The FDA has since supplemented the regulation with *Guidance for Industry: Content and Format for Pediatric Use Supplements.*

Although efficacy supplements are subject to specific review targets under the FDA's user-fee program, the applications receive one of the following six classifications:

SE1 (highest priority): A supplement proposing a new indication or a significant modification to an existing drug indication.

SE2: A supplement proposing a new dosage regimen, including an increase or decrease in daily dosage, or a change in frequency of administration.

SE3: A supplement proposing a new route of administration.

SE4: A supplement proposing a comparative efficacy or comparative pharmacokinetic claim naming another drug.

SE5: A supplement proposing a change expected to significantly affect the size of the patient population to be given the drug by broadening or narrowing the population.

SE6 (lowest priority): A supplement proposing a prescription-to-OTC marketing switch.

Editor's note: These classifications do not affect the review priority (i.e., applicable review time frame) assigned to efficacy supplements.

SNDAs Not Requiring Prior FDA Approval A sponsor may institute certain changes to an approved drug, its manufacturing process, or its labeling before submitting or obtaining FDA approval for an SNDA. When any of these changes are made, however, the sponsor must submit a supplemental application. The filing must "give a full explanation of the basis for the change, identify the date on which the change is made, and, if the change concerns labeling, include 12 copies of final printed labeling." Such changes include:

- changes that add a new specification or test method or that modify the methods, facilities (except a change to a new facility), or controls used to provide increased assurance that the drug will have the characteristics of identity, strength, quality, and purity that it purports or is represented to possess;

- labeling changes to add or strengthen a contraindication, warning, precaution, or adverse reaction;

- labeling modifications to add or strengthen a statement about drug abuse, dependence, or overdosage;

- labeling changes intended to promote the safe use of the product by adding or strengthening an instruction about dosage and administration;

- labeling changes to delete false, misleading, or unsupported indications for use or claims for effectiveness; and

- changes involving the use of a different facility or establishment to manufacture the drug substance, where: (a) the manufacturing process in the new facility or establishment does not differ materially from that in the former facilities or establishments; and (b) the new facility or establishment has received a satisfactory CGMP inspection within the previous two years covering that manufacturing process.

For such changes, the SNDA and its mailing cover should be marked: "Special Supplement-Changes Being Effected."

Changes Not Requiring SNDAs To avoid the submission of unnecessary SNDAs and the burdens that these applications would place on agency reviewing resources, the FDA exempts several types of minor changes from supplemental filing requirements. These modifications, however, must be reported and described in a sponsor's annual report. Exempted changes include:

- any modification made to comply with an official compendium;

- a change in the labeling regarding the description of the drug or the information about how it is supplied (changes in dosage strength or dosage form do not qualify);

- an editorial or other minor change in labeling;

- the deletion of an ingredient intended only to affect the drug's color;

- extension of the expiration date based upon full shelf-life data obtained from an approved protocol;

- a change in the container and closure system for the drug (except a change in container size for nonsolid dosage forms) based upon a showing of equivalency to the approved system under a protocol approved in the application or published in an official compendium;

- the addition or deletion of an alternate analytical method; and

- a change in the size of a container for a solid dosage form, without a change from one container and closure system to another.

Chapter 14

The FDA's Orphan Drug Development Program

Although orphan drugs represent only a minor percentage of the medicines prescribed in the United States, these products have gained an exceptionally high profile in recent decades. Early in the 1980s, for example, orphan drugs became not only the subject of major legislation, but the focus of an FDA office devoted solely to their development as well.

Regulatory, legal, and commercial controversies surrounding better-known orphan drugs, such as Genentech's human growth hormone and Amgen's erythropoietin, have done much to bring widespread attention to orphan products and industry efforts to develop and market these medicines. In part representing the government's response to these controversies, FDA regulations implementing the key elements of the orphan drug laws were released in December 1992.

Despite various legislative and judicial challenges, the FDA's orphan drug development program has stood largely intact over its 14-year history. The program was one of relatively few of the agency's drug approval-related activities that was not earmarked for reform under several FDA reform bills debated in the mid-1990s.[1] In addition, the U.S. orphan drugs program has been the model for similar programs in both Europe and Japan.[2]

The special problems and issues facing orphan product development are well documented. Orphan products are unique because they are potentially useful drugs, biologics, and antibiotics that have limited commercial value. There are several reasons why they may lack profit potential—for example, a product may be used to treat a disease with a small patient population, it may be used only in minute doses, or it may have an unfavorable patent status.

In the past, few companies were willing to invest in an experimental drug whose potential sales did not justify, or whose actual sales might not even recover, these expenditures. Individuals suffering from such rare conditions as Turner's Syndrome, central precocious puberty, acute graft v. host disease (GVHD), and cystinosis were caught between the medical reality that few others shared their plight and the economic reality that a drug's development can cost more than $200 million.

However, thanks to orphan drug legislation and the FDA's own efforts to shepherd these products through the development process, the 1980s and 1990s brought no dearth of firms willing to invest in orphan products. A recent study by the Tufts Center for the Study of Drug Development found that, in the first 13 years of the FDA's orphan drug development program, the agency granted 631 orphan designations involving 450 different drugs, 121 of which have been approved.

The FDA and Orphan Drugs: A Brief History

During the late 1970s, government leaders became increasingly concerned that the therapeutic abilities of many drugs went unexplored while millions of patients with one of an estimated 5,000 rare or orphan diseases went untreated. A 1979 report by the FDA-organized Interagency Task Force on Significant Drugs of Limited Commercial Value stated that, "whenever a drug has been identified as potentially life-saving or otherwise of unique major benefit to some patient, it is the obligation of society, as represented by government, to seek to make that drug available to that patient." The formal government response to the problem came several years later in the form of the Orphan Drug Act of 1983, a law that provides incentives for manufacturers to develop and market orphan products, including drugs, antibiotics and biologics.

Responsibility for administering the law was given to the FDA's Office of Orphan Product Development (OPD), which was founded in 1982. Today, the 20-person office continues to encourage orphan drug development by awarding financial incentives available under the law to sponsors of qualifying products, coordinating the efforts of investigators and drug companies, acting as a mediator between orphan sponsors and the FDA's drug and biologic review divisions, administering a grant program, and performing other promotional and educational activities.

The Importance of Orphan Drug Designation

The incentives offered under the Orphan Drug Act are seen as the keys to the development of future orphan products. The law provides major financial and marketing incentives to companies and investigators willing to research and develop qualified products. But before outlining the orphan product incentives themselves, it is worthwhile discussing orphan drug designation, a status that drugs must attain to become eligible for the most valuable incentives.

Tax advantages and marketing exclusivity are perhaps the two most important incentives that the U.S. Congress made available to orphan product sponsors through the Orphan Drug Act of 1983. Since Congress did not want these incentives to be awarded indiscriminately, it wrote into law that only products meeting specific criteria would be eligible for the two principal benefits.

Today, there are at least five basic eligibility criteria for orphan drug designation. To be eligible, a product:

- Must be a drug, biologic, or antibiotic. Medical devices, medical foods, and other products do not qualify for designation.

- Must have a sponsor that is testing or is planning to test the product for use in a "rare disease or condition." According to the Orphan Drug Act, a rare disease or condition is one that: "A) affects less than 200,000 persons in the United States, or B) affects more than 200,000 persons in the United States but for which there is no reasonable expectation that the costs of developing and making available in the United States a drug for such disease or condition will be recovered from sales in the United States for such drug." The under-200,000 provision applies not only to diseases or conditions with a total patient prevalence of less than 200,000, but to subpopulations of more common diseases as well. The FDA insists that sponsors of orphan products for such indications be able to test the product in,

299

and clearly label the product for, use in the relevant subpopulation. For prophylactic products such as vaccines and blood products, the figure of 200,000 applies to the number of patients receiving the product *per year*.

- Must not have been previously approved under a new drug application (NDA) or product license application (PLA) for the disease or condition for which the sponsor is seeking orphan status. In other words, eligible products include both new chemical entities (NCE) —substances never before approved as medicines in the United States—and products that have been approved for any indication other than the indication for which the sponsor is seeking orphan designation. When granted by the FDA, designation applies only to the subject product for use in the specific rare disease or condition.

- Must be shown to have an adequate pharmacologic rationale for use in the orphan indication. This requirement is not one that the FDA enforces rigidly. Dr. Marion Finkel, former director of the FDA's Office of Orphan Products Development, stated in a 1984 speech that "a plausible hypothesis backed by some experimental evidence would be sufficient for orphan drug designation."

- Must not be the subject of a submitted marketing application prior to the filing of an orphan status request. This requirement was added in mid-1988 through the Orphan Drug Amendment Act of 1987. The amendment was an attempt by Congress to reserve marketing exclusivity and tax incentives for those firms whose initial intentions were to develop orphan drugs, and to withhold the incentives from companies that pursue designation simply as an afterthought to optimize the profitability of their products.

Obtaining Orphan Drug Designation Congress gave the FDA the authority to determine which drugs meet the criteria outlined above. To have its product designated, a firm must submit to the FDA an application called a *Request for Designation of a Drug as an Orphan Drug*.

Orphan Drug Designation and Approval Statistics, 1990–1996							
	1990	1991	1992	1993	1994	1995	1996
Orphan Designation Applications Received*	132	84	77	72	81	71	77
Orphan Designations Made*	88	81	58	65	58	57	60
# of Orphan Drug Approvals	12	24	14*	13*	11*	9*+	23*

* drugs and biologics
+ New Molecular Entities only

Source: FDA

The FDA's 1992 orphan drug regulations specify nine basic submission requirements for designation requests. According to these regulations, a sponsor must submit two copies of a completed, dated, and signed designation request that contains the following:

- A statement that the sponsor requests orphan-drug designation for a rare disease or condition, which must be identified with specificity.

- The name and address of the sponsor; the name and address of the sponsor's primary contact person and/or resident agent, including the person's title, address, and telephone number; the drug's generic and trade name (if any); and the name and address of the source of the drug if it is not manufactured by the sponsor.

- A description of the rare disease or condition for which the drug is being or will be investigated, the proposed indication or indications for the drug, and the reasons why such therapy is needed.

- A description of the drug, and a discussion of the scientific rationale for the use of the drug for the rare disease or condition, including all data from nonclinical laboratory studies, clinical investigations, and other relevant data that are available to the sponsor, whether positive, negative, or inconclusive. Copies of pertinent unpublished and published papers are also required.

- When the sponsor of a drug that is otherwise the same as an already-approved orphan drug seeks orphan-drug designation for the same rare disease or condition, an explanation of why the proposed variation may be "clinically superior" to the first drug (see discussion below).

- When a drug is under development only for a subset of persons with a particular disease or condition, a demonstration that this patient subset is medically plausible.

- A summary of the regulatory status and marketing history of the drug in the United States and in foreign countries (e.g., IND and marketing application status and dispositions; the specific uses under investigation in each country; the indication(s) for which the drug is approved in foreign countries; and any "adverse regulatory actions" that have been taken against the drug in any country).

- Documentation, with appended authoritative references, to demonstrate: (1) that the disease or condition for which the drug is intended affects fewer than 200,000 people in the United States or, if the drug is a vaccine, diagnostic drug, or preventive drug, that the persons to whom the drug will be administered in the United States are fewer than 200,000 per year as specified in federal regulations, or (2) for a drug intended for diseases or conditions affecting 200,000 or more people, or for a vaccine, diagnostic drug, or preventive drug to be administered to 200,000 or more persons per year in the United States, that there is no reasonable expectation that costs of research and development of the drug for the indication can be recovered by sales of the drug in the United States (e.g., cost data, a statement and justification of future development costs the sponsor expects to incur, and an estimate of, and justification for, the expected revenues from drug sales during its first seven years of marketing).

- A statement as to whether the sponsor submitting the request is the "real party in interest" in the development and the intended or actual production and sales of the product.

Drug sponsors may request orphan drug designation any time prior to the submission of a marketing application for the product. Once a request for designation is submitted, the FDA's OPD has 60 days to issue a decision. In most cases, the office handles the review itself, although it may refer certain technical or scientific questions to one of the agency's drug or biological product review divisions. Within 14 months of a drug's designation, and annually thereafter, the sponsor must submit to OPD a brief progress report that includes a short account of the progress of drug development, the investigational plan for the coming year, and any changes that may affect the product's orphan-drug status.

When OPD denies these designation requests, the reasons range from poorly prepared designation request documents to the selection of invalid subpopulations. Before sponsors submit designation requests, OPD officials recommend that companies educate themselves about designation request submission requirements, and have a defined rationale for the use of a drug for a selected indication, a reasonable strategy for the product's development, and a highly specific indication and patient population that can be studied and for which the drug can be labeled if ultimately approved.

The practical advantages of orphan drug designation essentially are limited to tax incentives and marketing exclusivity. Although some believe that designation makes FDA drug reviewers more aware of a specific orphan drug, there are probably no real advantages during the drug approval process (see discussion below). FDA staffers claim that many sponsors are surprised to learn that orphan drug designation itself affords no competitive advantages. For example, a drug's designation does not stop another firm from requesting and obtaining a designation for the same drug and indication. Also, the seven-year marketing exclusivity is awarded to the first designated orphan drug to obtain marketing approval, not designation.

There seem to be few, if any, disadvantages to obtaining orphan drug designation. Having to prepare a designation request and having general information published about the drug upon designation are, in many cases, small inconveniences when compared to the benefits designation offers.

Still, some drug firms do not pursue designation when developing a product that would qualify as an orphan drug. In some cases, these firms do not seek orphan designation because they view it as their corporate responsibility as health-care companies to develop these products. Others speculate that companies, knowing that orphan drugs may prove useful in additional, more profitable ways, do not want the possible public relations burden of profiting from a drug developed using public monies.

A Look at Orphan Drug Incentives

Currently, the Orphan Drug Act and the FDA offer orphan drug sponsors four primary incentives: marketing exclusivity, tax credits, protocol assistance, and grants and contracts.

Marketing Exclusivity Marketing exclusivity may be the single most important incentive to orphan drug sponsors. Under the law, the first sponsor to obtain marketing approval for a designated orphan drug is awarded a seven-year period of marketing exclusivity for the product. During this period, no other sponsor can obtain FDA approval for the drug for the orphan indication. The agency can, however, approve identical versions of the drug for other indications.

The rewards of marketing exclusivity are linked directly to FDA approval. Although orphan designation makes a drug eligible for exclusivity, that exclusivity is not awarded until a product's NDA is approved. Therefore, several identical products could be designated for the same orphan indication, but only the first company to receive approval will obtain marketing exclusivity rights.

Marketing exclusivity has at least two main advantages over traditional patent protection. First, designation and product approval are virtually the only eligibility requirements for exclusivity. The product need not be new or unobvious, or meet any of the criteria used in determining a drug's patent eligibility. Because of this, natural substances and other products that are unable to receive any form of patent protection are eligible for marketing exclusivity.

The second significant advantage marketing exclusivity has over patent protection is that its life begins on the date of approval. Although a patent award grants a 17-year monopoly, a drug's patent life begins on the date the patent is awarded, and several years of that life are generally lost during the drug testing and evaluation process. Since exclusivity is awarded upon approval, its seven-year life is not eroded during product development.

While marketing exclusivity may be the most important orphan drug incentive, it is also the most complex. In the past, some critics have argued that the FDA's inability or unwillingness to deny marketing approval to drugs that are similar in structure to drugs that have already been awarded marketing exclusivity has unfairly denied orphan product innovators the protection afforded to them under the Orphan Drug Act.

In fact, the FDA's criteria for determining when two orphan drugs designated for the same indication are considered identical have been tested at least three times, most recently in 1996. During the late 1980s, the FDA faced a pair of widely publicized cases involving two human growth hormone products and two erythropoietin products. The issue, in both cases, involved the FDA's then-unpublished criteria for differentiating between medical compounds, particularly biologics and biotechnology products, for the purposes of marketing exclusivity.

Then, in December 1992, the FDA's orphan drug regulations first established the conditions under which the agency would consider two drugs to be the same and, therefore, take action to block the approval of the second designated product:

"(i) If it is a drug composed of small molecules, a drug that contains the same active moiety as a previously approved drug and is intended for the same use as the previously approved drug, even if the particular ester or salt (including a salt with hydrogen or coordination bonds) or other noncovalent derivative such as a complex, chelate or clathrate has not been previously approved, except that if the subsequent drug can be shown to be clinically superior to the first drug, it will not be considered to be the same drug.

(ii) If it is a drug composed of large molecules (macromolecules), a drug that contains the same principal molecular structural features (but not necessarily all of the same structural features) and is intended for the same use as a previously approved drug, except that, if the subsequent drug can be shown to be clinically superior, it will not be considered the same drug. This criterion will be applied as follows to different kinds of macromolecules:

(A) Two protein drugs would be considered the same if the only differences in structure between them were due to post-translational events, or infidelity of translation or transcription, or were minor differences in amino acid sequence; other potentially important differences, such as different glycosylation patterns or different tertiary structures, would not cause the drugs to be considered different unless the differences were shown to be clinically superior.

(B) Two polysaccharide drugs would be considered the same if they had identical saccharide repeating units, even if the number of units were to vary and even if there were postpolymerization modifications, unless the subsequent drug could be shown to be clinically superior.

(C) Two polynucleotide drugs consisting of two or more distinct nucleotides would be considered the same if they had an identical sequence of purine and pyrimidine bases (or their derivatives) bound to an identical sugar backbone (ribose, deoxyribose, or modifications of these sugars), unless the subsequent drug were shown to be clinically superior.

(D) Closely related, complex partly definable drugs with similar therapeutic intent, such as two live viral vaccines for the same indication, would be considered the same unless the subsequent drug were shown to be clinically superior."

These regulations established the concept of clinical superiority, and made it the criterion upon which the agency could base its approval of a second designated drug that is otherwise identical to, and is marketed for the same indication as, a previously approved designated orphan drug. To be considered clinically superior, a drug must offer a "significant therapeutic advantage" over the existing product. According to FDA regulations, this advantage can be based upon evidence of greater effectiveness, improved product safety in a significant segment of the target population, or, in exceptional cases, "a major contribution to patient care."

The FDA's application of these provisions was challenged in early 1996, when Berlex Laboratories filed suit to block the agency's approval of Biogen's Avonex (interferon beta), a competitor to Berlex' Betaseron (interferon beta), which was already marketed as a treatment for relapsing/remitting multiple sclerosis. Based on what is viewed as a safety advantage—fewer injection site reactions—the agency approved Avonex, stating that "a small demonstrated improvement in efficacy or diminution in adverse reactions may be sufficient to allow a finding of clinical superiority." In late 1996, the U.S. District Court dismissed the Berlex suit.

Tax Credits Designated orphan drugs are eligible for a 50 percent tax credit for funds spent on clinical development. Therefore, a firm can subtract directly from its annual tax bill one-half of the money spent on the clinical testing of an orphan drug.

However, there are several important limitations to the tax credit incentive:

- Sponsors can receive credits only for clinical testing conducted within the United States. The one principal exception to this is a situation in which the sponsor must go outside the United States to find the patients necessary to conduct the trial.

- The credits can be used only for clinical testing actually paid for and conducted by the sponsor. For example, a sponsor could not receive credits for another company's testing that is referenced in the sponsor's drug application.

- The credits are available only for products that are formally designated by the FDA.

- The credit can be applied only to testing conducted for the orphan indication for which a drug is designated.

• Tax credits do not apply to nonclinical testing. OPD staffers claim that this can be a problem, since basic animal toxicity and carcinogenicity testing alone can cost well over a million dollars.

Through the enactment of the Small Business Job Protection Act of 1996, Congress addressed what was, at least for many biotechnology and other fledgling companies, perhaps the most notable limitation to the Orphan Drug Act's tax incentives: Originally, tax credits were only beneficial to companies that were profitable. Under previous law, orphan product tax credits could be applied against taxes on profits, but could not be used to increase a company's losses or carried forward into a year in which the company would post profits.

Tax code revisions made under the Small Business Job Protection Act permit companies to carry forward tax credits into a year in which they can be applied against profits. The law's provisions allow credits to be carried forward for 15 years.

The orphan drug tax credit provisions must be reauthorized periodically by Congress. At this writing, Congress was considering legislation that would make the provisions permanent.

Protocol Assistance Protocol assistance is an incentive for which orphan designation is unnecessary. If a sponsor can show the FDA that a drug will ultimately be used for a rare disease or condition, the agency provides written recommendations on the nonclinical and clinical studies needed for the product's approval.

To obtain protocol assistance, a sponsor must submit a formal request providing information on the drug, including its intended use, available test data, regulatory and marketing status, and proposed testing plans. The FDA's 1992 orphan drug regulations specify 16 content requirements for such requests. OPD staffers warn that, unless sponsors ask specific questions in these requests, firms are likely to receive extremely vague recommendations. Protocol recommendations are made by product review divisions within CDER.

FDA Grants and Contracts The Orphan Drug Act authorizes the U.S. Congress to appropriate funds for grants and contracts to physicians, companies, and others who are developing orphan drugs. In fiscal year 1997, the Office of Orphan Product Development was granted $11 million for such purposes.

More common than contracts, grants are awarded to university-based investigators and some smaller companies, particularly biotechnology firms, for the clinical testing of orphan drugs. Contract funds, on the other hand, are available to investigators and companies that agree to conduct testing for a drug or in a therapeutic area of particular interest to the FDA.

The FDA Approval Process: Advantages for Orphan Drugs?

Generally, orphan products receive no preferential treatment in terms of testing and submission requirements, and face the same safety and effectiveness criteria and review processes as undesignated products. FDA staffers do claim, however, that the agency will modify the drug testing and approval process for orphan products when appropriate. In the past, issues such as the availability of patients with orphan conditions and the lack of competitive therapies have forced the agency to consider alternative testing requirements and review criteria.

NDAs submitted for orphan products are reviewed within one of the FDA's drug review divisions. There, reviewers evaluate products strictly on the basis of safety, efficacy, and risk-benefit analyses. Although the product's status as an orphan drug may appear to be of little or no benefit, OPD staffers do work to make agency reviewers more sensitive to the special issues that orphan products present.

One advantage that many orphan drugs have over other products is that they often receive prioritized reviews. This is related not to the fact that the products are designated orphan drugs, but that they are frequently the only treatments available for certain conditions. Because of this, the FDA generally classifies them as high-priority drugs, and expedites their review. However, the FDA has denied at least one petition requesting that all orphan drugs automatically receive the FDA's highest review priority. In 1996, for example, 2 of the 7 NME orphan drugs approved by CDER were not classified as priority products.

Historically, approval times for orphan drugs have compared favorably with those of conventional drugs, according to FDA statistics (see exhibit below).

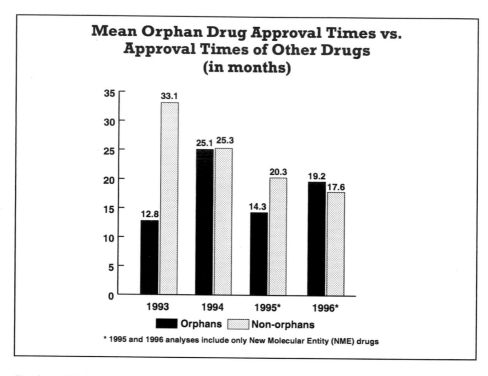

Mean Orphan Drug Approval Times vs. Approval Times of Other Drugs (in months)

■ Orphans ▨ Non-orphans

* 1995 and 1996 analyses include only New Molecular Entity (NME) drugs

During 1996, however, CDER approved NDAs for 7 orphan NMEs in an average of 19.2 months compared to 17.6 months for all NME-NDAs approved in that year.

What is the OPD's role in the review of an orphan drug? The office actively monitors the progress of orphan reviews, but has no formal authority in product approvals or real influence in the decisions of FDA reviewers. However, OPD staffers do attend FDA-sponsor meetings and act as mediators to help resolve special regulatory problems presented by orphan drugs.

References

1. Shulman, S.R. and Manocchia, M. (Tufts Center for the Study of Drug Development), *The U.S. Orphan Drug Program: 1983-1995*. In press.

2. Ibid.

Chapter 15

CDER's Bioresearch Monitoring Program

Since its regulatory decisions are based directly on research data, CDER has a vested interest in the accuracy and validity of clinical and nonclinical study results. Under CDER's Bioresearch Monitoring Program, agency investigators conduct on-site inspections of laboratories, clinics, and offices where scientific data are developed and stored.

Specifically, CDER inspects clinical investigators, drug firms, IRBs, and nonclinical laboratories to ensure: (1) that data submitted in product applications are accurate and valid; and (2) that the rights and welfare of human subjects are protected in clinical studies. During these inspections, FDA investigators evaluate how well sponsors, monitors, contract research organizations, IRBs, and clinical and nonclinical investigational site staff have fulfilled their various responsibilities and commitments under GCP, study protocols, and other standards and regulatory requirements.

While clinical investigators are the focus of most CDER bioresearch inspections, there are several reasons why inspection results are of great importance to clinical trial sponsors. First, drug sponsors are ultimately responsible for the conduct of clinical studies, and FDA inspections are designed to determine how well sponsors perform in that role. Secondly, these inspections, should they uncover serious problems, can result in the agency's rejection of data essential to a drug's approval.

Like virtually all other CDER drug review and compliance efforts, the Bioresearch Monitoring Program has been affected by the agency's prescription drug user fee program. Since the center faces mandated deadlines for NDA reviews, preapproval bioresearch monitoring inspections must be conducted within short time frames so that inspection results may be evaluated promptly. The compressed inspectional time frames have presented new challenges for FDA field investigators.

In addition, CDER reviewers and clinical investigations staff have been forced to carefully scrutinize the need for various inspectional assignments. Therefore, although inspectional activity may have risen in recent years because the agency is approving more NDAs, the number of studies and sites inspected per application may be lower today than in the past.

A Brief History of the Bioresearch Monitoring Program

The origin of the FDA's authority to inspect research data and related records lies in the Food, Drug and Cosmetic (FD&C) Act. The law states that every person required to maintain records must, upon the FDA's request, allow access to clinical data for review and copying. FDA regulations and Form FDA-1572 *Statement of Investigator*, which clinical investigators sign before undertaking the study of an investigational drug, state that "...the investigator will make such records available for inspection and copying."

Because of physicians' importance in the development and collection of clinical safety and efficacy data, inspections of investigators represent the core of CDER's Bioresearch Monitoring Program. FDA inspections of clinical investigators began in 1962, although only three inspections were conducted by 1965. The agency expanded its efforts in the years following and established a four-person office to organize and conduct inspections. Since government authorities outside the FDA believed that only physicians should inspect other physicians, however, inspectional activities were limited (i.e., only seven or eight inspections were conducted annually).

By 1972, the U.S. government had gained a new respect for the importance and abilities of FDA inspectors. As a result, the FDA initiated a survey of 162 commercially sponsored clinical investigators, 70 noncommercial clinical investigators, and 15 manufacturers. The results of this multi-year study, and increased FDA staff and budget, led to the founding of the agency's Bioresearch Monitoring Program in June 1977.

Although this chapter focuses on clinical investigator and sponsor/monitor compliance activities, today's Bioresearch Monitoring Program consists of five separate compliance inspection programs, each designed to evaluate the activities of a key entity in the conduct of a scientific study:

- Clinical Investigator Compliance Program;

- Sponsor/Monitor Compliance Program;

- Institutional Review Board (IRB) Compliance Program;

- Nonclinical Laboratory Compliance Program (for information on the inspection of nonclinical laboratories, see Chapter 3); and

- *In Vivo* Bioequivalence Compliance Program

These inspectional programs are managed by three branches within CDER's Division of Scientific Investigations: the Clinical Investigations Branch, the GLP and Bioequivalence Investigations Branch, and the Human Subject Protection Team.

The Clinical Investigator Compliance Program

As stated previously, inspections of clinical investigators represent the core of CDER's Bioresearch Monitoring Program. CDER has three separate investigator inspection programs:

- Study Oriented Inspection Program;

- Investigator Oriented Inspection Program; and

- Bioequivalency/Bioavailability Inspection Program.

Study Oriented Inspection Program Formerly called the Data Audit Program, the Study Oriented Inspection Program is a routine surveillance effort that involves the inspection of about 400 clinical investigators per year. During these inspections, which are conducted during an NDA's review, an FDA field inspector looks at the conduct of the study and performs a data audit. In evaluating the investigator's conduct of a clinical study, the inspector considers several factors:

- what the investigator, each of his/her staffers, and others did during the study;

- the degree of delegation of authority;

- when and where specific aspects of the study were performed;

- how and where data were recorded;

- how the drug substance was stored and accounted for;

- the monitor's interaction with the physician;

- evidence that proper informed consent was obtained from subjects; and

- evidence that IRB approval was obtained for studies performed.

Targeting Investigators and Studies for Data Audits

Inspection assignments for the data audit program are made by an application's reviewing medical officer in consultation with CDER's Division of Scientific Investigations. To determine which clinical investigators and studies should be inspected, the FDA uses a stratified sampling system that has the following priorities (listed in descending order):

1) studies important to the evaluation of a pending NDA;

2) studies submitted in support of new claims in supplemental NDAs;

3) important studies submitted in support of over-the-counter (OTC) drug claims;

4) studies conducted under maturing INDs;

5) studies conducted to upgrade labeling claims for old drugs found to be less than effective; and

6) studies conducted under noncommercial INDs.

In the typical audit, data submitted in an NDA are compared with the on-site records that should support their validity. On-site records to which an FDA inspector must be given access include a physician's office records, hospital records, and various laboratory reports. Records obtained prior to the initiation, and following the completion, of the study may be reviewed and copied.

Because of the inspectional program's nature, CDER's Clinical Investigations Branch (CIB) does not publicize its criteria for selecting studies and sites for routine inspections. Obviously, however, a particular study's importance to the approval decision will have a direct bearing on its likelihood of being inspected.

The branch also uses a sampling method for determining the number of sites within a particular study to be inspected, although the number is often influenced by other factors, including a protocol's complexity. CDER drug reviewers and CIB staff will also consider the number of patients at a site (i.e., sites with the most patients), the number of adverse experiences reported (i.e., sites with far fewer or greater reports), and the number of dropouts at a site. At this writing, CDER was developing an internal policies and procedures manual to describe the study and site selection and assignment process.

When the FDA has targeted key clinical studies and sites for inspection, agency staffers send a field inspector an "assignment package," which includes copies of a representative case report form (CRF), case report form tabulations, the protocol, and other pertinent information. The assignment package will indicate the number of subject records to be inspected at the site. If the field inspector discovers potential problems, he or she can then inspect other site records.

Due to the nature of physicians' work and schedules, inspections are made by appointment. Therefore, investigators are alerted as to which study is to be audited, and are given the opportunity to locate, collect, and organize all relevant records.

Because sponsors increasingly are relying on foreign data in their drug applications, CDER is now conducting significantly more inspections of foreign clinical investigators per year. In fiscal year 1996, for example, CDER conducted double the number of foreign site inspections than it had in any previous year. From 1980 through mid-1996, the center had conducted 190 foreign inspections, almost 60 percent of which were undertaken since 1993.

Cumulative Results of CDER Study Oriented (Surveillance)[1] Inspections of Clinical Investigators (6/1/77–3/20/97)

4910 surveillance inspections have been issued since 6/1/77*

4764 have been received to date. Of these:

Cancellations	322	Reviewed	4335
Washouts	123	Under Review	30

Classifications (New classification structure as of 1/1/94)	No.	% of 4305
Number of investigators in full compliance; no deficiencies noted (NAI)	966	22
Number of investigators with objectionable practices that do not represent major departures from regulations (VAI)	2972	70
Number of investigators where objectionable conditions or practices represent significant departures from regulations (OAI)**	337	8

Most Common Deficiencies*

Inadequate patient consent form	2134	50
Failure to adhere to protocol	1330	31
Inadequate and inaccurate records	1105	26
Inadequate drug accountability	854	20

Other Deficiencies

Failure to keep IRB informed of changes, progress	316	7
Inappropriate follow-up of adverse reactions	125	3
Unapproved concomitant therapy	115	3
Problems with records availability	110	3
Failure to obtain IRB approval if necessary	100	2
Failure to list additional investigators on Form 1572	81	2
Failure to obtain patient consent****	49	1
Inappropriate payment to volunteers	28	1
Submission of false data	24	1
Inappropriate delegation of authority	12	-
Commercialization of drug	10	-
Use of drug before obtaining IND status	4	-
Subjects receiving simultaneous investigational drugs	5	-

[1]Note: Previous category of "surveillance," inspections is changed to "study-oriented" but the new category is not exactly parallel.

*Included are 68 biologics inspections conducted between 10/1/85 and 1/1/88. **Includes warning letters as of 1/1/94. ***One inspection may contain no deficiencies or several deficiencies. Therefore, the total of percentages will not equal 100. ****FY 77-80 summary contained a category "problems with patient consent" that has been included under "inadequate patient consent form."

Source: FDA

The most common locations of these clinical trial site inspections include Canada (48 inspections), United Kingdom (27), France (18), and Germany (13). CDER generally will inspect a foreign-based investigator only when data from that foreign site are pivotal to a drug's approval.

"Investigator Oriented" Inspection Program The "investigator oriented" site inspection is, in most respects, similar to the study oriented, or routine, inspection. Investigator oriented inspections are not routine, however, and may be initiated for one or more of several reasons:

- the investigator is suspected of impropriety;

- the investigator is responsible for a large volume of work, particularly if that work involves different medical disciplines;

- the investigator has done work outside his or her specialty;

- the investigator reports effectiveness for a drug that appears to be too optimistic when compared to the reports of other physicians studying the same drug;

- the investigator reports no toxicity or few adverse reactions when other physicians report numerous reactions of a certain type;

- the investigator seems to have too many patients with a given disease for the locale or the setting in which he or she practices;

- the investigator reports laboratory results that are consistent beyond the usual biologic variation or that are inconsistent with results submitted by other investigators;

- representatives of the sponsor have reported to the FDA that they are having difficulty obtaining case reports from the investigator, or that they have found the investigator to be deficient in some other manner;

- a routine audit revealed problems too serious to be handled by correspondence; or

Cumulative Results of CDER Investigator-Oriented (For Cause)[1] Inspections (6/1/77–3/20/97)

478 for cause inspections have been issued since 6/1/77*

469 have been received to date. Of these:

Cancellations	9	Reviewed	448
Washouts	6	Under Review	6

Classifications (New classification structure as of 1/1/94)†	No.	% of 434
Number of investigators in full compliance; no deficiencies noted (NAI)	109	25
Number of investigators with objectionable practices which do not represent major departures from regulations (VAI)	136	30
Number of investigators where objectionable conditions or practices represent significant departures from regulations (OAI)**	203	46

Most Common Deficiencies***	No.	%
Inadequate patient consent form	187	44
Failure to adhere to protocol	225	53
Inadequate and inaccurate records	225	52
Inadequate drug accountability	120	28

Other Deficiencies		
Failure to keep IRB informed of changes, progress	60	14
Unapproved concomitant therapy	47	11
Submission of false data	47	11
Problems with records availability	39	9
Inappropriate follow-up of adverse reactions	30	7
Inappropriate delegation of authority	21	5
Failure to list additional investigators on Form 1572	13	4
Subjects receiving simultaneous investigational drugs	11	3
Failure to obtain IRB approval if necessary	11	3
Use of drug before obtaining IND status	6	1
Failure to obtain patient consent*****	5	1
Commercialization of drug	3	1
Inappropriate payment to volunteers	0	–

[1]Note: Previous category of "for cause" inspections is changed to "investigator-oriented" but the new category is not exactly parallel.

* Included are 68 Biologics inspections conducted between 10/1/85–1/1/88. ** Includes warning letters as of 1/1/94.

*** One inspection may contain no deficiencies or several deficiencies. Therefore, the total of percentages will not equal 100. **** There are 22 missing or incomplete files for which no deficiencies could be abstracted. ***** FY 77-80 summary contained a category "problems with patient consent" that has been included under "inadequate patient consent form." † new classification structure as of 1/1/94.

Source: FDA

- the FDA receives letters or phone calls claiming violations of subject's rights, variations in protocol, or some other violation or noncompliance.

Investigator oriented inspections are usually conducted by a Clinical Investigations Branch reviewer and a field investigator. Although the procedures used parallel those of routine inspections, the inspection team probably reviews more data. For instance, the inspection team will probably evaluate more case reports—sometimes for the entire study—and may audit studies of more than one drug. Patient interviews may be conducted when there are questions as to whether a subject participated in a study, whether the subject had the condition being studied, or whether informed consent was obtained.

Bioequivalency/Bioavailability Inspection Program Bioequivalency/bioavailability inspections involve the inspection of both a clinical and an analytical facility. According to FDA staffers, these inspections are more important for the verification of biopharmaceutic data submitted for generic drugs than for new drugs. An FDA field inspector and an FDA laboratory scientist qualified in the evaluation of analytical techniques conduct this audit.

During the inspection of a biopharmaceutic facility, where a drug is administered to, and blood samples are then taken from, human volunteers, the inspection team will verify that IRB approval was given for the study and that all regulatory requirements were met. The inspector might review such records and factors as drug accountability records, prescreening laboratory data, the presence of medical supervision, the handling of biological samples, and the assessment of situations in which the health and safety of the subjects are placed at risk.

In the analytical audit, the inspection team reviews standard operating procedures for the technology utilized, the status of the samples to be analyzed, qualifications of the personnel performing the analyses, raw documentation of the reported results, and the presence of quality control techniques such as the use of standard curves.

Post-Inspectional FDA Actions At the conclusion of all three types of inspections, the FDA inspector conducts what is called an "exit interview" with the clinical investigator. During this exchange, the two individuals discuss the inspector's findings, which will be reported to the FDA in the form of an Establishment Inspection Report (EIR).

In some cases, the inspector may leave the investigator with a written statement of his/her observations on Form FDA-483, the *Inspectional Observation Form*. This statement identifies the relevant deviations from regulations, which may include protocol deviations, IRB noncompliance and inadequate informed consent. The inspection results are discussed in detail with the clinical investigator, whose responses are recorded as part of the EIR. CDER provides a detailed discussion of the Clinical Investigator Compliance Program in its *Compliance Program Guidance Manual for Clinical Investigators* (7348.811).

The Sponsor/Monitor Compliance Program

Historically, CDER's Sponsor/Monitor Compliance Program has not been one of the center's most active monitoring programs. FDA officials claim that this is due to several factors, including relatively broad regulations on sponsor requirements and CDER's greater concerns about investigator activities and compliance. Agency officials also maintain that, in comparing an NDA's data tabulations with site records during investigator inspections, CDER is also indirectly inspecting the sponsor's records.

Nonetheless, CDER does initiate sponsor inspections to determine: (1) if a sponsor, a sponsor's employee, or a contract research organization (CRO) is monitoring a clinical investigation adequately; and (2) if the sponsor is fulfilling each of its requirements as outlined in existing federal regulations. The clinical sponsor and its research-related activities are the primary focus of inspections conducted under this program. It is worth mentioning, however, that the activities of two other entities, because they may assume some of the sponsor's responsibilities during a clinical study, may also be investigated by the FDA:

- *Clinical Monitors.* Monitors are those individuals selected by either a sponsor or contract research organization to oversee the progress of the clinical investigation. The monitor may be an employee of the sponsor, a contract research organization, or a consultant.

- *Contract Research Organization* (CRO). CROs are organizations or corporations that enter into contractual agreements with sponsors to perform one or more of the sponsor's duties in the clinical research process. Sponsors may delegate several of their responsibilities to a CRO, including the design of a protocol, the monitoring of clinical studies, the selection of investigators and study monitors, the evaluation of reports, and the preparation of materials to be submitted to the FDA.

CDER's Division of Scientific Investigations manages the sponsor/monitor compliance program, as it does each of the other bioresearch monitoring efforts. Staffers within this office decide which sponsors are to be inspected, what a particular inspection will consist of, and what actions the FDA will take in response to an inspector's report.

Most of CDER's activities regarding sponsors/monitors can be classified as what some agency officials call "information-gathering investigations." In many cases, the center initiates these investigations when it needs specific information from sponsor/monitor records (e.g., randomization reports) to address an issue or question raised during a clinical investigator inspection. These information-gathering efforts are not designed as comprehensive inspections, but as quick, focused reviews directed at specific records.

Formal "routine surveillance" inspections of sponsors and monitors are becoming less common. CDER conducts about 20 surveillance inspections annually. "For cause" inspections, which are even less common, are performed when there are indications that a sponsor is not fulfilling its responsibilities.

In general terms, a drug sponsor can be selected for a surveillance inspection if the company is the sponsor of a pending NDA or active IND (i.e., an IND under which a firm is conducting clinical studies).

After determining which firms satisfy these criteria, the FDA's Division of Scientific Investigations forwards an inspection assignment to the relevant FDA regional office—the office that oversees the district in which the sponsor's headquarters are located. The assignment package tells an FDA field inspector the name and address of the sponsor, and provides instructions on which study or studies are to be investigated.

The Inspection of Drug Sponsors Sponsor inspections take place at the company's headquarters, and generally involve the evaluation of records from recently conducted or active studies. According to the FDA's *Compliance Program Guidance Manual for Sponsors, Contract Research Organizations, and Monitors* (7348.810), the field inspector evaluates at least six elements of a clinical study: (1) the selection of and directions to a monitor; (2) test article accountability; (3) assurance of IRB approval; (4) the adequacy of facilities; (5) continuing evaluation of data; and (6) records retention.

Monitor Selection and Directions. In this aspect of the inspection, the FDA investigator determines if the clinical monitor is adequately qualified, and whether the sponsor has given the monitor sufficient direction. Specifically, the inspector must determine:

- whether at least one individual has been charged with monitoring the progress of the investigation (if there are two or more monitors, the inspector must determine how the responsibilities are divided);

- what training, education, and experience qualify the monitor to oversee the progress of the clinical investigation;

- whether written procedures have been established for the monitoring of the clinical investigation; and

- whether the sponsor has assured that the monitor has met his or her obligations.

Test Article Accountability. The inspector must evaluate whether the sponsor maintained adequate drug accounting procedures before, during, and, if applicable, after a clinical investigation. The inspector is instructed to make six separate determinations:

- whether the sponsor maintained accounting procedures for the test article, including records showing: (1) the shipment dates, quantity, serial, batch lot or other identification number of units sent; (2) the receipt dates and the quantity of returned articles; and (3) the names of investigators;

- whether the records are sufficient to allow a comparison of the total amount of the drug shipped against the amounts used and returned by the investigator;

- whether all unused or reusable supplies of the test article were returned to the sponsor when either (1) the investigator discontinued or finished participating in the clinical investigation, or (2) the investigation was terminated;

- if all unused or reusable supplies of the test article were not returned to the sponsor, a determination of the alternate disposition of the test article and a description of how the sponsor determined the manner in which the investigator accounted for unused or reusable supplies of the test article dispensed to a subject and not returned to the investigator;

- whether the alternate disposition was adequate to ensure that humans or food-producing animals were not exposed to experimental risk; and

- whether records were maintained for alternate disposition of the test article.

Assurance of IRB Approval. For a clinical investigation subject to IRB approval, the FDA inspector must determine whether the sponsor maintains documentation showing that the clinical investigator obtained IRB approval before any human subjects were allowed to participate in the investigation.

Ascertaining the Adequacy of Facilities. The FDA inspector must determine whether the monitor assessed the adequacy of all facilities used by the study investigator (e.g., office, clinic, hospital).

Continuing Evaluation of Data. The inspector must examine records to evaluate the clinical sponsor's efficiency in reviewing data submitted by the investigator and in responding to reports of adverse reactions. In this aspect of the inspection, the investigator must make six determinations:

- whether the sponsor reviews all new case reports and other data received from the investigator regarding the safety of the test article within ten working days after receipt;

- whether all case reports and other data received from the investigator are periodically evaluated for effectiveness as portions of the study are completed (included in this determination are the practices of the monitor);

- what actions are taken in response to incomplete case report forms;

- whether there is a system for tabulating the frequency and character of adverse reactions;

- whether existing evidence indicates that the sponsor's present data receipt system is operating satisfactorily; and

- whether any deaths occurred among study subjects, and what actions were taken to determine whether the deaths were related to the use of the test article.

Record Retention. Finally, the inspector must determine the sponsor's compliance with whichever of the following two record retention requirements is applicable: (1) records must be retained for a period of two years after a drug's marketing application is approved; or (2) records must be retained for a period of two years following the date on which the sponsor discontinues the shipment and delivery of the drug for investigational use and so notifies the FDA.

Chapter 16

Accelerated Drug Approval/Accessibility Programs

During the 1980s and early 1990s, the AIDS crisis thrust the FDA into a crucible of victim desperation and public and political pressure. Ultimately, the realities and politics of AIDS spurred the FDA to develop and implement several plans under which promising new therapies could reach desperately ill patients more quickly.

From 1987 through 1992, the FDA developed and implemented four principal drug access programs: the treatment IND, a mechanism that provides patients with access to promising experimental-stage drugs for serious and life-threatening diseases; parallel track, a plan that provides patients suffering from AIDS or AIDS-related diseases with early access to experimental-stage therapies; an accelerated drug development program for drugs designed to treat life-threatening and seriously debilitating diseases; and an accelerated drug approval program for therapies designed to treat serious or life-threatening illnesses.

In developing such programs, the FDA has acknowledged that the traditional drug development process is a compromise in many respects, and that the system can be particularly costly to those in dire need of new therapeutic alternatives. After all, it is during this process that potentially valuable drugs are often withheld from patients who may need them while clinical testing and the NDA review move forward. While critics have charged that some aspects of the drug approval process are unethical and even cruel, the FDA continues to hold that the randomized, placebo-controlled clinical trial remains the single most efficient vehicle for determining whether new drugs are safe and effective.

For at least two reasons, the desperation and public pressure that prompted government action began to abate at least somewhat in the early 1990s. First, victims of AIDS and AIDS-related conditions had several approved therapeutic options to treat their conditions. Secondly, increasing numbers of experts began to question the wisdom of providing early and expanded access to therapies whose risks and benefits have not been characterized in traditional drug development processes. In 1992, for instance, at least one study questioned the relevance of the surrogate endpoints on which the approval of the first AIDS therapies were based.

Further, some agency advisors pointed to several patient deaths during a Phase 2 trial involving the hepatitis B treatment fialuridine (FIAU) as both a warning about the dangers of expanded access plans and a confirmation of the value of traditional drug development schemes. Although FIAU was not used in an expanded access program, members of the FDA's Antiviral Drugs Advisory Committee pointed out that, if the drug had shown early activity against AIDS, it might have been used in such a scheme. Five trial-related deaths might have become dozens or even hundreds under an expanded access program they speculated during a 1993 meeting. One member of the committee, which reviews AIDS treatments as well, suggested that the pendulum had begun to swing away from early drug access and expedited development plans and back toward conventional drug development programs.

In the mid-1990s, other factors seemed to undermine the appeal of these programs. For example, with CDER approving new drugs in an average of 18 months, and AIDS treatments in an average of less than 6 months, some companies may no longer consider participation in these programs necessary to ensure rapid approvals.

Despite this, the FDA's four initial expanded access and accelerated development/approval programs stand largely as they did when introduced. In most cases, however, they are now less active than they were in previous years.

On March 29, 1996, the FDA added a fifth formalized program to expedite the development and approval of desperately needed new drugs. In response to mounting criticism over the imbalance of resources targeted to AIDS drug reviews versus those targeted to other life-threatening illnesses, the FDA established what it called the Oncology Initiative. This program brought several reforms that some analysts estimated would reduce cancer drug development times by at least a year and cut average oncology drug review times from 12.4 to 6 months (see discussion below).

The Treatment IND

Although the FDA had been pressured to reform clinical testing methodologies in the past, the unique issues posed by AIDS demonstrated the shortcomings of the drug development process as never before. As Burroughs Wellcome's AZT, or Retrovir, emerged as the first therapy to show promise in treating AIDS, victims of the disease not fortunate enough to be enrolled in clinical trials refused to die silently in the name of science. The intense public debate that followed was often bitter, but was not unproductive. After early clinical studies of AZT showed promising results, the FDA quickly approved what it called a treatment IND, under which more than 4,000 patients were allowed access to AZT while the drug underwent final FDA review.

The realities of AIDS first brought formal changes to FDA regulations on May 22, 1987, when the agency published a final rule allowing the treatment use and sale of investigational drugs intended to treat desperately ill patients. Specifically, the regulations were "intended to facilitate the availability of promising new drugs as early in the drug development process as possible...to patients with serious and life-threatening diseases for which no comparable or satisfactory alternative drug or other therapies exist."

In many respects, the treatment IND was a compromise that attempted to satisfy those who believed that the desperately ill should have unlimited access to an emerging therapy, and those who believed that a developmental-stage drug should be withheld from patients outside the clinical trial setting until such testing is completed and is judged to have demonstrated the drug's safety and effectiveness. Under a treatment IND, desperately ill patients gain access to a promising drug while the all-important clinical development and FDA review of a drug continue.

Although it was the AIDS crisis that eventually brought the FDA to formalize the treatment IND as it is now known, agency officials point out that the treatment IND has its roots in the 1960s and 1970s. At that time, applications commonly referred to as "compassionate INDs" were used to make unapproved antiarrhythmics, calcium channel blockers, and beta blockers accessible to patients intolerant to other therapies. In the early 1980s, FDA regulations formally recognized the treatment IND, allowing its use in cases in which: (1) there was sufficient evidence of safety and effectiveness; (2) the potential benefits outweighed the risks; and (3) the medical condition under study was a serious disease with no satisfactory therapies.

The 1987 regulations took a relatively loose concept and, for the first time, defined the treatment IND's purpose, established more specific criteria for FDA approval, and described how and when the treatment IND could be used. The regulations specify the point in a product's development at which treatment use may begin, a key factor since preapproval accessibility was the primary goal of the treatment IND.

To qualify for treatment use under the FDA's treatment IND program, a drug must meet four principal criteria. According to federal regulations, "FDA shall permit an investigational drug to be used for a treatment use under a treatment protocol or treatment IND if: (i) The drug is intended to treat a serious or immediately life-threatening disease; (ii) There is no comparable or satisfactory alternative drug or other therapy available to treat that stage of the disease in the intended patient population; (iii) The drug is under investigation in a controlled clinical trial under an IND in effect for the trial, or all clinical trials have been completed; and (iv) The sponsor of the controlled trial is actively pursuing approval of the investigational drug with due diligence."

The second criterion noted above deserves a brief discussion, primarily because the entire treatment IND concept is designed for desperately ill individuals with no therapeutic alternatives. Responding to concern about its interpretation of the "no comparable or satisfactory alternative drug or other therapy available" requirement for treatment IND eligibility, the FDA has clarified that this standard is met "when there are patients who are not adequately treated by available therapies, even if the particular disease does respond in some cases to available therapy. This criterion would be met, for example, if the intended population is for patients who have failed on an existing therapy (i.e., the existing therapy did not provide its intended therapeutic benefit or did not fully treat the condition); for patients who could not tolerate the existing therapy (i.e., it caused unacceptable adverse effects); or for patients who had other complicating diseases that made the existing therapy unacceptable (e.g., concomitant disease making available therapy contraindicated) for the patient population."

In reality, FDA regulations provide for two different treatment IND vehicles: one for drugs designed to treat immediately life-threatening illnesses, and the other for drugs intended to treat serious diseases. The timing of, and FDA criteria for granting, treatment INDs for the two types of indications differ considerably.

Treatment Use for Immediately Life-Threatening Conditions

Under the May 1987 regulations, the FDA defined "immediately life-threatening disease" as a stage of a disease in which there is a reasonable likelihood that death will occur within a matter of months or in which premature death is likely without early treatment. The agency claimed that it would apply a common sense definition so that death within more than a year would not normally be considered immediately life-threatening, but that death within several days or even several weeks would fall under the definition.

For illustrative purposes, the FDA identified in the regulations nine diseases that would "normally" be considered immediately life-threatening: advanced cases of AIDS, advanced congestive heart failure (New York Heart Association Class IV), recurrent sustained ventricular tachycardia or ventricular fibrillation, herpes simplex encephalitis, most advanced metastatic refractory cancers, far advanced emphysema, severe combined immunodeficiency syndrome, bacterial endocarditis, and subarachnoid hemorrhage (see listing below of treatment INDs approved).

Provided that a drug meets the four principal criteria outlined above, the FDA may only deny a treatment IND "if the available scientific evidence, taken as a whole, fails to provide a reasonable basis for concluding that the drug: (A) May be effective for its intended use in its intended patient population; or (B) Would not expose the patients to whom the drug is to be administered to an unreasonable and significant additional risk of illness or injury." The rather vague efficacy standard was discussed just briefly in the regulation's preamble, which stated that, "...the level of evidence needed is well short of that needed for a new drug approval—and may be less than what would be needed to support treatment use in diseases that are serious but not immediately life-threatening."

One of the more hotly debated aspects of the treatment IND regulations was the timing of treatment programs for drugs used against immediately life-threatening conditions. Some regarded the FDA's criteria as too liberal, and claimed that these criteria allow general accessibility before a drug development program can be expected to provide sufficient evidence of safety and/or effectiveness. The FDA, however, held to the provisions of its early proposals, and allows drugs for immediately life-threatening conditions to be "made available for treatment use...earlier than Phase 3, but ordinarily not earlier than Phase 2."

But the FDA stresses that available scientific evidence, rather than simply the phase of development, is more important to its decision-making process: "FDA expects that data from controlled clinical trials will ordinarily be available at the time a treatment IND is requested. However, FDA is committed to reviewing and considering all available evidence, including results of domestic and foreign clinical trials, animal data, and, where pertinent, in vitro data. FDA will also consider clinical experience from outside a controlled trial, where the circumstances surrounding an experience provide sufficient indication of scientific value."

Treatment Use for Serious Conditions The FDA's criteria for granting treatment INDs for serious conditions were considerably less controversial than those for immediately life-threatening illnesses. Interestingly, however, the FDA provided no specific definition of "serious" in either the treatment IND proposal or final rule. The agency did give examples of serious conditions: Alzheimer's disease, advanced multiple sclerosis, advanced Parkinson's disease, transient ischemic attacks, progressive ankylosing spondylitis, active advanced lupus erythematosus, certain forms of epilepsy, nonacidotic or hyperosmolar diabetes, and paroxysmal supraventricular tachycardia.

To qualify for treatment use, drugs intended to treat serious illnesses must meet a tougher, if more vague, safety and effectiveness standard than that described above for life-threatening conditions. The FDA "may deny a request for treatment use...if there is insufficient evidence of safety and effectiveness to support such use."

Considering this requirement, it is not surprising that treatment INDs for serious illnesses are more likely to be granted later in the clinical development process than are therapies for immediately life-threatening conditions: "In the case of serious diseases, a drug ordinarily may be made available for treatment use...during Phase 3 investigations or after all clinical trials have been completed; however, in appropriate circumstances, a drug may be made available for treatment use during Phase 2."

Designated Treatment INDs: June 1987-February 1997
(drugs and biologics)

Generic (Trade Name)	Sponsor	Indication	Designation Date
Cytomegalovirus immunoglobulin[b,o]	Mass. Dept. of Public Health	Prevention of cytomegalo-virus infections in certain renal transplant patients	10/19/87
Ifosfamide[c,e,o] (Ifex)	NCI/BMS	Testicular cancer (in conjunction w/mesna)	12/24/87
Mesna[c,o] (Mesnex)	NCI/Asta	Hemorrhagic cystitis (in conjunction w/ifosfamide)	12/24/87
Trimetrexate[e,o] (Neutrexin)	NIAID/Warner-Lambert (licensed to U.S. Bioscience)	PCP	2/12/88
Clomipramine (Anafranil)	Ciba Geigy	Severe OCD	6/3/88
Selegiline[o] (Eldepryl)	Somerset	Parkinson's	6/16/88
Pentostatin[c,e,o] (Nipent)	NCI/Warner-Lambert	Hairy cell leukemia	7/28/88
Teniposide[c,o] (Vumon)	NCI/BMS	Refractory acute lymphoblastic leukemia	10/7/88
Gancyclovir[e] (Cytovene)	NIAID/Syntex	Cytomegalovirus retinitis	11/28/88
Aerosolized Pentamadine Isethionate[e,o] (Nebupent)	Lyphomed/Fujisawa	PCP (AIDS) [new formulation]	2/3/89
Levamisole HCL[c] (Ergamisol)	NCI/Janssen	Colon cancer (in conjunction w/ 5-flurouracil)	5/4/89
Erythropoietin[b,o] (Eprex)	Ortho	AIDS-associated anemia [new indication]	6/27/89
Colfosceril Palmitate[e,o] (Exosurf neonatal)	Burr. Wellcome	Neonatal respiratory distress syndrome	7/26/89
Didanosine/ddI[a] (Videx)	NIAID/BMS	AZT-intolerant AIDS-related Complex	9/28/89

–continued–

Generic (Trade Name)	Sponsor	Indication	Designation Date
Beractant[b,e,o] (Survanta)	Abbott	Neonatal respiratory distress syndrome	9/29/89
Zidovudine/AZT[a] (Retrovir syrup)	Burr. Wellcome	AIDS in children [new indication]	10/26/89
Alglucerase[b,e,o] (Ceredase)	NINDS/Genzyme	Gaucher's disease	11/7/89
Fludarabine Phosphate[c,e,o] (Fludara)	NCI/Triton Biosciences*	Chronic lymphocytic leukemia	11/24/89
Baclofen Intrathecal[d,o] (Lioresal)	Medtronic	Spasticity in oral baclofen-intolerant MS/SCI patients [new formulation]	3/7/90
Sargramostim/ GM-CSF[b,o] (Leukine)	Immunex	Neutropenia due to bone marrow transplant	9/24/90
Zalcitabine/ddC[a,o] (Hivid)	Hoffmann La Roche	AZT-intolerant ARC/AIDS patients	5/30/91
Perfosfamide/4-HC[o] (Pergamid)	Scios-Nova	Ex vivo treatment of bone marrow	6/14/91
Oxandrolone[o] (Oxandrin)	Gynex**	Boys with constitutional delay of puberty [new indication]	10/17/91
Atovaquone[e,o] (Mepron)	Burr. Wellcome	PCP	11/8/91
Tacrine (Cognex)	Warner-Lambert	Alzheimer's disease	12/02/91
Rifabutin[e,o] (Mycobutin)	Adria	Prophylaxis of myco-bacterium avium complex	3/6/92
Cladribine/2-CDA[c,o] (Leustatin)	Ortho	Hairy cell leukemia	3/6/92
Paclitaxel[c] (Taxol)	BMS	Ovarian cancer	7/15/92
Oxandrolone[o] (Oxandrin)	Gynex**	Girls with Turner's Syndrome [new indication]	10/21/92
Copolymer-1[o] (Copaxone)	Teva Marion Partners	Multiple sclerosis	1/5/93

–continued–

Generic (Trade Name)	Sponsor	Indication	Designation Date
Metformin (Glucophage)	Lipha	Non-insulin dependent diabetes mellitus	9/10/93
Vinorelbine (Navelbine)	Burr. Wellcome	Non-small cell lung cancer	4/14/94
Human Growth Hormone[b,e,o] (Serostim)	Serono	AIDS-associated wasting/ weight loss	12/20/94
Gemcitalbine HCl (Gemzar)	Lilly	Locally advanced or metastatic pancreatic cancer	1/27/95
Atorvastatin (Lipitor)	Warner-Lambert	Homozygous familial hypercholesterolemia or severe refractory hypercholesterolemia	2/9/95
Riluzole[o] (Rilutek)	RPR	Amyotrophic lateral sclerosis (ALS)	6/20/95
Cell Therapy[b,o] Autologous Peripheral Blood Lymphocytes	Cellcor	Treatment of metastatic (Stage IV) renal cell carcinoma	9/15/95
Cidofovir[b] (Vistide)	Gilead	Relapsing cytomegalovirus retinitis	9/1/95
Carmustine Wafer[o] (Gliadel)	Guilford/RPR	Recurrent malignant glioma- intracranial therapy	10/27/95
Insulin-like Growth Factor IGF[o] (Myotrophin)	Cephalon/Chiron	Protein-based therapeutic treatment of amyotrophic lateral sclerosis	6/24/96
Nelfinavir mesylate (Viracept)	Agouron	Protease inhibitor for use by patients for whom other treatments have failed	9/12/96
Progestereone Vaginal Gel (Crinone)	Columbia Research Labs	In vitro fertilization	2/7/97

a=accelerated approval; b=biological; c=group C cancer drug; d=device; e=Subpart E designation; o=orphan drug designation. * Berlex acquired Triton Biosciences in 1990; ** Gynex merged with Bio-Technology General in 1993.

Source: Shulman, SR, Tufts Center for the Study of Drug Development, June 1997

Obtaining FDA Permission for Treatment Use Both drug sponsors and practicing physicians may pursue FDA approval for a treatment use. The sponsor of a drug's IND may do so through a treatment protocol, while "licensed practitioners" must submit a treatment IND.

According to FDA regulations, a sponsor-submitted treatment protocol must provide:

- the intended use of the drug;

- an explanation of the rationale for use of the drug, including, as appropriate, either a list of what available regimens ordinarily should be tried before using the investigational drug, or an explanation of why the use of the investigational drug is preferable to the use of available marketed treatments;

- a brief description of the criteria for patient selection;

- the method of administration and the dosages of the drug; and

- a description of clinical procedures, laboratory tests, or other measures designed to monitor the effects of the drug and to minimize risk.

Additionally, a treatment protocol must "be supported" by an informational brochure for each treating physician, technical information relevant to the safety and effectiveness of the drug for the intended treatment purpose, and a commitment by the sponsor to ensure the compliance of all participating investigators with informed consent requirements.

Like a traditional IND submission, a treatment protocol becomes active 30 days after the FDA receives the protocol, or on earlier notification by the FDA that the treatment use may begin. Of course, treatment protocols are also subject to clinical holds any time after submission.

If a practicing physician wants to obtain for treatment use a drug whose sponsor will not establish a treatment protocol for this purpose, the practitioner must submit his or her own treatment IND. Such applications must contain:

- a cover sheet (Form FDA 1571);

- information on the drug's chemistry, manufacturing, and controls, and prior clinical and nonclinical experience with the drug (when not provided by the sponsor either directly or through the incorporation-by-reference of information in the existing IND);

- a statement of the steps taken by the practitioner to obtain the drug from the sponsor under a treatment protocol;

- treatment protocol containing all the information required for such a submission (see discussion above);

- a statement of the practitioner's qualifications to use the investigational drug for the intended treatment use;

- the practitioner's statement of familiarity with information on the drug's safety and effectiveness derived from previous clinical and nonclinical experience with the drug; and

- the practitioner's commitment to report to the FDA safety information in accordance with current regulations.

The licensed practitioner who submits a treatment IND is the "sponsor-investigator" for such an IND, and is responsible for meeting all applicable sponsor and investigator responsibilities. Like standard INDs and treatment protocols, treatment INDs may be initiated 30 days after submission or upon early notification by the FDA.

The Sale of Investigational Drugs The FDA's treatment IND regulations also contain provisions that allow sponsors to sell investigational drugs under some conditions. However, drug sponsors may not "commercialize an investigational drug by charging a price larger than that necessary to recover costs of manufacture, research, development, and handling of the investigational drug."

According to federal regulations, a sponsor may charge for an investigational drug under a treatment protocol or treatment IND, provided that: "(i) There is adequate enrollment in the ongoing clinical investigations under the authorized IND; (ii) charging does not constitute commercial marketing of a new drug for which a marketing application has not been approved; (iii) the drug is not being commercially promoted or advertised; and (iv) the sponsor of the drug is actively pursuing marketing approval with due diligence."

At least 30 days prior to selling an investigational drug, a sponsor must notify the FDA in writing and, with this notification, include a certified statement that the requested price is not greater than the amount necessary to recover costs associated with the drug's manufacture, research, development, and handling. If the FDA does not contact the sponsor within the 30-day review period, the sponsor is free to begin selling the drug.

A sponsor may also sell a drug in any clinical trial, provided the sponsor can gain the FDA's prior approval. To obtain this approval, the sponsor must provide an adequate explanation of why sale of the drug is necessary to either begin or continue a trial.

Unfortunately, the final regulations give few details on how a company can show that the sale of a drug is necessary or how this necessity should be determined. The regulation's preamble states that "charging for investigational drugs during a clinical trial would normally not be allowed.... FDA believes that cost recovery is justified in clinical trials only when necessary to further the study and development of a promising drug that might otherwise be lost to the medical armamentarium. The agency believes that this situation is most likely to arise in the context of new products derived through biotechnology which are produced by small, medium and large firms alike."

The FDA has approved the sale of several investigational products under the treatment IND program. A 1995 Tufts Center for the Study of Drug Development study found that 9 of the first 33 drugs granted treatment IND status were also approved for sale during development, including Serono's Serostim, Teva/Lemmon's Copolymer-1, Gynex' Oxandrin, Warner-Lambert's Cognex, Genzyme's Ceredase, Lyphomed/Fujisawa's Nupent, Somerset's Eldepryl, and Massachusetts Department of Public Health's Cytomegalovirus immunoglobulin.

Although more than three dozen treatment INDs have been granted, the submission and approval of treatment INDs have diminished somewhat since 1991 (see listing above). Since that time, the agency has granted 17 treatment INDs. The reasons, many believe, are related partly to continuing industry ambivalence toward the IND program, perhaps because of issues related to the potential costs, complexities and liabilities associated with expanded access. And while the agency still recommends treatment INDs to some sponsors, it is also obvious that the FDA has not been as aggressive in recruiting treatment INDs since Frank Young, M.D., who was the FDA commissioner when the program was introduced, left the agency in late 1989.

The FDA's Accelerated Drug Development Program (Subpart E)

By mid-1988, the FDA had successfully implemented several initiatives designed to make drugs more accessible through both preapproval availability plans and speedier reviews. At that time, the treatment IND regulations were in effect, and seven experimental therapies had been available to patients with AIDS, cancer, Parkinson's disease, and other life-threatening conditions. In addition, the agency had established a new level of review priority for all AIDS products, and had created a new drug review division to focus on evaluating these therapies. The FDA credited such initiatives with the rapid availability and review of AZT, which the FDA approved only 107 days after the submission of Burroughs Wellcome's NDA.

In August 1988, then-Vice President George Bush, in his capacity as the chairman of the Presidential Task Force on Regulatory Relief, asked the FDA to build on these "successes" by developing procedures for expediting the marketing of new therapies intended to treat AIDS and other life-threatening illnesses. In the two months that followed, FDA officials met with representatives from other government agencies, AIDS groups, and consumer, health, and academic organizations to obtain input on developing this program.

The FDA released such a plan on October 21, 1988: its Interim Rules on Procedures for Drugs Intended to Treat Life-Threatening and Severely Debilitating Illnesses, or Subpart E procedures. The interim rule, which the FDA claims is based on its experience with AZT, is described by the agency as an attempt "to speed the availability of new therapies to desperately ill patients, while preserving appropriate guarantees for safety and effectiveness. These procedures are intended to facilitate the development, evaluation, and marketing of such products, especially where no satisfactory therapies exist. These procedures reflect the recognition that physicians and patients are generally willing to accept greater risks or side effects from products that treat life-threatening and severely debilitating illnesses than they would accept from products that treat less serious illnesses. These procedures also reflect the recognition that the benefits of the drug need to be evaluated in light of the severity of the disease being treated. The procedures apply to products intended to treat acquired immunodeficiency syndrome (AIDS), some cancers, and other life-threatening and severely debilitating illnesses."

Like the treatment IND, the FDA's accelerated development plan was announced with considerable fanfare and, in turn, was met by some degree of skepticism. Even officials within the FDA review units responsible for the approval of AIDS and cancer therapies claimed that the plan's primary elements—close sponsor consultation and an accelerated clinical testing scheme—were already common practice.

But because it provides for a drug's approval before its sale, the accelerated development program has three key advantages over the treatment IND, according to the FDA: (1) no limitations are put on the pricing or profitability of FDA-approved drugs; (2) consumers who buy FDA-approved drugs are eligible for third-party reimbursement, for which patients under treatment INDs cannot qualify; and (3) FDA approval confers some liability protection to manufacturers.

Essentially, there are four key components to the FDA's expedited development plan: (1) early and increased FDA and sponsor consultation aimed at formulating agreements on the design of preclinical and clinical studies needed for marketing approval; (2) the "compression" of Phase 3 clinical trials into Phase 2 testing; (3) the FDA's adoption of a modified medical risk-benefit analysis when assessing the safety and effectiveness of qualifying drugs; and (4) the use of Phase 4 postmarketing studies to obtain additional information about drug risks, benefits, and optimal use.

Eligibility for Accelerated Development Eligibility was perhaps the most fascinating aspect of the interim regulation when it was first released. Recognizing the great opportunities that expedited approval could offer, the drug industry quickly turned to the agency for guidance on which products might qualify for the plan.

In general terms, the expedited approval program applies to new drugs, antibiotics, and biologics under study for treating life-threatening or severely debilitating diseases. As is true for every other regulation, the scope of this interim rule is subject to FDA interpretation, which the agency bases on two primary definitions:

- *Life-Threatening Conditions.* For the purposes of the plan, "life-threatening" illnesses include: "(1) Diseases or conditions where the likelihood of death is high unless the course of the disease is interrupted; and (2) Diseases or conditions with potentially fatal outcomes, where the end point of clinical trial analysis is survival." Any disease whose progression is likely to lead to death, particularly in a short period (e.g. six months to one year), would also fall under this definition, as would any "condition on which a study is to be carried out to determine whether the treatment has a beneficial effect on survival (e.g., increased survival after a stroke or heart attack)."

- *Severely Debilitating Conditions.* The FDA has defined "severely debilitating" illnesses as "diseases or conditions that cause major irreversible morbidity," such as severe function deficits in multiple sclerosis, Alzheimer's disease, or progressive ankylosing spondylitis, and blindness due to cytomegalovirus infection in AIDS patients. The agency cautioned that accelerated approvals would be relevant only for studies that "will examine the treatment's capacity to prevent or reverse what would otherwise be irreversible damage such as putting ankylosing spondylitis into remission and stopping joint damage and deformity, or preventing blindness."

Despite these definitions, eligibility remained a widely discussed issue in the months following the interim rule's publication. To help educate industry as well as its own staff, the FDA completed a retrospective review of approximately 200 new molecular entities (NME) approved during the 1980s to determine which of these would have been eligible under the new rules. The agency also reviewed its existing inventory of approximately 10,000 drug INDs, and reportedly contacted the sponsors of qualifying drugs.

The Cornerstone of Accelerated Development: Early FDA-Sponsor Consultation Despite serious questions about whether the agency should involve itself in the research process, FDA officials have maintained that early consultation is the single most critical element of this program. The FDA believes that the insights it has gained in reviewing both acceptable and unacceptable drug applications could prove invaluable to sponsors, and that close consultation will allow the agency to share its expertise in the planning and design of both preclinical and clinical development programs.

According to the FDA's interim rule, FDA-sponsor consultations would take two forms:

- *Pre-Investigational New Drug Application (IND) Meetings.* Prior to an IND submission, the sponsor may request a meeting "to review and reach agreement on the design of animal studies needed to initiate human testing. The meeting may also provide an opportunity for discussing the scope and design of Phase 1 testing, and the best approach for presentation and formatting of data in the IND."

- *End-of-Phase 1 Meetings.* In the FDA's ideal accelerated drug development program, Phase 3 clinical trials are "compressed" into Phase 2 studies, which then provide the data on which the drug is to be approved. Therefore, after Phase 1 data are available, the sponsor may again request a meeting to "review and reach agreement on the design of Phase 2 controlled clinical trials, with the goal that such testing will be adequate to provide sufficient data on the drug's safety and effectiveness to support a decision on its approvability for marketing."

Restructuring Clinical Trials In attempting to use data derived from Phase 2 trials as the basis for the final approval of a new drug, the FDA brought about, in theory at least, a reasonably significant departure from the traditional drug development and approval path. Interestingly, however, the FDA drug review divisions responsible for evaluating AIDS and cancer therapies claimed to have approved desperately needed new drugs based upon Phase 2 clinical data well before the plan's introduction.

Under the accelerated development scheme, Phase 3 trials are "compressed" into Phase 2 studies, with Phase 1 trials taking on the significance of conventional Phase 2 studies. According to the interim rule, "to increase the likelihood that phase 2 testing can provide sufficient results, sponsors could need to plan phase 2 studies that are somewhat larger and more extensive than is currently the norm, including a mode for replication of key findings. Moreover, to avoid missing an effect by using too little drug, or to avoid studying a dose that proves toxic, it may be necessary to study several doses in the first formal trials, an approach that may require a larger study but can plainly save time, thereby enabling physicians to treat patients with life-threatening illnesses more rapidly. However, it should be appreciated that if a drug has only minor or inconsistent therapeutic benefits, its positive effects may be missed in this stage of clinical testing, even if the drug ultimately proves to be beneficial following more extensive phase 3 trials."

On the issue of the quantity of data needed for approval, the FDA has stated that, in most cases, two pivotal Phase 2 studies will be necessary: "…the agency cautions that persuasively dramatic results are rare and that two entirely independent studies will generally be required." The approvals of the first AIDS drugs under the accelerated program, however, indicated that the FDA was willing to base the approval of desperately needed drugs on a single pivotal study.

Other Provisions of the Interim Rule The FDA's interim rule contains key provisions in several other areas, including the following:

- *Treatment IND.* The accelerated approval plan was not meant to eliminate the need for treatment INDs. In fact, when the preliminary analyses of Phase 2 results appear promising, the FDA may ask the sponsor to submit a treatment IND, under which the test drug could be made available while the sponsor prepares, and the FDA reviews, the NDA.

- *FDA Risk-Benefit Analysis.* According to the interim rule, the "FDA will consider the seriousness of the disease being treated in balancing risks and benefits…. Clearly, for a life-threatening illness, a relatively high level of known risks and some uncertainty about potential risk from the drug can be acceptable in exchange for the improved survival provided by effective drug treatment for a condition that, if left untreated, would result in death. Similarly, for the same life-threatening illnesses, evidence of effectiveness must be weighed against risks of the drug and the knowledge that death would result in the absence of treatment."

- *Phase 4 Testing.* Although FDA officials state that approvals granted under the accelerated plan are in no way conditional on sponsor willingness to conduct postmarketing testing, the agency says that it "...may seek agreement from the sponsor to conduct certain postmarketing (phase 4) studies to delineate additional information about the drug's risks, benefits, and optimal use. These studies could include, but would not be limited to, studying different doses or schedules of administration than were used in phase 2 studies, use of the drug in other patient populations or other stages of the disease, or use of the drug over a longer period of time."

With little recent data available on the accelerated development program, it is difficult to know how active the agency and industry have been in this area. According to a 1995 Tufts Center for the Study of Drug Development study, the FDA approved 28 drugs under the Subpart E regulations from October 1988 through December 1994. However, the study also showed that only 4 of these 28 drugs were approved in 1993 and 1994, 2 of which were for different dosage forms of Fujisawa's Prograf (tacrolimus).

By most accounts, the Subpart E program has become less relevant given the agency's successes under the prescription drug user fee program. In addition, the agency now routinely works with sponsors of all drugs so early in the development process that the accelerated development program's focus on early sponsor-FDA interaction is probably no longer viewed as a worthwhile incentive to participate.

Accelerated Drug Approval Program (Subpart H)

With its 1988 accelerated drug development program in place, the FDA wanted to take "additional steps...to facilitate the approval of significant new drugs...to treat serious or life-threatening diseases." The agency did so under a final regulation (Subpart H) published in December 1992.

Unlike the FDA's accelerated development program, which focused largely on expediting the drug testing process, the Subpart H regulations focused on accelerating the agency's review and approval of promising therapies. The regulations attempted to do so by modifying the criteria on which the agency can base marketing approval for desperately needed new drugs, and by giving the agency greater authority regarding the study and use of the drugs following approval.

Specifically, the accelerated approval program allows the agency to base marketing approval on a drug's effect on a surrogate endpoint or on a clinical endpoint other than survival or irreversible morbidity. According to the regulation, "FDA may grant marketing approval for a new drug product on the basis of adequate and well-controlled clinical trials establishing that the drug product has an effect on a surrogate endpoint that is reasonably likely, based on epidemiologic, therapeutic, pathophysiologic, or other evidence, to predict clinical benefit or on the basis of an effect on a clinical endpoint other than survival or irreversible morbidity. Approval under this section will be subject to the requirement that the applicant study the drug further, to verify and describe its clinical benefit, where there is uncertainty as to the relation of the surrogate endpoint to clinical benefit, or of the observed clinical benefit to ultimate outcome. Postmarketing studies would usually be studies already underway. When required to be conducted, such studies must also be adequate and well controlled."

In its April 1992 regulatory proposal for the accelerated approval plan, the FDA discussed the benefits of not requiring companies to study the effects of desperately needed new drugs on primary endpoints (i.e., mortality or morbidity). "Approval of a drug on the basis of a well-documented effect on a surrogate endpoint can allow a drug to be marketed earlier, sometimes much earlier, than it could if a demonstrated clinical benefit were required... Approval could be granted where there is some uncertainty as to the relation of that endpoint to clinical benefit, with the requirement that the sponsor conduct or complete studies after approval to establish and define the drug's clinical benefit."

Ironically, it was controversy over the use of surrogate endpoints that led FDA officials to begin considering possible improvements in the accelerated approval program in the mid-1990s.[1] At FDA advisory committee meetings and in communications to the agency, it was the AIDS community itself that had begun to question the wisdom of basing approval on largely unvalidated surrogate endpoints.

Despite such concerns, the FDA's accelerated approval program has been perhaps the most active of the agency's expedited development and review initiatives in recent years. According to data from the Tufts Center for the Study of Drug Development, 15 of the 20 drugs approved under Subpart H were approved in 1994, 1995, and 1996 (see listing below).[2] In addition, drugs reviewed under Subpart H represent 6 of CDER's 10 fastest approvals since 1963.[3] Not surprisingly, these 6 products were all AIDS-related therapies.

Eligibility for Accelerated Approval Under the FDA's regulations, the accelerated approval program "applies to certain new drug and antibiotic products that have been studied for their safety and effectiveness in treating serious and life-threatening illnesses and that provide meaningful therapeutic benefit to patients over existing treatments (e.g., the ability to treat patients unresponsive to, or intolerant of, available therapy, or improved patient response over available therapy)."

Although the agency stated in its April 1992 proposal that it would apply the terms "serious" and "life-threatening" as it had in its treatment IND program and other programs, the FDA did discuss their application once again in the context of the accelerated approval plan. "The seriousness of a disease is a matter of judgement, but generally is based on its impact on such factors as survival, day-to-day functioning, or the likelihood that the disease, if left untreated, will progress from a less severe condition to a more serious one. Thus, acquired immunodeficiency syndrome (HIV) infection, Alzheimer's dementia, angina pectoris, heart failure, cancer, and many other diseases are clearly serious in their full manifestations. Further, many chronic illnesses that are generally well-managed by available therapy can have serious outcomes. For example, inflammatory bowel disease, asthma, rheumatoid arthritis, diabetes mellitus, systemic lupus erythematosus, depression, psychoses, and many other diseases can be serious for certain populations or in some or all of their phases."

From the implementation of the accelerated approval program in October 1991 through year-end 1996, the agency approved 20 drugs under Subpart H (see listing below). According to the Tufts Center for the Study of Drug Development, the average review time for these drugs was 7.7 months.

FDA's Accelerated Approvals (Subpart H)
October 1991-December 1996

eric (Trade)	*Sponsor*	*Indication*	*FDA Review Phase*
,danosine/ddI (Videx)	BMS	Advanced HIV in patients intolerant to zidovudine	6.4 months
Zalcitabine/ddC (Hivid)	Roche	Combination therapy with zidovudine in advanced HIV infection	7.6 months
Interferon Beta (Betaseron)	Chiron/ Berlex	Treatment of ambulatory patients with remitting/relapsing multiple sclerosis to reduce the frequency of clinical exacerbations	13.1 months
Clarithromycin (Biaxin)	Abbott	Treatment of disseminated mycobacterial infections due to Mycobacterium avium and Mycobacterium intracellulare	13.8 months
Pulmozyme (DNASE)	Genentech	Treatment of cystic fibrosis	9.0 months
Stavudine/D4T (Zerit)	BMS	Treatment of adults with advanced HIV infection-alternative therapy	5.8 months
Zalcitabine/ddC (Hivid)	Roche	Monotherapy for treatment of HIV and a revision of the combination therapy with zidovudine	11.6 months
Zidovudine/AZT (Retrovir)	B. Wellcome	Combination therapy with zalcitabine in advanced HIV infection	5.5 months
Dexrazoxane (Zinecard)	Pharmacia	Cardioprotection from doxorubicin toxicity in breast cancer patients	9.7 months
Bicalutamide (Casodex)	Zeneca	Treatment for advanced prostate cancer	12.6 months
Lamivudine (Epivir)	Glaxo- Wellcome	HIV infections in adults	4.3 months
Liposomol Doxorubicin HCl (Doxil)	Sequus	Treatment of Kaposi's sarcoma in patients with disease that has progressed on prior combination chemotherapy or in patients intolerant to such therapy	14.5 months

FDA's Accelerated Approvals, October 1991-December 1996 *(continued)*

Generic (Trade)	Sponsor	Indication	FDA Review Phase
Saquinavir (Invirase)	Hoffmann-LaRoche	Treatment of advanced HIV infection	3.1 months
Ritanovir (Norvir)	Abbott	Treatment of late-stage HIV	2.4 months
Protease Inhibitor (Crixivan)	Merck	Treatment of advanced HIV infection	1.4 months
Docetaxel (Taxotere)	Rhone-Poulenc Rorer	Treatment of breast cancer for patients who fail to respond to standard treatment	5.4 months
Irinotecan HCl (Camptosar)	Pharmacia & Upjohn	Second line treatment for colorectal cancer	5.5 months
Nevirapine (Viramune)	Boehringer Ingelheim	Treatment for patients with HIV-1 who have experienced clinical or immunological deterioration	3.9 months
Flutamide (Eulexin)	Schering-Plough	Early-stage prostate cancer	6.0 months (to be confirmed)
Midodrine (ProAmatine)	Roberts	Orthostatic hypotension	11.5 months

Source: Shulman and Brown, *The Food and Drug Administration's Early Access and Fast Track Approval Initiatives: How Have They Worked?*, Tufts Center for the Study of Drug Development, 1995

The Parallel Track Program

In mid-1989, National Institute of Allergy and Infectious Diseases (NIAID) Director Anthony Fauci, M.D., publicly proposed a new experimental drug accessibility plan called "parallel track." As proposed, the plan would allow the availability of experimental AIDS therapies earlier than ever in clinical development.

The federal government officially unveiled the parallel track program in April 1992 as a plan "intended to make promising new investigational drugs for AIDS and other HIV-related diseases more widely available as early as possible in the drug development process." The approach called for AIDS drugs to be made available after the completion of Phase 1 studies to subjects who are unable to enroll in the controlled trials or are unable to benefit from current therapies. Although similar to the treatment IND concept, parallel track is a more liberal mechanism in that it can provide for expanded drug access when the evidence of a drug's effectiveness cannot meet the threshold necessary to qualify for a treatment IND.

There are other, if more subtle, differences between the two experimental access programs. While the treatment IND requires approval at the commissioner's office level, parallel track is technically a protocol amendment, which needs the approval of review division directors. Also, sponsors can submit their parallel track proposals for review by the AIDS Research Advisory Committee of the National Institute of Allergy and Infectious Diseases in addition to the FDA.

In October 1992, Bristol-Myers Squibb's AIDS drug Zerit (stavudine) became the first drug made available under parallel track. The company established the parallel track arm during Phase 2/3 trials, and at a time when the controlled trials were enrolling rapidly. Just six weeks into the parallel track program, the company's controlled trials were fully enrolled, while the parallel access arm had enrolled several hundred patients. Ultimately, more than 13,000 patients received the drug under the parallel track program. Two earlier expanded drug access programs—for Hoffmann-La Roche's Hivid (zalcitabine or ddC) and Bristol-Myers Squibb's Videx (didanosine or ddI)—were said to be the models for the parallel track program.

Since this time, however, the parallel track program has failed to attract willing industry participants. Although some companies have discussed parallel track programs with the FDA, Zerit remains the only drug made available in the program's five-year history.

While it is generally acknowledged that AIDS patients have many more therapeutic options than they did in the early 1990s, FDA officials are uncertain why the program has not been more active. Like the treatment IND program and any other expanded access plan, however, parallel track access can be extremely expensive. In addition, since parallel track drugs would be made available even earlier in drug development, it is likely that many sponsors and AIDS patients have been reluctant to participate in this program.

The Oncology Initiative

The FDA's most recent accelerated drug development and approval program is its Oncology Initiative, which was implemented in March 1996. Introduced as "a uniform policy" rather than as a regulation, the Oncology Initiative comprises four separate elements, each of which the FDA claimed to have the authority to implement immediately:

- *Accelerated Approval for Cancer Drugs.* "To speed the availability of cancer drugs, FDA may now rely on partial response (such as measurable but incomplete shrinkage of a tumor) to a therapy, in addition to the current criteria such as a patient's survival and improved quality of life," the agency stated. "While the predictive value of partial responses may still be a matter of discussion and study for all types of cancer patients, FDA has concluded that for patients with refractory malignant disease or for those who have no adequate alternative, clear evidence of anti-tumor activity is a reasonable basis for approving the drug. In these cases, studies confirming a clinical benefit may appropriately be completed after approval. By basing accelerated approval on surrogate markers such as tumor shrinkage for patients who have no satisfactory alternative therapy, and by allowing more definitive data on survival or other criteria to be developed after marketing approval, FDA believes that many cancer therapies will reach patients sooner." Under the policy, the agency will also apply the accelerated approval provisions to certain products intended to remove a serious or life-threatening toxicity of cancer treatment.

In effect, this aspect of the Oncology Initiative simply extends the accelerated approval process (Subpart H) to cancer drugs. While the FDA points out that the accelerated approval program has been applicable to promising drugs for cancer patients who do not benefit from or cannot tolerate available therapy, the agency stresses that, in the past, "this approval mechanism has not been frequently utilized, largely because general agreement on reasonable surrogate endpoints has been lacking." Post-approval studies would be required for most drugs approved on the basis of tumor shrinkage and for all products that remove treatment-associated toxicities.

- *Expanded Access for Drugs Approved in Other Countries.* Under this aspect of the Oncology Initiative, the FDA plans to contact the

U.S. sponsor and encourage the company to pursue an expanded access protocol "whenever a cancer therapy for patients who are not curable or well-treated by currently available therapies is approved by a recognized foreign regulatory authority." To qualify, a drug must be in a controlled clinical trial in the United States and be approved by "an identified regulatory agency in a foreign country." Although the FDA did not identify any "recognized" regulatory authorities, it does state that the authorities must have "review practices, review standards, and access to specialized expertise in the evaluation of agents for use in cancer treatment that are sufficient to allow FDA to conclude that a marketing approval action by that authority is likely to provide an adequate basis for proper consideration of an expanded access protocol for U.S. patients."

In considering such expanded access protocols, the agency will accept an English-language version of the data submitted to the foreign regulatory authority. The expanded access protocols should be directed at the "same general type of patient condition and similar dosage and schedule" as approved by the foreign regulatory authority.

- *Cancer Patient Representation at FDA Advisory Committee Meetings.* The FDA will expand the "consumer member" concept in the context of its advisory committees, each of which typically includes a consumer member. "Because cancer is not one disease but many, FDA will now include a person who has experienced the specific cancer on each cancer-therapy advisory committee... FDA will now ensure that an individual who has personal experience with the specific cancer being studied be included as an ad hoc member of each cancer therapy committee."

- *Clarification of the FDA's Policy for Studies of Marketed Cancer Products.* To reduce the number of unnecessary INDs submitted by clinical investigators, the agency clarified its policy on INDs for studies of marketed drugs and announced that it would now refuse to accept INDs for exempt studies of marketed drugs. The agency states that it will not accept an IND for a study of a lawfully marketed drug if: (1) the study is not intended to support approval of a new indication or a significant change in product labeling or advertising; (2) the study does not involve a route of administration or dosage level or use in a patient population or other factor that significantly increases the risks (or decreases the acceptability of the risks) associated with the use of the product; and (3) the study meets the requirements for IRB and informed consent and does not commercialize the investigational product. The agency also clarified that it will not view a drug company's act of providing a marketed drug free of charge for an investigator-initiated study as constituting a promotional activity. In mid-1997, the Division of Oncology Drug Products (DODP) was developing a guidance document to further clarify the policy regarding the criteria for exemption.

During the Oncology Initiative's first year, DODP granted accelerated approvals to two drugs: Taxotere (docetaxel) in May 1996 for the treatment of patients with locally advanced or metastatic breast cancer who have progressed or relapsed following doxorubicin chemotherapy; and Camptosar (irinotecan) in June 1996 for the treatment of patients with metastatic colorectal cancer whose disease has progressed following 5-fluorouracil (standard) chemotherapy. DODP claims that the initiative has attracted "enormous interest," and that the division participated in over 100 formal meetings with oncology product sponsors.

In following up on the expanded access component of the Oncology Initiative, DODP has written to regulatory authorities in 24 "major" countries to request a list of all cancer or cancer-related therapies approved in each country during the past 10 years. As of May 1997, the division had received responses from 15 countries and identified 44 drugs marketed in one or more of the countries but not yet approved in the United States. According to the agency, "no further action is indicated for a number of these drugs, which are not needed for patients in the U.S. due to the availability of other similar or superior drugs. Reviews of available information on several products are not yet final, but at present all products that appear to potentially provide a significant benefit in cancer treatment can be accessed by U.S. patients, either in the marketplace or through an established IND-special exception mechanism."

References

1. Shulman, S.R. and Brown, J.S. (Tufts Center for the Study of Drug Development), *The Food and Drug Administration's Early Access and Fast-Track Approval Initiatives: How Have They Worked?* Food and Drug Law Journal, 1995, pp. 503-531.

2. Ibid.

3. Hewitt, P. (Tufts Center for the Study of Drug Development). Data from Tufts Center for the Study of Drug Development Marketed Drugs and Expedited/Accelerated Datasets, March 1997.

Index

OTC drug labeling, 226
prescription drug labeling, 224-226

Drug Master Files (DMF), 68-69, 185

-E-

Emergency Use IND, 53

End-of-Phase 2 meeting, 133-135

Environmental Analysis Report, 70, 188

-F-

FDA Advisory Committees, 16, 247-259
CDER use of, 253-255
functioning of, 255-258
influence of, 258-259
membership of, 250-252

FDA Ombudsman, 237

FD&C Act: *see Federal Food, Drug and Cosmetic Act*

Federal Food Drug and Cosmetic Act, 4-6, 136

Final Printed Labeling: *see Drug Labeling*

-G-

Good Clinical Practices, 149-164
informed consent requirements, 161-164
investigator responsibilities, 158-159

IRB responsibilities, 159-161
sponsor responsibilities, 150-158

Good Laboratory Practice, 8, 39-49, 74-75
applicability of, 40-41
FDA enforcement of, 46-49
history of, 40
major provisions of, 41-46
typical violations of, 48

Good Review Practices, 206

Good Manufacturing Practice; *see Current Good Manufacturing Practice*

-I-

ICH: *see International Conference on Harmonization*

IND: *see Investigational New Drug Application*

Informed Consent: *see Good Clinical Practices*

Institutional Review Board: *see Good Clinical Practices*

International Conference on Harmonization, 3, 20
effects on clinical testing, 114, 119
effects on nonclinical testing, 20
effects on postmarketing adverse experience reporting, 269-272

Investigational New Drug Application (IND), 8-9, 51-84
annual reports to, 82-83, 128

applicability of, 53-55
content requirements for, 55-75
emergency use IND, 53
FDA review of, 9-11, 102-112
information amendments to, 84
investigator IND, 53
regulatory reform's effect on, 2,
55, 67-68, 72
safety reports to, 78-82, 128
status categories for, 111-112
submission of, 75
treatment IND, 327-337
types of, 52-53
updating requirements for, 76-84

Investigator IND, 53

Investigator's Brochure, 60-63

IRB: *see Good Clinical Practices*

-L-

Labeling Requirements: *see Drug
Labeling*

-M-

MedWatch Program, 80

-N-

NDA: *see New Drug Application*

New Drug Application, 13, 165-204
amendments to, 204
annual reports to, 263-264
application form for, 167, 176-179
archival copy of, 173-176

case report forms section of, 201
case report tabulations section of,
199-201
chemistry section of, 182-190
clinical data section of, 194-198
content requirements for, 171-
172, 176-202
debarment certification section
of, 202
FDA guidelines regarding,
169-171
FDA prioritization of, 229,
239-246
FDA review of, 14-16, 208-227
FDA-sponsor meetings regarding,
203-204
field copy of, 173-176, 188, 202
history of, 166-169
index of, 179
labeling section of, 179-180
methods validation package
section of, 189-190
microbiology section of, 193-194
nonclinical pharmacology/
toxicology section of, 190-192
patent certification section of, 201
patent information section of, 201
pharmacokinetics and bioavailability section of, 192-193
review copy of, 173-176
safety update section of, 198
samples section of, 189
sponsor rights during FDA review
of, 228-238
statistical section of, 198-199

summary of, 180-182
user fee cover sheet for, 202

Nonclinical Testing, 7-8, 17-36
    acute toxicity studies, 25-27
    carcinogenicity studies, 29-31
    chronic toxicity studies, 28-29
    FDA guidance on, 18-21
    FDA role in, 18
    genotoxicity studies, 33-35
    international harmonization
    efforts regarding, 20
    pharmacodynamics, 22-23
    pharmacokinetics, 23-24
    pharmacology studies, 22-24
    reproductive toxicity studies, 31-33
    special toxicity studies, 31
    subacute toxicity studies, 27-28
    toxicity studies, 24-36
    toxicokinetic studies, 35-36

Not-Approvable Letters: *see Action Letters*

-O-

Oncology Initiative, 13, 91, 144, 346-351

Orphan Drugs, 297-310
    approval times for, 309-310
    designation of, 300-304
    grants and contracts for, 308-309
    history of, 298-299
    marketing exclusivity for, 304-307

protocol assistance for, 308
tax credits for, 307-308

Over-the-Counter Drug Labeling: *see Drug Labeling*

-P-

Parallel Track, 346-347

Phase 1-4 Clinical Testing: *see Clinical Testing*

Pivotal Clinical Trials: *see Clinical Testing*

Postmarketing Requirements, 261-281
    adverse experience reporting requirements, 265-272
    general reporting requirements, 262-265

Preapproval Inspections, 213-214

Preclinical Testing: *see Nonclinical Testing*

Pre-NDA Meetings, 203-204

Prescription Drug User Fee Program, 2, 205, 228

Primary Endpoints: *see Clinical Endpoints*

Priority Drugs, 229, 241

Protocols: *see Clinical Protocols*

-R-

Refuse-to-File Actions, 210-213

-S-

Scale-Up and Post-Approval Changes Initiative, 287-290

SNDA: *see Supplemental NDA*

Standard Drugs, 229, 241

Subpart E Program: *see Accelerated Development Program for Drugs*

Subpart H Program: *see Accelerated Approval Program for Drugs to Treat Life-Threatening and Severely Debilitating Illnesses*

SUPAC: *see Scale-Up and Post-Approval Changes Initiative*

Supplemental NDA, 283-296
  regulatory reform and the, 284-285, 287-290
  when to submit, 285-286

-T-

Toxicity Testing: *see Nonclinical Testing*

Treatment IND, 53, 327-337

-U-

User Fees: *see Prescription Drug User Fee Program*